CW00501422

DARTMOOR PRISON

A Complete Illustrated History

VOLUME TWO – THE CONVICT PRISON 1850-PRESENT DAY

'At Her Majesty's Pleasure'

Ron Joy

HALSGROVE

First published in Great Britain in 2002

Copyright © 2002 Ron Joy

*All rights reserved. No part of this publication may be reproduced,
stored in a retrieval system, or transmitted in any form or by any means
without the prior permission of the copyright holder.*

British Library Cataloguing-in-Publication Data
A CIP record for this title is available from the British Library

ISBN 1 84114 201 8

HALSGROVE

Halsgrove House
Lower Moor Way
Tiverton, Devon EX16 6SS
Tel: 01884 243242
Fax: 01884 243325
email: sales@halsgrove.com
website: www.halsgrove.com

Printed and bound in Great Britain by Bookcraft (Bath) Ltd, Midsomer Norton

FOREWORD

I arrived at HM Prison Dartmoor on 18 June 2001. My impression of the prison would have been the same as that of anyone who has looked at this imposing granite building rising out of the moor.

As the 38th Governor, my agenda was to take it forward. One cannot however take a prison such as Dartmoor forward without understanding its past. This book does just that. Ron Joy has succeeded in creating the definitive work on the prison simply known as 'The Moor'. His personal insight and experiences led him on a trail of discovery. The book that resulted has been long in the making and is genuinely a labour of love on his part.

I hope you enjoy it as much as I have done, not just because it is a 'good read', but also as a superb insight into the past.

Graham L. Johnson
Governor, Dartmoor Prison
15 July 2002

Think gently of the erring
and do not thou forget,
However darkly stained by sin
He is thy brother yet.

Heir of the self same heritage
child of the self same god,
He hast but stumbled in the path
Thou hast in weakness trod.

From a poem written by a convict for his father.

CONTENTS

ACKNOWLEDGEMENTS

Many thanks to the following for their invaluable word-of-mouth recollections and access to private documents: Officer Dave Bone, last man to ride mounted patrol (pony patrol) at Dartmoor Prison; John Dymond, Australia, for information on William Dymond, warder Dartmoor Convict Prison 1873, later governor of an Australian prison; Officer C. Elcombe, last man to fire a rifle at Dartmoor Prison; Chilli Frampton, former officer circa 1932, later farm manager; Richard Elmer Johnson, information on Francis Dolphin, ex-1812 war prisoner; Chief Officer 1 Lenaghan, Dartmoor Prison; Marjorie Mace (Putt), information on Capt. Stacey, ex-1812 war prisoner; Stan Mutton, officer circa 1932; Mr Tiley, ex-steward Dartmoor Prison (joined 1904); Officer Pinney, circa 1932 Dartmoor Prison; Joan and Stan Von Sternberg, USA information on Fort Sewell; Cyril Penny, officer circa 1932; Chief Officer 1 Dennis Sutton re German prisoners; Reg Gauci re transported convicts.

INTRODUCTION

After the departure of the French and American prisoners from Princetown in 1815–16 the weeds grew in the deserted streets and Dartmoor was claiming back its own.

A small detachment of the Sappers and Miners Regiment was based at the barracks in order to take care of some maintenance in both the barracks and the war prisons, in an attempt to preserve their viability. The owner, the Duchy of Cornwall, continued to pay the necessary rates and expenses.

The huge numbers of cattle that had been kept in Butchery Field, sufficient to feed about 10 000 men plus many staff and families, were now removed and a silence descended. So ended a dreadful period in the history of Dartmoor.

Within a couple of years of the war prisons being closed, a House of Commons Committee began investigating prisons in London. Severe overcrowding and disease made these establishments desperate places.

Proposals were made to move 2000 convicts to the supposedly 'good' climate of Dartmoor at an estimated cost of £5000. A report to this effect was produced which suggested that the cutting of granite by convicts would cleanse the land and render it fit for cultivation, and that an iron railway might then transport the granite to Plymouth.

Thomas Tyrwhitt wrote to the Chamber of Commerce at Plymouth on 3 November 1818 in favour of the construction of a railway from Princetown to Plymouth. Having set his heart on opening up Dartmoor, he considered the report from the Committee added weight to his letter. Much to Tyrwhitt's disappointment, however, the House of Commons did not adopt the recommendations of the Committee's report but in 1820 it was announced that King George IV had sub-scribed £1000 and the necessary land for the removal of orphan children from the streets of London. They were to be housed in the former war prison at Dartmoor, 'under a system of religious, moral and industrial training to reclaim them from the habits of vice and immorality'.

King George IV was Prince of Wales and Duke of Cornwall during the con-struction of the war prisons. He, too, wanted to see Dartmoor opened up and perhaps he saw in these unfortunate waifs and strays the opportunity for cheap labour. This is certainly implied in his term 'industrial training'. Luckily for the orphans, the scheme was never carried out and the war prisons decayed further in Dartmoor's harsh climate.

But after three Acts of Parliament, the floating of loans and large public sub-scriptions led to the horse tramway being brought to Princetown at a cost of £66 000. This tramway opened on 26 September 1823, its main use being to convey granite from the quarries on Dartmoor to Plymouth.

Meanwhile, the prison church was locked up, maintenance at the prison slowly came to a halt and the building began to fall apart rapidly without constant and skilled maintenance needed in an environment such as that of Dartmoor. Nettles filled the churchyard, grass grew in the streets of Princetown, and the prison yard, too, was choked with weeds. Indeed, in 1970 when part of the prison was shut off for the building of a small store, after just three months the grass was waist high on a hitherto stone-strewn, vegetation-free, piece of land.

Maintenance was carried out in a small way by the Duchy of Cornwall in order to preserve these dark, satanic buildings, but the decay rapidly escalated. Some of the floors had fallen in, no doubt due to the leaking walls and roofs being left unrepaired and under constant bombardment from the high rainfall of Princetown.

In 1831, the Revd Mason wrote a letter to the barrack sergeant complaining that very little maintenance had taken place on the prison buildings which housed tenants, or on his church. In 1832 records show some repairs being carried out to the barracks and war prison. These were undertaken by the Sappers and Miners Regiment stationed in the barracks and were seen as a great help by the quarry workers and farm labourers occupying some of the prison buildings.

During this period it was commonplace for convicts to be treated with the most unreasonable savagery. They would be hanged for the most trivial of offences and, as there was little room for housing prisoners, they would often be transported to provide labour in the colonies. Transportation began with the Vagrancy Act of the sixteenth century which gave magistrates the power to order offenders to be transported to such places as the Privy Council saw fit.

A letter written by James I in 1619 directed that 100 dissolute persons should be sent to Virginia, and in an Act created by Charles II the term transportation was first used. In 1718 it became legal for contractors to be handed convicts who had escaped the death penalty. The contractor would then make arrangements with our North American colonies in Virginia and convey the convicts there for terms not exceeding fourteen years. There was high demand for cheap labour in the colonies at this time and thus the contractor was able to sell his convicts to those in need of workers. It was not entirely uncommon for innocent people to be kidnapped and sold as convicts. It is estimated that more than 40 000 prisoners were sent to Virginia, many of whom never returned.

During the American War of Independence many of these deported convicts were sent home to Britain where they were housed in old hulks and captured vessels belonging to the Royal Navy. Conditions aboard such ships were poor and those housed on them were subjected to barbaric acts of cruelty. Few people cared about the treatment of these prisoners as social conditions throughout the country were poor and the law-abiding populace themselves were subjected to hard living conditions. Tales of children working in mines and factories are familiar to us, and the plight of these youngsters, many of whom lost their lives, is illustrative of the standard of living during this period.

The British Government, at the behest of the great prison reformer John Howard, began to work on the production of plans for prison penitentiaries. These plans were put on hold following the exciting discovery of Australia by Captain Cook, and later the Government was able to order the deportation of convicts to this foreign land.

The first fleet of two frigates and nine transport ships anchored in Botany Bay in January 1788 in the new-founded colony of Australia. For a time, everyone was content. The criminals of which England had rid herself of were now working hard in a harsh environment to open up new land for the colonists. Soon, however, protests were being made from those establishing the colony in Australia. It seemed that Australia was so flooded by convicts that they had begun to take precedence over the settlers. The British Government became aware that alternative measures must be taken.

In 1835 the storm surrounding transportation was about to break and the Government was forced to agree that it must come to an end. A Parliamentary Committee condemned the practice and in about 1840 transportation to New South Wales ceased.

During the first four years following this, however, 16 000 convicts were still being sent to Australia, and Tasmania, in particular, was flooded with people. The small population of farmers could not cope with the number of convicts who had served their time, and who, not being allowed to go back to Britain, now demanded work. Trade was halted and Tasmania was close to being declared bankrupt. In 1846 transportation to the island would also be halted in order for some thought to be given to its future.

The Government then had to hire all available accommodation in England as all colonies except for Western Australia refused to accept transported criminals. The enormous pressure to find secure accommodation forced the Government to again assess the old war prisons on Dartmoor.

A letter dated 23 July 1834 states: 'Estimate to defray the charge of repairing two prison buildings at Dartmoor to be £7000.' This was signed by F.T. of Whitehall Treasury Chambers who held a detailed survey dated 21 January 1834 from Mr G.L. Taylor which read as follows:

> *My Lord,*
> *I have estimated the cost of altering one of the prison buildings at Dartmoor into 64 solitary cells, according to the plan of Mr Crawford, at the sum of £3000 – warming same by hot water = £500. A total of £3500 or two buildings to contain 128 cells at £7000.*
> *The cells in the seven buildings (war prisons) are intended to be each 14ft x 8ft 6ins in the clear (inside measurement), a central passage between cells 12ft wide, cells to be 10ft high on the ground floor and 9ft 6ins high on the upper floor.*
> *All the division walls to be 18ins thick, the central passage to be the whole height of the building, and lighted from the sides of the raised part of the roof. The upper-storey cells to be entered from an open gallery on each side about 3ft wide.*
> *The staircases and entrances will be required to be altered as shown on the plans, if the buildings are divided as shown on the plans each of the long buildings will contain on the ground floor 30 cells, and on the upper floor 34 cells, together 64 cells.*
> *If all seven buildings are alike they will contain together 448 cells, the infirmary building will contain on the ground floor 31 cells, together 62 cells.*
> *The petty officers' prison will also contain 62, making a grand total of 572 cells. Each cell to have double doors to prevent the prisoners talking to each other across the passages, and as the prisoners are to be confined in absolute solitude, each cell should have a small privy constructed therein, on the self-acting principle, with a constant supply of hot water from a general reservoir.*

This was written in 1834. Convicts had to wait until 1980 – one-hundred-and-fifty years later – for this privy and hot water to be made available!

A more detailed survey was ordered and here follows the report made by G.L. Taylor. This information is illustrative of how much the prison had deteriorated in just twenty-five years since the opening date:

The Dartmoor Prison Survey *by G.L. Taylor.*

The Octagonal Rooms [top of main drive]
Originally lookout rooms, the struts of the roofs are in process of decay from damp – and when they give, the roofs which are supported by them will do so too – the ends should be scarfed.

No. 1 prison [now F]
The gable end, stairs, platforms and all timbers in and connected to them are

decayed, the girders on the south wall need scarfing – the plate at the foot of the lower frame has the lead out of it in places, it should be secured by new flashings, or all the queen posts will rot with the wet.

No. 2 and No. 6 prisons [No. 2 demolished 1906, No. 6 now old kitchen]
These are the newest prisons and in best order, but the gables and all woodwork connected therewith are damp and decayed – the floors of these two are boarded, the rest lime ash on shingle. The privies of No. 2 and No. 6 have their roofs slated, the rest are decayed having been of Purbeck Stone. Most external doors decayed and hinges rusted. Floors require partial repairs.

No. 3 prison [under sports hall]
Gables damp and platforms decayed, floors partly decayed – attic floors are lime and ash, leaks require stopping here, privy roofs gone.

No. 4 prison [now church]
Centre gable and stairs as last generally good except above. Small repairs to floors and gables would make it tenable. Privy roofs decayed.

No. 5 prison [demolished under C-wing]
As last.

No. 6 prison [now old kitchen]
The SE angle much exposed, six girders are gone in walls, and plates decayed, platform of stairs gone and all bond timbers at that end.

No. 7 prison [demolished now under A-wing]
SW long front about ten girders decayed at ends, should be scarfed and plates cut out, gables very damp, landings attached are all gone and stairs and privy roof all gone. The gables are covered in moor stone copings and cornices at the level line which let in wet at joints and at top – the masonry is generally bad and the stone porous so that the walls are constantly damp.

Petty officers' prison [now hospital/classrooms]
East entrance the south wall timbers in it, decayed, and all floors attached are decayed – the walls are very damp where chimneys are, in all instances.

Infirmary [now workshops]
Opposite building west of entrance S wall damp, and all attached timber decayed. Battening all decayed on this side and all plastering decayed. Walls at chimney breasts are very bad.

Matrons' house [now former visits building]
Dispensary etc. and ground floors all gone and upper floors at chimneys also rotted away.

Agent's house [now officers' mess]
Ground floors all gone and opposite buildings (surgeon's house) are occupied by John Ledger (keeper).

Turnkeys' houses
Are in a very bad state.

Barracks [1–10–11 remain]
Floors generally bad; the roofs in tolerable preservation but require attention particularly at the lower plate of the Louvre. The staircase platform of all the prisons are decayed from being attached to the walls which are wet in the south and west the timbers in and attached to them are entirely decayed.
G.L. Taylor, 21 January 1834

In the *Exeter and Plymouth Gazette* dated 1835, the following extract appeared:

On 1 August the Home Secretary Lord John Russell met two commissioners and a surveyor at the Dartmoor Prisons of War to inspect them and the military barracks, offices etc., previous to their being adapted to a penitentiary for convicts on the solitary system, i.e., one convict per cell.

It was determined that No. 4 prison [now old Church of England chapel] should be immediately repaired and sub-divided into cells for imprisoning trans-ports, and rendering their labour productive by cultivating the soil and teaching them trades.

The No. 4 prison will at first be occupied by convict artificers, carpenters, smiths and the like who will be employed under a superintendent in putting in repair the six other prisons – which will make this intended extensive establishment capable of securing some 5000 prisoners.

In 1837 Colonel Jebb, Surveyor General of Prisons, visited the war prisons and barracks and reported favourably on them being used for long-term offenders, but it was still to be over a decade before this happened.

In 1846 the British Patent Naphtha Company applied for a lease of some of the buildings and was granted use of the old infirmary buildings which are now the workshops. A trestle bridge was built over the boundary wall, where today's builders-operatives' yard is situated, enabling peat to be carried from the peat grounds at the Blackabrook head to the peat distillation plant in the old infirmary. Naphtha was intended to be an alternative to coal gas, used in lighting and heating, but the naphtha produced at Princetown was extremely smoky and could not be sold easily, leading the company to bank-ruptcy after a few years. Later the production of gas from peat would be more successful thanks to the tremendous workforce made up of convicts. It became a hugely economical system.

The Duchy steward was constantly organising repairs to all buildings, while straying cattle were kept clear of the prison burial grounds that held nearly 2000 prisoners, though the bones of French and American prisoners were later exposed as the wind and rain eroded the soil covering their shallow graves.

Quarrymen and tin miners were notoriously difficult; those living in Duchy accommodation at Princetown were hard-working, hard-living, hard-fighting men who suffered appalling conditions and wages and undoubtedly made the rent collector's task almost impossible. This job was given to an old barrack sergeant called John Ledger who is recorded as living in the surgeon's house in G.L. Taylor's survey. It is reputed that Ledger threatened to shoot one tenant with a long gun (musket). What a task he had! But he succeeded well and went on to be landlord of the oldest, most respected public house in Princetown, the Plume of Feathers, which, having been built in 1785, preceded the prison.

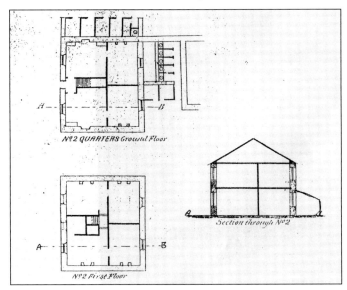

Left: *No. 2 barrack block, barrack sergeants' quarter.*
Above: *Plume of Feathers. John Ledger, the old prison buildings' keeper, was the landlord of the Plume at one time.*

The Duchy of Cornwall knew that one day the war prisons were likely to be reopened as a convict prison and thus it was in its best interests to spend money on repairs and prevent the buildings from slipping into a ruinous state and eventual total destruction. Estimates would have been made as to the cost needed for repairs and such an estimate appears in Taylor's report.

This was highly optimistic, of course, as the procedure for obtaining funds was a long-drawn-out business, a system little changed during the author's time as a principal officer (works). All plans and estimates for work had to be submitted three years ahead as a proposed estimate, twelve months ahead as a provisional estimate, then six months in advance as a positive estimate. This last six-monthly estimate then had to be vetted – and usually pruned – by head office before funds would be issued for the following six months' work. Taylor's recommendations of 1834 became a 'proposed' estimate in 1836 but nothing was finalised and the work would not be fully implemented until the Government finally decided to reopen Dartmoor Prison to house convicts more than a decade later.

Chapter One
DARTMOOR PRISON OPENS

In September 1850, after the Government had finally agreed to reopen Dartmoor to take convicts, the No. 3 prison was repaired by free workmen and the old petty officers' prison was readied for warders and military guards.

On 1 November 1850 a detachment of the 4th Regiment of Foot under the command of Ensign Hall marched into Princetown. On the following day, the soldiers were sent to Hill Quarries to await the arrival of 59 convicts from Millbank, Plymouth. These convicts were carried to Princetown aboard the Plymouth & Dartmoor Railway, accompanied by Deputy Governor Morrish and eight warders. Almost two weeks later, on 14 November, the first governor, Captain Gambier arrived with a further 95 convicts and escorts of warders.

The work of converting the old war prisons into a convict prison commenced and continued for many years. The ruined leat which took water to the buildings was repaired to provide decent water for the establishment. The leat was taken from a feeder of the Walkham at a place called Spriddle Lake, then ran to the reservoir outside the prison gates, a distance of approximately four miles. From the round tower at the reservoir, water could be diverted via a number of valves, to all prison and barrack buildings. The maintenance of the leat has been imperative since this time to the successful running of the convict prison.

The move into the prison was not an entirely smooth one. The miners and quarrymen who had previously rented the barracks were evicted to make room for the troops and warders, leaving families without accommodation. The infirmary was under the control of the British Patent Naphtha Company which refused to give the building up until the lease expired on Lady Day. Despite these problems, work was carried out at an impressive rate and by the end of December 1850 sufficient emergency repairs had been completed. Permanent occupation by convicts was now granted and it was estimated that 1300 convicts would eventually be held at Dartmoor. These estimates proved to be accurate.

With the development of the new convict prison came the decision to rename the prison buildings. Instead of the previous system of clockwise numbering, the buildings were to numbered in a counterclockwise direction. The old petty officers' prison, which became the barracks when Americans were held at Dartmoor, was renamed No. 1 convict prison, the present use being the lower and upper classrooms and hospital. No. 7 war prison was to become No. 2 convict prison, the present site being A-wing. The No. 6 war prison became No. 3 convict prison, presently the old kitchen, and No. 5 war prison became No. 4 convict prison, now under C-wing. The No. 4 war prison became the Church of England chapel and No. 3 war prison became No. 5 convict prison. This building was later demolished and the gymnasium was built on the foundations. The No. 2 war prison was also demolished and is now underneath the all-weather sports field. The No. 1 war prison became No. 6 convict prison and penal prison, today F-wing (see Appendix Four).

Convict prisons Nos 1 and 3 were fitted out as open dormitories with hammocks to house over 700 invalid prisoners. These were later converted into corrugated iron cells. No. 3 held 382 men in hammocks. No. 2 and No. 4 were gutted and four tiers of corrugated iron cells were built back-to-back.

The two rows of corrugated cells were built in the centre of the building with a passage around the outside to ensure that no convict was in contact with the outside walls and windows. The sketches are not drawn to scale and do not show the correct number of cells as there were in fact two rows of 16.

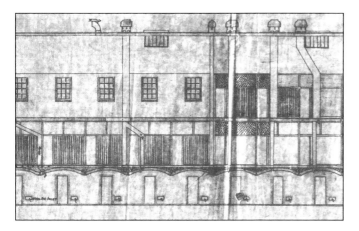

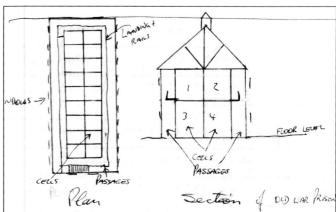

Above: *The author's illustration of convict No. 1 block, (now hospital/classrooms) showing corrugated iron cells with perforated iron sheets above doors for ventilation to right of elevation.*
Above right: *The author's plan of how iron cells were built in the old war prisons i.e. back-to-back and away from outer walls for security.*

The cells did not have windows but instead a gap underneath the door for ventilation, and despite the strong draughts this created, they were reputedly warmer and preferable to the wet stone cells built from 1860 onwards. Convicts were able to talk to their neighbours and any small amount of heat generated would soon build up to a reasonable temperature. This was impossible in the stone cells which remained damp and cold until the 1960s when a heating system was installed by Johnson & Baxter, contractors from Plymouth. The author and Number 26 party cut holes in the walls for heating pipes and rebuilt them once the pipes were installed. The last of the corrugated cells were demolished along with the remaining No. 5 war prison building in 1915. The present C-wing was then built on the site.

In 1850 there were 109 members of staff at Dartmoor Prison. This figure seems extraordinarily low in comparison to modern times, especially bearing in mind that a prisoner in the 1850s was often very violent and would attack or injure a member of staff if at all possible. Today the staff at Dartmoor Prison numbers more than 300.

The following article, taken from the *Plymouth, Devonport & Stonehouse Herald* of 2 November 1850, describes the circumstances of the arrival of the first prisoners at Dartmoor:

The prisons at Dartmoor are being put into repair for the reception of convicts, and it is said that when the whole arrangements are carried out that several thousand prisoners will be sent to the spot.
The authorities, having experienced great difficulty in coming to a conclusion on secondary modes of punishment, have now determined to try the efficacy of imprisonment and hard labour on the bleak hills of the Forest of Dartmoor.
On Friday 1 November the first batch of prisoners was brought down by the mail train, and left at the late Laira Station, where an escort of the 4th Regiment under the command of Ensign Hall was in readiness to receive them, and from that place were conveyed in wagons via the Dartmoor Railway to the prisons at Dartmoor.
The convicts will, we learn, at first be occupied in repairing and fitting up the remainder of the war prisons. When the work is fully accomplished and the full number sent down the prisoners will be employed under the strictest surveillance in cultivating certain parts of the moor.

Each year the governor of Dartmoor Prison presented a report to head office on the year's work. This included reports by various heads of departments within the prison. The first governor's report for 1850–51 was made by Captain Gambier and stated the following:

> *Many of the warders on their appointment had no conception of the kind of duties they undertook to perform, and others were quite unaccustomed to either exercise authority or submit to discipline – many have resigned or have been dismissed and now a body of zealous, active and trustworthy men are established here, though there are a few who I fear will not be able, satisfactorily, to discharge their duties. I consider a prison officer employed on public works should possess far different qualifications to one who is an officer in a closed prison. This is particularly the case at Dartmoor where he will be employed in charge of convicts on the open moors cutting turf or superintending the operations of reclaiming the land.*
>
> *Under such circumstances it is necessary that he should exercise the utmost vigilance, activity and intelligence in seeing that his men are properly distributed at their work, and in taking care to keep them all in view at all times. The class of men who are best qualified for such duties are pensioned NCOs, because from their previous habits they not only exercise a watchful vigilance over their different gangs, but they are also obedient to any instruction they may receive.*

The living conditions for both staff and convicts in 1850 are made clear in the following extract taken from the governor's order book:

> *At the opening of the prison on Wed. 6 Nov. Mr Bullen will take charge of A-wing as principal warder with Warders Creasley, Silvester and Banchron.*
>
> *Warder Crane will take charge of the inner entrance until further notice. Warders Bentley and Clark will assist during the reception of the prisoners in taking them to their cells – afterwards pumping or cleaning or whatever may be required. Warder King will assist in cleaning the offices and will go to the post and do whatever else may be required, Watchman Martin will take charge of the yards coming on duty at 6pm and going off at 6am. In going his rounds he will see to the apparatus fires and the fires in the boiler house.*

The working day during these troublesome times was a long one. The following is taken from the same governor's order book and dates from 4 November 1850:

> *The following shall be the routine of duty until further orders:*

5.30 – 6.00am	*The bell in the centre hall to be rung by the officer on duty for officers and prisoners to use.*
6.00 – 7.15am	*Light gas, sweep out cells, examine prisoners' beds and clothing, clean corridors.*
7.15 – 7.30am	*Serve out breakfast.*
7.30 – 7.50am	*Officers to breakfast.*
7.50 – 8.00am	*Officers muster in central hall.*
8.00 – 9.00am	*Chapel.*
9.00 – 1.00pm	*Exercise and pumps and other work.*
1.00 – 1.15pm	*Serve out dinner.*
1.15 – 2.15pm	*Officers at dinner.*
2.15 – 5.00pm	*Exercise and pumps and other work.*
5.00 – 5.30pm	*Officers on extra duty (tea). Prisoners at work in cells and pumps.*
5.30 – 6.00pm	*Warders roll call in their divisions, move all cell doors and report whether all prisoners are present. If any absent the cell and Reg. No. of each prisoner absent, and the name of the officer in charge.*
6.00 – 7.30pm	*Prisoners at work in cells and officers frequently going around to inspect the prisoners at work.*
7.30 – 8.00pm	*Serving out and at supper.*
8.00 – 8.30pm	*Prisoners at work in cells and officers inspecting.*
8.30 – 9.00pm	*Reading or writing in cells.*
9.15pm	*Turn off gas.*

The officers when on their divisions are expected to see each prisoner at least once every hour commencing at 5.30am to 9.30pm.
The night duty in the interior will be taken by the warders in rotation commencing on the 5th with Warder Cheasley from 10 – 2 and Warder Silvester from 2 – 6.
Until further orders all officers will be expected to sleep in the prisons and no lease can be given until the arrangements are more complete.
The above routine is to be considered as outline only of the duties which is to be filled up as circumstances may require.
From chapel and exercise the prisoners will keep their caps with the peaks pulled down to prevent their features being seen by the other convicts – and keep five paces apart from each other. No prisoner is to leave his cell without his label on his breast, which label is to be taken off and hung on the hook above the prisoners head at chapel.
No officer is to quit the prison on any occasion or on any pretext whatsoever with any key belonging to the prison in his possession.
Before quitting the prison he shall deposit his key or keys in the key box in the inner porters room.
Every officer whether sleeping in the prison or not is to deposit his keys in the above box.
Until further orders the key box is to be taken into the governor's house at the hour of locking the prison gates V12 at 10 o'clock pm.

The pumps that are mentioned so often in the governor's report are 'cranks'. The prisoners had to 'pump air'. One of the reasons for this was to build up their strength so that they would be strong enough to work in the colonies if sentenced to transportation.

Document in Prison Archives explaining what the 'pumps' are and detailing prison life in general. Source unknown.

THE CONVICT PRISON, DARTMOOR

We lately gave some account of the large prison at Prince's Town, Dartmoor, for convicts under sentence of penal servitude; and we now present a second series of Illustrations, including those of some prisoners working as tailors, others as carpenters, and one doomed to turned a crank, according to his estimated strength, from 10,500 to 14,500 times a day, with no better effect of utility than "grinding the air." This last-mentioned exercise is felt to be most humiliating, and is only imposed, as an occasional penance, upon those prisoners who have wilfully misbehaved themselves and broken the rules of the establishment. For the rest, whether employed in the granite-quarries, on the farm, or in the workshops indoors, they have no real sufferings to endure beyond the irksomeness of strict discipline and enforced labour, which must indeed be very disagreeable to persons of idle, lawless, and irregular previous life. The regulations enforced at the Dartmoor prison with reference to the daily routine, the hours of work and rest, the food dietary, and the division of classes, with their allotment to different occupations, were precisely explained in our former notice of this subject. Among the features common to this and to other prisons and Houses of Correction is the peep-hole, with an iron lid, in the door of each cell, through which the warder can quietly look in and see the solitary inmate, if he has any suspicion that mischievous practices are attempted, or if he hears any unusual noise. Every prisoner, moreover, has to rise at five o'clock in the morning, to wash and dress himself, and then to clean out his cell: so that it may be necessary to look in and see that they are stirring betimes. Their breakfast, dinner, and supper are taken in the cells: after which they may read, if they can, the books lent them from the prison library, or they may write letters; while those who cannot read and write may learn of the prison schoolmaster, during two hours of the evening. All lights are extinguished at eight o'clock. By good conduct and industry, a convict may get one fourth of the term of his sentence remitted, and may earn a grant of money, to the amount of £3, with which to start in life when he comes out. We have already described the buildings at Prince's Town, which were originally erected for the French prisoners of war seventy or eighty years ago. The mortality among them was not excessive, but there is a burial-ground for those who died here, with a monument erected by Captain W. J. Stopford in 1865. Some of the American prisoners of war are interred in a separate inclosure.

Chapter Two
ESCAPES

T he first convicts to escape from Dartmoor made their departure on 10 December 1850, just one month after the opening. At the 6am morning roll call prior to going off duty from No. 1 convict prison, Warder Jameson found that three men were missing. The men, John Broderick, John Thompson and Charles Webster, had ripped up the floorboards and climbed into the basement which is now the lower classrooms. Tools and materials were, and still are, stored in this basement. The men forced an outer door open and scaled the boundary wall adjacent to it using a plank of wood found in the store. Once the alarm had been raised, police scoured the neighbouring towns and villages in search of the convicts.

Four days later a constable in Ashburton arrested Thompson in the town. Another constable met Broderick and Webster on the London road, a mile outside Ashburton. He seized Broderick but Webster fled and was never seen again. Thompson and Broderick gave the prison a detailed account of the time they were away from Dartmoor. The men had made straight for Plymouth hoping to lose themselves in a large town. Later they described how whilst walking in Plymouth they had met three policemen, none of whom suspected a thing.

The runaways then came to a toll house which was still in operation, perhaps the one at Halfpenny Bridge, Stonehouse, and as they could not pay the half-penny toll were forced to turn back. The men headed out into open country, towards Ashburton, begging food from the people that they met but were unlucky as the only sustenance they received was a small amount of milk from a farmer. At this point they were sighted by their pursuers and fled. They spent the night wet, cold and miserable in a bog. The following three nights were spent more warmly in a haystack.

Following an enquiry at the prison it was decided that the two night-warders were at fault for not keeping full supervision of the prisoners. They were dismissed immediately and their families evicted from the prison quarters. All of their possessions were placed on the street by prison staff that day.

The two recaptured prisoners, Thompson and Broderick, were transferred to other prisons. This was a safety measure which recognised that the men now had too much knowledge about the layout of the buildings under the infirmary which could be passed on to other convicts who, in turn, might want to plan an escape.

During 1851 it was common for convicts to be able to leave the prison to assist artisan officers. Known today as trades' officers, these were uniformed men requiring assistance in carrying out work on the prison and quarters. They now also train convicts in certain skills thus equipping them with a trade by which to earn a living following their release.

On 17 February 1851 a convict called Gordon Taylor was employed as a painter in the barracks which housed warders and military guards. Taylor managed to slip away unnoticed by the principal officer or anyone else in charge until news of a man running across the moors reached the prison. Eventually he was captured by the Plymouth police and his subsequent sentence for escaping was transportation to Bermuda.

Did Taylor ever return from Bermuda? It would appear that the odds were against him. Following a gruelling Atlantic crossing on a convict ship, aboard which many people would have died, the hard work and heat of the colony would have proved a struggle. The malaria-ridden plantations and the liberal use of the cat-o'-nine-tails would have been a long way from the task of painting of a prison barracks on Dartmoor.

On 15 April 1851 two prisoners called John Jones and John Catton ran away from their work party in the afternoon. They kept themselves well hidden for a few days, and on 19 April robbed a man at Moretonhampstead, then were never seen again. What happened to them? Did they emigrate? Where did they go? The mind runs riot when hearing of such events!

A convict named John Bell was working out on quarters near the church when he made a dash for it. He was eventually captured in Exeter. On 1 May 1851 William Tegg became the first prisoner to be buried in an unmarked grave at St Michael's Church cemetery. He was thirty-three years old.

Trusted prisoners were allowed to work outside the prison without the benefit of a warder escort. One such convict was J. Hartley who walked away from his work party and the task he had been given on 22 August 1851. He was found by Farmer Dodd of Whitchurch, hidden in his farm buildings. The farmer received a reward of £5 for the capture of Hartley.

A noteworthy escape from Dartmoor Prison in these early days was that of Thomas Clutch who managed to slide between the bars of a window on the ground floor of No. 3 prison. He ran to the boundary wall which was in desperate need of repointing, climbed it like a monkey, and was gone. Clutch, like all of those mentioned before him, was one of many early escapees from Dartmoor.

Convicts were often subjected to work tasks which involved hard labour. One such task was the quarrying and dressing of stone. They would have to transport stone in handcarts, breaking it for use on the roads. A particularly hard task was reclaiming land for the farm. As a uniformed works' officer some time in 1971, the author was given the task to work with two prisoners in the rebuilding of some manholes on the Mis Tor Leat route. In order to do this we had to trench some boggy areas and drain the water into the prison leat. I had heard about trenching land from some of the pre-1932 officers and was eager to get some first-hand experience. If the same problem was to arise in the future it would be useful to know how to deal with the labour.

The three of us began trenching and I mucked in with the two men, my object being to excavate a trench about three-feet deep in the bog. This would then be laid with stones in the bottom and back-filled to form a drain known on Dartmoor as a French Drain. Within the first foot of digging we encountered water and this was to stay with us the whole time we were excavating. The ground that we were shovelling was peat which is a black, gooey mess. It refused to leave the shovels without being scraped off and very soon we were wet through from the waist down. Our clothes became extremely heavy, especially my thick serge uniform which I had on underneath my overalls. The material quickly rubbed skin off various parts of my legs. After four hours I called quits. I had had enough; the skin was worn off the sides of my knees and was extremely sore. We had managed to get to three-feet deep and lay stone down but the task had proved too much for us.

As a former building-trades worker I am very used to working out of doors in all weather and was amazed to find this task, which we were really only playing at, so difficult. The two convicts in my charge were very pleased when I called a halt. One can imagine the convicts of 1850 working under the control of sadistic warders and assistant warders for long, long hours year round. This would have included all the biting winters which were prevalent from 1850–1950. Our four-hour trenching experience was performed in bright sunshine, albeit knee-deep in black peat-water!

In the 1850s food would have been taken out with the work party at 7am, under the supervision of ruthless ex-army NCOs who were now warders. These men would themselves have been subjected to fierce discipline and be marched out to the lands that needed reclaiming all over the prison estates. The lunch-time meal would be of cold food and there was no sitting down for the meal break. The convicts were permitted to erect a corrugated iron screen about eight-feet high and 12 feet along. Huddled on the lee side of the screen in an effort to avoid the biting wind, they would eat their paltry meals.

Convicts having their meal during a break from hard labour on the prison estates. The men were not allowed to sit down to eat.

After a short period the screen would be laid down flat and the men would go back to their work until 'cease labour' was called. Wet, cold, tired and hungry they then would commence the march back to their cold cells and a meal before bed. The convicts were subject to search at all times and would often be called back out of their cells for this purpose. Sometimes searches were made while a convict was labouring and all kinds of articles might be planted by vindictive staff. A convict who was disliked by warders could easily be found guilty of possessing prohibited articles, regardless of how they had got there.

When the convict had had his supper, he was liable to be called out of his cell at the whim of a warder, especially if he had a particular grudge against the man. One convict is reported to have been called out of his cell for a haircut six times in one week despite being desperately tired and in need of rest. A convict's life could be made all the more unbearable by a warder punishing any so-called assault with the cat-o'-nine-tails.

Prisoners were punished in all manner of ways, with bread and water replacing regular meals or a meal being missed entirely, and the 'cat' of course. If an officer's hat was knocked slightly askew it would be deemed an assault on that officer and thus the cat-o'-nine-tails would follow.

In addition to this physical punishment the work rate was kept very high and life became intolerable for the convicts. In 1851 records show that approximately a third of all prisoners were punished. One wonders what the actual figures were, as even in 1968, more than a century later my training principal officer would say, 'Give the b____ nothing and then take that away.'

Imagine digging trenches for hours on end in the waterlogged ground. The men were working from October to December at 1400 feet above sea level with poor food, scant shelter and a lack of suitable clothing or footwear. The farm report for 1 October 1851 to 31 December 1851 is indicative of just how hard the convicts were forced to work:

In three months:

32 acres trenched two-feet deep.
7 acres drained three-and-a-half-feet deep.
268 yards of wall built five-feet high.
100 yards of wall built three-and-a-half-feet high.
3 acres of planting and trenching.
770 yards of new road.
450 yards of old foundations within the prison grounds removed.
Crops chiefly flax, hemp, turnips, mangel wurzels and oats.

Recalling the small area of trenching our small work party had covered, it makes the heart sink. These men had covered 32 acres. There were no comforts. Work finished, the men would march back to their prisons where they would remain cold and wet. Even on sunny days footwear would become soaked by the peaty ground and with no means to dry them out, they would be put on damp and cold the following day. In the freezing winters of the 1850s this would have been torturous.

It is important to note that the lifestyle of the staff at the prison was not a particularly pleasant one. They too would be standing in the biting wind for hours at a time and their living conditions were not too favourable. In the report from the heads of department, extracts from which appear earlier, the governor's report of 1851 included the following statement from the chaplain:

The first agricultural labour commenced 20 Feb. 1851 [three months after opening] *about 500 convicts work out on the hills. A school should be established for the children of warders. Staff are to co-operate in these plans by increasing the weekly payments of the children, or by other means.*

The demands placed on the staff to pay for their children's schooling would have excluded many children, most likely girls, from getting any form of education. Staff wages were meagre and large families would have found it difficult to survive.

Chapter Three
TRANSPORTATION 1851–1868

Convicts at Dartmoor Prison would have been given similar notices to that handed out at Pentonville Prison with regard to transportation. Prisoners from Dartmoor were transported to Van Diemen's Land from 1851 and many to Western Australia from 1851–68. Others were also sent to Gibraltar and Bermuda.

NOTICE.

PRISONERS admitted into Pentonville Prison will have an opportunity of being taught a Trade, and of receiving sound Moral and Religious Instruction. They will be transported to a Penal Colony, in Classes, as follows :—

FIRST CLASS.

Prisoners who shall, when sent from this Prison, be reported by the Governor and Chaplain to have behaved well.

These, at the end of 18 months, will be sent to Van Diemen's Land, to receive a Ticket of Leave, on landing, which, until forfeited by bad conduct, will, in that Country, confer most of the advantages of freedom. In Van Diemen's Land, labor being in great demand, and wages being therefore high, the Prisoner's knowledge of a trade, and the possession of a Ticket of Leave, will enable him, with industry and continued good conduct, to secure a comfortable and respectable position in Society. Prisoners who obtain Tickets of Leave may also, by industry and good conduct, acquire, in a short time, means sufficient to enable their families to follow them.

SECOND CLASS.

Prisoners who have not behaved well.

These, also, at the end of 18 months, will be transported to Van Diemen's Land where they will receive a Probationary Pass, which will secure to them only a limited portion of their earnings, will admit of their enjoying only a small portion of liberty, and will subject them to many restraints and privations.

THIRD CLASS.

Prisoners who have behaved ill.

These will be transported to Tasman's Peninsula, a Penal Colony, occupied only by Convicts and the Military Guard, there to be employed on the Public Works, in Probationary Gangs, without wages, and deprived of liberty; and their families will not be permitted, under any circumstances, to follow them.

Prisoners will see how much depends on their own conduct during their confinement in this Prison. According to their behaviour and improvement here, will be their future condition in the Colony to which they will be sent.

Notice given to prisoners at Pentonville, London. Dartmoor transportees to Van Diemen's Land would have been given a similar notice, however no such examples survive at Dartmoor Prison.

The following letter was sent from Dartmoor Governor M. Gambier to Colonel Jebb on 17 July 1853:

To Col Jebb CB
I beg to report for your information that having made the necessary arrangements with the Commander in Chief at Plymouth to supply boats, I have this morning dispatched the 40 convicts to Laira Station for embarkation on board the Sibella *[?] convict ship, to complete their probation on Public Works at Gibraltar.*

The governor's report dated 31 March 1851 (end of year) makes interesting reading, especially regarding the movements to and from the hulks and other prisons. Transportation to the colonies is also recorded. The following report was produced five months after the prison opened and records the numbers of arrivals from different prisons:

Remains 31 Dec. 1850	174
Received during year from Millbank	232
Pentonville	72
Portland	2
Hulk Justicia	22
Hulk Stirling Castle	30
Hulk Warrior	10
Hulk York	40
Bath Prison	5
Bedford Prison	26
Leicester Prison	42
Preston Prison	20
Reading Prison	28
Wakefield Prison	45
Invalids from Shorncliffe	152
Hulk Defence	239
Total	1176

The 239 men from the Hulk Defence were accompanied by the proportionate number of staff.
Disposed of:

Sent abroad with tickets of leave to Western Australia	13
Van Diemen's Land	49
Public Works Gibraltar	11
Further probation Van Diemen's Land	17
Removed to Millbank for misconduct	10
Pentonville	5
Hulk Defence	2
Hulk Justicia	5
Hulk Warrior	3
Hulk York	20
Derby Gaol (pardoned)	1
Discharged with free pardon	8
13 escaped, 7 brought back, 6 missing	
Died	10
Total disposed of	160

Roll on 31 March 1851 = 1176 – 160 = 1016

In 1852 the number of transported convicts was still high. For example, 329 men were sent to Van Diemen's Land with tickets of leave and 10 men to Western Australia, one man embarked for Public Works to Van Diemen's Land and 100 men to Western Australia. The total for this year was 570 men transported overseas, 30 of them going to Bermuda. The last record the author could find was for 1867 for men sent to Western Australia, who would have arrived in 1868. In 1869 seven men were sent back to Dartmoor from Perth. It is estimated that almost 160 000 people were transported from the United Kingdom between 1787 and 1868, with at least 13 000 females included in this figure. The governor's report from 1851 offers the following explanation on how the prisoners at Dartmoor were readied for their experiences overseas:

> *Convicts are undergoing a probationary period of discipline previous to execution of their sentences of transportation and the object is not only to create habits of continuous and persevering industry and to render them more useful to a colony but to reduce the cost of their detention by a judicious application of their labour.*

The early years were very successful for the directors of convict prisons. There was a high return from the labour of the convicts and, in the meantime, these same men were being trained to work hard for long periods in preparation for being sent to the colonies in Australia, Tasmania, Bermuda, Gibraltar and elsewhere. The high returns were paid for both by the hard-working prisoners and the devoted warders and ancillary staff.

Security was provided by the army detachment and discipline was kept at high levels by the warders. The barracks sergeant was in charge of the soldiers in the 11 barracks situated opposite the church, down Barrack Road. The army officers were stationed in the luxury of the officers' mess which was built at the same time as the prison in 1809. This later became the Duchy Hotel and then the prison officers' mess from 1941–91. It is now the High Moorland Visitor Centre. The author spent the first twelve weeks of his prison service career in room 10 of the Duchy Hotel awaiting a vacancy in official quarters so that his family might join him on Dartmoor from North Devon.

Below: *Dartmoor Prison officers' mess, now the High Moorland Visitor Centre.*

WORK DONE DURING 1851–52

The tradesmen and artisans continued the massive task of repairing the old war prisons. Conversions went on apace, as did the construction of new roads and the cutting and transporting of peat for fuel. During this time, special service prisoners (modern-day 'red-bands') would wear a blue jacket instead of the customary brown. If a red collar was attached to the blue jacket this signified a prisoner was allowed to work outside the prison without the escort of an officer. In those days no visitor was allowed on prison roads and these men would never have come into contact with a person not from the prison.

If the convict wore a blue jacket without a red collar he would be allowed to work inside the prison without an escort. The modern red-bands, who are allowed to move and work within certain areas, are not a new idea but actually experience the same prison rules as the blue-jackets.

During the years 1851–52, 67 acres of land were drained and trenched at two-feet and three and-a-half-feet deep. The space between drains would have been 16 to 24 feet. Sewage from the barracks and officers' quarters was directed to fields around the barracks and this treatment yielded one ton of hay per acre after a few months of spreading. During 1852 the hay crop was 30 tons.

Between 4 May and 20 October 1852, 1920 tons of peat were cut for fuel. This would have been as the result of hard labour and with the help of the prison peat railway which carried peat from the bogs some distance from the prison. The turf sheds were at the terminus of the railway which had a bridge over the boundary wall in what was the building operator's yard. It would then be taken into the gasworks, which is now the blacksmiths' shop. The photograph shows a broken wheel and parts of the small railway found on the peat lands by leat staff in the 1970s.

The broken wheel from a railway wagon found on the prison peat grounds.

Governor Gambier carried on in office for a second year. On 9 January 1852 the prison roll was 1016 men, with a further 679 received during the year and 562 lost to transportation, death or pardon. By 31 December 1852 there were 1133 men. During 1852 a tremendous amount of building work was completed in addition to repairing and renovations to the old war prisons. The farm built 2832 yards of new walls and repaired 8000 yards of old walls, 1584 yards of new roads were constructed and 2420 yards of old roads restored. Work was pursued with the utmost endeavour in all areas.

The farm kept detailed records of its work and of its stock. For example, in 1852 it had six horses, ten cows, six calves and a hundred pigs. Milk was supplied to the prison daily and butter was made and then sold to officers. The horses were used for carting goods, not for working on the land. All ploughing and harrowing was done by teams of convicts who also had to carry out the removal of huge granite stones. Their labours left a lasting legacy; it is a pleasure to see the well-kept fields and walls around the prison.

Above and right: Stones carved by prisoners with Queen Victoria's VR emblem and the date they were quarried. The 1852 stone – the year of the mutiny – is set in a wall on the main road to Tavistock and the 1853 stone is in a wall in Barrack Road.

JANUARY 1852 MUTINY

A convict named Slidders who was confined to a separate cell in No. 2 prison tried to cut his way out of the cell using the metal heel of his boot. As a result, from that day to this, any convict put in a separate cell, now called a segregation unit, is not allowed to wear boots during his incarceration. Not content with this, Slidders planned to lead a mutiny, but another prisoner informed Governor Gambier who successfully quelled the potential unrest by addressing the prisoners. The convicts returned quietly to their work while Slidders was arrested and moved to the penal cells to be even more severely dealt with.

Dartmoor Prison was home to many invalid prisoners who were subjected to hard physical labour under warders who were far from sympathetic. Some men working in their cells were, in 1852, allowed to have their doors open throughout the day. They were to remain at labour within the cell but despite this the noise created by the chatting of prisoners was deemed too loud. On

15 June 1852 talking was forbidden and has remained so. On 17 June 1852 it was decided that cell doors would once again be closed; during the author's time in B2 hall the doors were always shut.

At this time, there was much outside interest in Dartmoor Prison. On 20 July 1852 it was visited by Queen Victoria's husband Prince Albert. While the Queen remained in Plymouth, the Prince Consort was ascending Dartmeet Hill in his coach and could hear the saluting guns of the Plymouth garrison heralding the Queen's arrival in the city. The Prince made a close inspection of the prison and the convicts behaved well.

On 8 November 1852 a convict called Barrow escaped from the gasworks building at the terminus of the railway line. To break out of the gasworks compound, Barrow climbed the gas-house chimney and crossed the trestle bridge that conveyed the peat wagons into the prison over the boundary wall. The military sentry who was stationed permanently on the trestle bridge never saw Barrow and only later was the usual alarm raised throughout the county.

Barrow must have lain low for several days because on 10 November the clothes locker of the night officers' quarters was broken into and some clothes stolen. It was later discovered that these clothes were pawned in Plymouth on 16 November. The convict was never seen again and, quite possibly, lived the rest of his life as a free man – crime free.

August 1852 saw the change of the military guards. Such changes took place at short intervals over a period of a few months. The new guards were the 7th Regiment Royal Fusiliers with Captain Brown in command. The regiment was commanded in Plymouth by Lt-Col. Lacy Yeo who was later killed in the Crimean War along with 572 members of the illustrious regiment.

The governor's report for 1852 contains further information about the transportation of convicts to various destinations. The total number of departures for that year was 554, including one man sent to a lunatic asylum. The number of arrivals was slightly greater at 679.

The expenditure by the prison in 1852 was £30 365.17s.8¼d. minus the rent paid by officers which was £323.11s.6d. The net expenditure was £30 042.6s.2¼d. The accuracy of this figure down to a farthing is remarkable.

The year 1853 began with heavy snowstorms. In January and February blizzards hit Princetown and on 13 February meat wagons travelling from Tavistock were snowed up at Merrivale. A hundred convicts were sent out into the blizzards to cut a road through. But the appalling weather had more tragic results for three members of the 7th Regiment Royal Fusiliers. A report in the *Plymouth & Devonport Weekly* on Thursday 17 February 1853 recorded the story:

Corporal John Penton, Private George Driver and Private John Carlin belonging to No. 7 company (Capt. Brown) 7 Regiment Fusiliers stationed at Dartmoor Prison unfortunately lost their lives in the snow on Dartmoor on Saturday night. The two Privates, who only left the military hospital last week, marched up from HQ St George's Square early on Saturday morning under the charge of Corporal Ramsden, who conducted them ten miles further to the Dousland Barn Inn where they came under the control of Corporal Penton.
Snow having fallen all day, the landlord advised them not to proceed but the Corporal said they must obey orders and the three men marched on. It is surmised from the positions in which their hats and knapsacks were scattered that they passed through the first snowdrifts on the margins of the moor two miles from the Inn and reached the Devil's Bridge a mile and a half further.
There they could not proceed and retraced their steps to the first snowdrift, which by that time had become impassable, and there they unhappily perished.
John Smith of No. 3 Company who returned to Devonport on Saturday states that

he and Penton were four hours in the morning coming from Dousland Barn (five miles) being at times up to their arms in snow which was in some parts eight-feet deep. He endeavoured to dissuade Penton from returning the same evening. It appears that the Corporal was despatched with two invalid soldiers who were to proceed to Plymouth, at which he was to receive two men in exchange and to escort them to Princetown from Dousland. On his arrival at Dousland he was strongly persuaded not to attempt crossing the moor that night, as the weather was so boisterous and the snow very deep, the drifts in many places reaching a depth of 20 to 25 feet, and the thermometer 25 degrees below freezing point.

But the Corporal would proceed on his journey announcing that 'he had his orders and must abide by them' therefore, in consequence and at a place called Double Waters, the two privates strayed slightly from the road and had evidently fallen down exhausted, and were thus frozen to death, they were found near each other, one lying on his side, the other on his back.

A strict search was made for the Corporal who was still missing, but without avail until eleven o'clock on Tuesday when he was discovered lying on his face, about 200 yards from the back of the Duchy Hotel in Princetown, quite dead. [This spot is now called Soldiers' Pond.]

Soldiers' Pond where one of the Royal Fusiliers perished in 1853 trying to get back to his barracks at Princetown.

It is conjectured that after his two companions fell he endeavoured to reach this place to obtain assistance, and was so near his destination when he fell and thus perished almost within sight of his home.

The soldiers were found about three o'clock on Sunday afternoon, the Corporal was twenty three years of age and had been married about a month.

From 500 to 700 convicts are busily employed cutting roads through the snow, so as to enable provisions to be brought here. On Saturday these things had to be carried by the prisoners on their backs and then brought over the snow at a very imminent risk.

The three fusiliers were buried side-by-side in one grave beside the south wall of the churchyard. Set in the wall above them is a slate memorial tablet which was paid for by the privates of the regiment. Inside St Michael's Church in Princetown is a marble tablet with the following inscription:

Sacred to the memory of Corporal Joseph Penton, Privates Patrick Carlin and George Driver of the 7th Royal Fusiliers who lost their lives in a snowstorm on the neighbouring moor on the 12 February 1853 when in execution of their duty. This tablet is erected in token of his admiration of their conduct as soldiers (In braving danger in preference to disobeying orders).

By their commanding officer Lt Col Lacy Yeo of the 7th Royal Fusiliers.

Just after this tragic accident the 7th Regiment Royal Fusiliers landed in the Crimea at the head of the Light Division, still commanded by Lacy Yeo who had recorded his tribute to the three men lost on Dartmoor. By the end of the Crimean War, Yeo and 572 other members of the regiment were also dead.[1]

[1] *The Fusilier,* the Journal of the Royal Regt of Fusiliers (5th 6th 7th 20th) Vol. 5, No. 6, June 1987.

One of their enemies in the Crimea had been the bitter cold for which they were ill equipped. Perhaps as they froze in that inhospitable climate they thought of the time they had stood before the frozen graves of Penton, Carlin and Driver at St Michael's Church, Princetown.

Memorial on the wall of St Michael's Church graveyard of the three Royal Fusiliers who died in the blizzards of 1853.

Chapter Four

PRISON LETTERS

The prison holds a ledger in which a copy of each piece of correspondence is kept. Each item of outgoing correspondence would be copied by a clerk and inserted into the ledger which covers the period from 9 February 1852 to 18 August 1854. There would have been perhaps three or four ledgers in existence before this one but none of them has been found. The letters within are a valuable source of information about the current affairs of the prison at that time. Staff were often deemed unsuitable for their duties, as this letter sent on 7 January 1853 from Governor Gambier to Colonel Jebb illustrates:

I beg to report for your information that I have this day been compelled under my sense of duty to suspend Warder Calib Rourke from duty and order him instantly to quit the prison for absenting himself from duty at 7.45 o'clock pm yesterday evening. When on duty at 8.30 this evening was found in a helpless state of intoxication laying in filth in one of the local beer houses in Princetown. This officer's conduct has been of a disgraceful character – I beg you to recommend his immediate dismissal.
He joined the prison on 14 May last year and has previously been reported for absenting himself from duty.
He acknowledges the above report to be quite correct, I beg to add this officer is in receipt of a pension of 6d per week for service in the marine artillery.

A letter to Colonel Jebb dated 30 July 1853 illustrates how worried Gambier was about deaths at Dartmoor Prison:

I deem it my duty to forward to you the enclosed letter which Dr Campbell has written to me. The mortality of convicts has been considerable at Dartmoor since the commencement of this year and the medical officer has drawn my attention to the probability of additions to the number already dead by the close of 1853.

The following letter from Governor Gambier on 5 August 1853 is addressed to Captain Witty:

I have to report for your information that two convicts 1759 William Potter and 1943 Thomas Hall attempted to escape by running away from the gang to which they were attached. They were employed outside the prison breaking stone and repairing the road leading from Princetown to the prison. This morning (at about 5 o'clock) they were immediately pursued and captured by the officers and brought back to the prison. I immediately investigated into all the circumstances attending this attempt and I am of the opinion that no blame is attached to the officers of the gang, or to the sentry who was posted with them, with this exception, Warder Pascoe who was in charge of the gang, in his anxiety to execute a good quantity of work laid out the gang, allowed his men to be extended over too great a space of ground, thus rendering the supervision of the gang more difficult. I beg to add however that I have always found this officer most attentive to his duties and very intelligent. With regard to the prisoners I beg to state from their being brought before me, I ordered them to be placed in 4lb leg-irons with the distinctive yellow dress and to be sent out to work again, which they subsequently refused to do. I have therefore had them placed in the cells pending your decision, I have to request

your authority for continuing the irons. The conduct of these two prisoners has been good in this prison and in other prisons, but I find they have both been previously transported.
Reference to the prisoner 1759 William Potter I am given to understand that he attempted to escape from Gibraltar while undergoing his previous sentence, but having nothing authentic relative to it, I beg to add both prisoners are invalids and the medical officer informs me they are unfit to undergo corporal punishment. I shall therefore feel obliged by your instructions and I enclose the statements of the officers by which you will observe that Officer Crawford discharged his musket at the prisoners which did not take effect.

Letter of 4 February 1854 from Governor Gambier to John Hackett:

I hereby give you notice to quit the government quarters now occupied by No. 2 mess room in the barracks on or before the 12 o'clock this day, as you have ceased to be an officer of this prison and is required by your successor.

Letter to Captain Whitby from Governor Gambier dated 15 February 1854:

In reference to the enclosed list of convicts returned with the necessary corrections made, I beg to appraise you that the following men, viz:
1961 George Power
1989 Joseph Gardner
2244 William Aitken
2245 William Thomas
Will be included in the list now being prepared of convicts for removal to Western Australia and Gibraltar.

On 28 December 1853 Governor Gambier sent the following to Joseph Kimball Esq., surgeon superintendent of the convict transport ship, the *Sea Park*:

I enclose a letter addressed to a convict serving at the convict establishment at Freemantle, Western Australia, being a reply to a letter posted to me from the convict, and I should be much obliged by you having the goodness to oblige me by delivering it on your arrival in the colony.

The following letter comments on the effects that cold weather had on the old muskets. It was written by Governor Gambier to Colonel Jebb on 2 June 1853:

In reply to your letter of the 1st Inst. respecting the supply of ammunition, I beg to state that about 50 muskets are in daily use, 20 of which are double-barrelled. The charges are, in dry weather, being withdrawn about once per week, and in wet weather generally being the 2nd or 3rd day, that during the late severe weather both barrels and nipples kept full of snowdrift, and had to be withdrawn, sometimes twice a day.
With respect to the purpose of your letter I beg to suggest that not less than 2000 rounds be demanded, 1000 to be buckshot and the other musket cartridge. With respect to pistol ammunition we are not in want at present.

So the snow and cold weather made the life of military guards at Dartmoor Prison extremely difficult. The year 1853 continued with tremendous hardships for staff and convicts alike. Convicts slept in cold unheated cells. Those sleeping in hammocks were literally ten inches apart and covered the entire open floor of a room. The following letter from Governor Gambier is dated 5 August 1853 and is to Captain Witty:

I am glad to find that I shall be getting a little better men in exchange for those to go to the Stirling Castle. There is no reason whatever why you should not fill up all the vacancies, namely 88, provided you give me the proper staff as sanctioned by the estimate for 1274 men. This would involve an increase of one warder and eight assistant warders, I refer you to my letter to Mr Friend from this end date 14 February 1852.

But I beg to add that if I leave it to you I will readily take in the full number of prisoners namely 1274 on my present staff leaving the additional officers open until Col Jebb returns from Scotland, so as to give the Col time and as little trouble as possible.
With respect to the distance of a hammock from centre to centre when hung on hooks 2ft 4ins apart, it is of course somewhat dependent on the size of the man occupying the hammock, the average distance between hammocks is ten inches, that is between hammocks when occupied.

Convicts continued to attempt escaping from the labour and conditions of the prison. The prospect of freedom, even knowing the severe punishment following capture, was deemed attractive. Invalid prisoners were forced to work on outside parties attempting tasks of gruelling and physically demanding work. The letter from Governor Gambier to Captain Whitty that explains the attempted escape by two invalid convicts, detailed earlier, is indicative of the conditions in which these men were forced to work.

The letter regarding convicts William Potter and Thomas Hall informs us of the work these men were carrying out. They were breaking granite rocks down to a very small size with sledgehammers in order to repair roads. This work was obviously beyond their physical ability. As the doctor in the letter states they were unsuitable for flogging, they must have been in a terribly bad way. Doctors in prisons in 1852 would have had little sympathy for men that they thought were 'trying it on'.

The leg-irons placed on the men weighed four pounds and it would have been impossible for the men to wear these and carry out hard labour. The irons would have been left in place for a considerable length of time as the letter requesting their continuance would have to come from Head Office. It was common for permission to continue the use of leg-irons to be granted so the abominable contraptions were worn for long periods. The irons were rivetted to the prisoner making it impossible to remove them and attempting to sleep in a hammock with them still attached must have been very painful.

In the letter Gambier continues by saying that Officer Pascoe was an intelligent officer, yet he blamed him for spacing the men too far apart in order to achieve a greater work output. If the work output had been lower, Pascoe would again have been blamed so he was, in effect, in an impossible situation. It was common for officers to be used as scapegoats for mishaps within the prison, particularly the more innocent members of staff.

Recent closure of the Royal William Victualling Yards signalled the end of an era. In 1853 Dartmoor Prison received much of its food ration from the yards. It was also the establishment which maintained the Plymouth fleet. The following letter dated 22 August 1853 is from the governor's journal:

To Captain Superintendent, Royal William Victualling Yard, Devonport.
Having received a supply of pork and biscuits from the Royal William Victualling Yard Devonport, and anxious the accounts for the prison be passed through the books, I shall feel obliged if to you having the goodness to cause the charge for the said articles against the prison to be made out and forwarded to me at your earliest convenience.

The welfare of convicts' families was not uppermost in the minds of the prison staff. The following letter was sent by Governor Gambier to Captain White and is dated 27 December 1853:

I beg to forward the usual list of duplicates of 106 convicts embarked for Sea Park for tickets of leave in Western Australia, and for convicts embarked in the same ship for Public Works in the same place.
The whole number (106) left this prison this morning at about 8.45 for the combined officer escort to Laira for embarkation.

These letters give an interesting insight into the responsibilities of governors.

Towards the end of 1853 Mr Watts, the engineer, made an application for the post of foreman of works. The previous position of clerk of works was to be dispensed with. The post of foreman of works, and later senior foreman, continued for almost one-hundred-and-thirty years until 1981 when the post of chief officer 1 (works) was introduced at Dartmoor. The clerk of works' post was reintroduced to the prison, this being the author's role for some years. This involved overseeing some quite major works and also letting tenders for contractors to complete work at the then short-staffed prison. This staff-shortage lasted from the 1960s until the 1990s.

In 1853, goods, uniforms and equipment were in short supply for the military. The following letter testifies to this. It was written by Governor Gambier to Captain Shelton, commanding the detachment of the 93rd Highlanders, dated 2 December 1853:

I beg to acknowledge the receipt of your letter of the 1st Inst. I really regret that the oilskin leggings reported by you as being inserviceable, I have none in store to exchange for them. I have asked the steward to have them repaired and repainted which will occupy about a fortnight.

It is surprising that a few pairs were not in storage as one would have thought that with guards constantly on duty in freezing temperatures and wet weather, oilskins would have been kept in sufficient quantity. The prison leat which provided water from 1809 up until the 1990s would fill up with snow causing the water supply to stop. The convicts would then have to shovel snow from the ditches to free the supply. Staff and convicts would be soaked to the skin following such tasks and their treatment on return to the prison was atrocious. Cold cells greeted the convicts; warders were little better off for their superiors treated them very poorly. The unheated barrack quarters were icy, vault-like buildings and the clothing of soldiers, warders and convicts alike was totally unsuitable. Family life for the staff was truly terrible thanks to poor pay, scant medical treatment and the application of barbarous discipline.

Ironically, perhaps, Dartmoor Prison has been a meteorological weather station providing information about the weather on the moor since 1875. The records show that in 1853 there were only 157 days of fair weather and 208 days when rain or snow fell. During my service at the prison, 1968–92, part of my duties was as the official meteorological officer, having been trained at the Met. Office at Bracknell. I used to take the maximum and minimum of various temperatures, for example, wet, dry, ground, and provide details of cloud type and height, wind direction and speed, visibility, amount of rainfall, present and past weather, to name a few. Having checked various records it seems to be the norm at Dartmoor that there will be more than 200 days in the year on which precipitation is recorded.

Governor Gambier's report on 1 January 1854 is interesting reading regarding the use of gas produced by the prison gasworks. There were 364 gas burners in the prison, each of which consumed four cubic feet of gas per hour. This amounts to 1456 cubic feet per hour. Taking into account the terrible weather during the winter months, this works out at 10 600 cubic feet of gas per day. In order to make this amount of gas, the peat-cutters had to be very busy. Four tons of peat turf were consumed on a single December day, 2.5 tons for heating the apparatus and 1.5 tons for producing the gas. Gas produced during the whole year was 2 032 600 cubic feet, the average daily use being 5569 cubic feet, although in reality the gas heating and lighting was only used for seven or eight months of the year. Bedtime was at 8pm so after this time, no lighting would have been required. Gas consumption was recorded in 1853–54 as religiously as such details were kept during my tour of duty as electrical mechanical engineer. The use of fuels and any savings that could be made were always of paramount importance.

The combination of strong gales and buildings in excess of 80-feet high meant that during my time as principal officer (works), our roofs would blow off with shattering rapidity. The governor's report of 1 January 1854 goes on to say that repairs to the roofs were made regularly owing to boisterous winds and heavy snowfalls. When the author was a basic-grade officer part of my duty was the roofing repairs. At one time myself and a fellow officer had to erect scaffolding on what is now G-wing in order to replace some sheets which had blown from the roof. While we were doing so the wind increased and snow began to fall. Because of the extreme heights we did not use convicts to assist us and so, while they were safe and dry in their cells, we were battling against strong gales and a blizzard trying to hang on tight and repair the sheets while our ladders were lifted up by the wind.

The great difference between repairs made in 1853 and 1970 was that my colleague and myself were able to go home following our work to be greeted by a warm house and suitable quantities of hot food. The workers of the 1800s would have had no such luxury, instead returning to dark, cold barracks with a single peat fire over which to dry damp clothes. Not surprisingly, wet uniforms would frequently be worn the following morning.

On 20 February 1854 Governor Gambier was transferred to Portsmouth Prison; later to become Director of Convict Prisons. His deputy at Dartmoor, Mr Morrish, was promoted to replace him, and in his first governor's report in 1854, stated that conversion of the old war prisons into the convict prison was now complete, accommodating 1200–1300 men. But work in and around the buildings still carried on apace.

The prisoners would work nine-and-a-quarter hours a day in spring, one hour more during the summer and two hours less during the winter. This was their actual working day and did not include breaks for food or the prayers held in the chapel before and after labour. The days were incredibly long and it seems strange that the chaplain devoted so much time to prayer when the first thing on the convicts' minds was probably rest.

The author's notes taken from the records of 1853 detailing convict tranfers (above) and peat consumption (right).

During this time, prisons Nos 5 and 6 were not used for housing convicts. Prison No. 5 was a carpenter's shop and was also used as a flogging shop for the convicts, as detailed in a letter to Dr Campbell from Governor Gambier the previous year:

The director having ordered me to the infliction of corporal punishment on convicts Coates and Henry Bedford, I propose having it done at 1pm this day in the old carpenter's shop. I shall feel obliged by your presence.

The director has instructed me to check the fitness of the prisoners to receive his punishment before having it inflicted, I shall feel obliged if you will have the goodness to furnish me with a certificate, I also beg to inform you that I am this day about to forward to the director my report on the two suicides of Lewis and Honway, and thus feel obliged by your furnishing me with a certificate to each of these.

The doctor's report for 1853 continues:

One man injured as a result of a charge going off at the quarry, he had the presence of mind to throw himself on his face, his back and extremities were riddled with pieces of rock, he made a good recovery.

Convicts at this time were treated very carelessly by warders, who expected them to lift enormous blocks of granite and 'pick out' misfired charges of powder from holes bored for that purpose in huge granite blocks. The picking out process caused quite a number of explosions and, of course, many serious injuries and several deaths. The men were 'only convicts' and were required to perform these tasks without question, failure to do so would result in punishment. Work in 1854 also focused on reclaiming land and repairing buildings under the newly appointed Governor Morrish. Deputy governor was Captain Furlong, the medical officer was Dr Campbell. The chaplain at this time, Revd Dobie was assisted by Revd Batchelor. The military guard of enrolled pensioners continued to give excellent service, the military experience of these men giving incalculable benefit.

Old oakum store being demolished, early 1990s.

Convicts, it has already been established, worked incredibly hard at the prison. One particularly detestable task was the picking of oakum, used in vast quantities by the Royal Navy; the oakum produced at Dartmoor was sold to Devonport Dockyards for caulking ships' timbers in order to render them waterproof. The work entailed pulling apart lengths of old tarred rope with bare hands and separating the individual strands, a horrible job that made the hands extremely sore.

Below: *Author's notes taken from official records of 1854 detailing convict transfers (below left) and oakum picking and the value of farm produce in 1864.*

Disposals for 1854 included:-

To Western Australia	75
Bermuda	16
Millbank Prison	8
Pentonville	2
Portsmouth	1
Stirling Castle Hulk	33
Lunatic asylum	1
Exeter Jail	1
Discharged free pardon	2
" on Licence	495
Expiration of Sentence	1
Escapes	2
Deaths	24
TOTAL	661

Oakum pickers

Quarter ending	cwt - qrs - lbs
31 March 1864	57 . 3 . 24
30 June 1864	61 . 3 . 1
30 Sept 1864	35 . 3 . 24
31 Dec 1864	60 . 1 . 0

Rate @ £5.0.0 per ton = £53 - 19 - 9

Farm produce supplied to prison

7217 gals of milk	@ 6d	£180 - 8s - 6d
286 lbs of Butter	@ 1/-	14 - 6 - 0
63 lbs Lard	@ 10d	2 - 11 - 8
Celery 23 cwt 1 qtr	@ 15/-	17 - 8 - 9
Parsnips 27 cwt	@ 3/0½ d	5 - 4 - 7
Cabbage 326 cwt	@ 3/8d	59 - 15 - 4
Onions 49 cwt	@ 9/0	14 - 15 - 9
Turnips 159 cwt	@ 30/-	11 - 18 - 6
Parsley 4 cwt 1 qtr	@ 20/-	4 - 5 - 0
Spinach 3 cwt	@ 5/-	0 - 15 - 0
Lettuce 1 cwt 2 qtrs	@ 10/-	0 - 15 - 0
Chives 1 cwt	@ 10/-	0 - 10 - 0

Veg supplied to Infirmary 3 - 2 - 2

1339 Tons of Peat @ 9/- £602 - 11 - 0

During refurbishment in 1970 by trades' officers and convict assistants it was discovered that some of the heating flues leading from the basement hot-air chambers were not supplying as much heat as they should. Upon investigation, we found that nearly all the heating flues were stuffed with unpicked pieces of rope, with only a small passage available for the hot air to rise. Convicts working in the cells had a fixed amount of oakum to pick each day as an absolute requirement and consequences could be dire if the quantity was not met. Yet, it seems, they had removed the grating from the heating vent in their cells and put unpicked lengths of oakum down the flue. These shafts, 15 feet in length from the ground-floor cells down to the heating chamber were gradually filled up and the unpicked oakum had lain there, undisturbed, for more than one-hundred years. The author and No. 26 party had the task of removing it all.

Many escape attempts were made from Dartmoor Prison though most of the convicts were caught fairly quickly. The turf grounds were an area of the prison where many such desperate attempts took place. Here men worked in appalling conditions with no food supplied until specific quantities of peat had been excavated. When captured the men would be flogged and remain working inside the prison for all time, and made to wear the distinctive yellow-striped suit – known as e-man's dress – still worn by all escapees today, as well as cross-iron weights for a long period.

The years passed excruciatingly slowly for the convicts from 1853 to 1855. The farm was worked extremely hard but the convicts preferred working out of doors with the animals. The animal population was growing fast and the amount of land cleared was quickly sown with a variety of crops. These included hay, barley, oats, potatoes, carrots, turnips, parsnip, cabbage, mangold and swedes. The hay crop, which was fertilised by sewage from the prison, did very well in 1855 and made more than 90 tons. Barley, or 'bere', also made a good stock with 25 acres sown. The farm's progress is reflected in the value of the goods handed over to the prison steward, the total of which was £223.4s.9d. This considerable amount of money was won by sheer hard work by staff and convicts alike.

The author's notes taken from official records concerning livestock (above) and the value of goods supplied (right).

The year 1856 saw Mr Morrish continuing as governor while the new chaplain was Mr Holderness and the medical officer Dr Jones. The conversion of No. 1 prison was completed and the cells occupied by prisoners with mental deficiencies. Walking into the lower classrooms today one can see the cells still have the inner wooden cell door in place as well as the iron external wicket door.

These 'weak-minded' prisoners would be fed through the bars of the outer gate with the inner wooden door opened only for meals.

The visiting room at the prison, which is now the staff information room, was very small at only 12-feet square but the number of visitors soon petered out as transport to the prison was near non-existent and costs extremely prohibitive. It was common for convicts to serve long sentences with no contact whatsoever with the outside world.

On 20 April 1854 enrolled pensioners relieved units of the army based at Dartmoor Prison. These pensioners provided fire-power in the event of attempted escapes and problems with inmates. Warders and assistant warders provided the day-to-day control and discipline of the prisoners, the pensioners being there mainly to shoot escaping prisoners.

In June 1857 the enrolled pensioners were finally withdrawn after almost three years of distinguished service to be replaced by a similar number of Civil Guards – one superintendent, two sergeants and 24 privates. They created a new arm of the prison service which proved beneficial both to the prison and the immediate locality as they were mainly local men, most of whom were younger ex-servicemen but with experience under their belt.

During 1857 and 1858 removals from the prison proceeded alongside a heavy programme of works within the prison itself. In one year there were 221 transfers to other prisons and 28 to the hulk *Defence.* In total there were 52 convicts sent to the colonies of Western Australia, Bermuda and Gibraltar and 24 prisoners died at Dartmoor, a total of 325 removals. Today, 24 deaths in one year would cause an enquiry (in 1994 Exeter Prison was heavily criticised for five deaths in one year) but in the late 1850s the figure passed unnoticed. Bear in mind that convicts could, at any time, use bedding strips to plait into ropes and hang themselves from cell bars.

Labour continued along the same lines throughout the 1850s with the main tasks being land clearance, quarrying, farm work, and building and conversions. In 1856–57, 1775 tons of peat were cut and 160 tons of hay produced with barley and oats covering 37 acres. In 1859 the work included the conversion of the late boys' school in the barracks into officers' quarters. There were also alterations made to the east guard barrack alongside the prison boundary wall where the French and American cemeteries now stand. Deaths in 1859 were again very high at 23, a sobering figure when one takes into account that these convicts were fit, healthy young men on arrival at Dartmoor.

In 1861 there were again changes among the staff with Captain R. Best succeeding Mr Bannister as deputy governor, Mr Lineham being appointed chief warder and Mr Roome as medical officer.

Above left: *Former petty officers' prison, now the Roman Catholic church.* Above: *Part of the petty officers' prison, now used as a hospital and classrooms.*

(1857) (1858) Removals were quite high as well.

Transfers to other Convict Prisons	221
" " the Hulk Defence	28
Embarkations to Western Australia on "CLARA"	15
" " " " "NILE"	19
" " Bermuda on AGRA	10
" " Gibralter on HARRIA MITCHELL	8
Deaths	24
	325

The author's notes taken from the official records of convict removals 1857–58 and 1856–57.

1856/57 Roll

Removals to Millbank	13
Pentonville	1
Portsmouth	45
"Warrior" hulk	12
Stirling Castle Hulk	28
Defence Hulk	17
To Western Australia	12
Lunatic asylums	6
Exeter Gaol	7
Discharged Free Pardons	9
" on Licence	307
" Medical Grounds	1
" Special Grounds	6
Escapes	4
Deaths	34
Total Removals	– 502

Receptions   + 580

So Roll was 937
Less Removals – 502
Plus Receptions of 435 / +580
Total Roll   1015

The roll in this year stood at 1065, with 18 deaths recorded. On Ash Wednesday news of riots at Chatham came to Dartmoor but had no effect on the convicts who were subjected to such severe discipline and control. During this period the men were occupied with works on the prison buildings in general and the officers' quarters in the barracks. Repairs were made to the chaplain's house and farm buildings. The reclamation of land continued, as did repairs to the peat tramway and the bridge.

Work on the chaplain's house and the conversion of the former public house at Rundlestone into two officers' quarters was completed in 1861. In 1862 major repairs were undertaken on Princetown Church by the convicts. On 31 December the governor's report states that Mr Lineham had resigned in November after eight years as chief officer 1 at Dartmoor Prison, to be succeeded by Mr Seeley who had been superintendent of the Civil Guard at Dartmoor for five-and-a-half years. Mr Seeley's position was succeeded by Mr Norman, an assistant warder at Chatham Prison.

At the end of 1863, during which year there were 17 deaths, work included:
1. New heating apparatus for No. 2 prison.
2. Extensive repairs to tramway to peat grounds and also to the bridge which carried the peat wagons over the wall (now 6 party area) to the gas-house.
3. Repairs to the peat wagons.
4. Improved ventilation to No. 2 prison.
5. Turf-cutting, peat, to No. 21 and No. 22 fields.
6. Turfing at Watern newtake.
7. Repairs to fences at Rundlestone.
8. New work at No. 24 field.
9. Setting up new signal post at Watern.
10. No. 6 prison was divided with corrugated iron sheets to form a new penal wing.

The gasworks produced 2 309 110 cubic feet of gas. The Met. report for the year showed 78.3 inches of rain, 183 fair days and 182 wet days.

On 29 October 1864 Governor Morrish, who had served for ten years, was transferred to Portland Convict Prison and replaced by Mr George Clifton.

During the changeover, extensive repairs were undertaken on the governor's house. A fire started in the servants' quarters at the top of the house, spreading rapidly to the roof so that when Governor Clifton arrived the roof was well alight and burning fiercely, a dramatic welcome!

A convict working on the building desperately tried to extinguish the fire but became seriously ill due, presumably, to smoke inhalation.

In 1990 the author was a principal officer (works) and clerk of works for the new prison officers' mess which was being built in the old governor's house. During these alterations I had to examine the roof to check its structural stability and found enormous amounts of evidence of the 1864 fire. Many of the timbers of the roof had been burnt half-way up the roof, showing the severity and extent of the blaze. Instead of replacing all of the roof timbers, which would be normal practice these days, pieces of new rafter had been nailed to the sides of those burnt – presumably for speed as the new incumbent was on site. If the roof timbers had been completely replaced it would have necessitated considerable extra work on the eaves, soffits and gutters.

It must have been extremely embarrassing for the staff at Dartmoor Prison to have their new boss's house burn down on the day that he arrived with his family. One wonders what Governor Clifton's thoughts about the competence of his future staff were as he arrived outside the blazing house!

A large amount of ash from the burning roof had filled parts of the eaves and soffits and lies between the roof timbers to this day, a permanent souvenir of the drama. In 1990, when I examined the old servants' fireplaces which were still in use, I was amazed to see just how easily fires could happen. A piece of turf falling from the unguarded fire would cause the whole dry-as-timber roof to go up in flames. It is a miracle that further fires did not break out between 1864 and 1964 as the roof was rebuilt without any measures for prevention.

Clifton and his family were taken to the Duchy Hotel in Princetown until repairs were finished on the damaged house. The sketch below shows the roof of the governor's house illustrating how these temporary repairs – the same ones I discovered one-hundred-and-thirty-six years later (!) – were made:

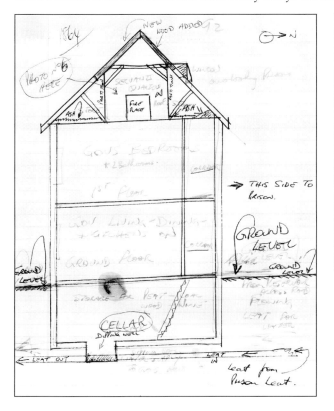

Left: *The author's sketch showing the servants' quarters in the roof of the governor's house where the fire of 1864 occurred.*
Above: *Photograph of the servants' bedroom where the fire started.*

In April 1864, 78 boys arrived from Parkhurst Prison and were put in B-ward of No. 1 prison. This is now the upper and lower classrooms and was, circa 1809, the old petty officers' prison. The two schoolmasters and one warder who accompanied the boys remained at Dartmoor Prison and became permanent members of staff. There was to be greater discipline employed than at Parkhurst and this was considered to be most beneficial for the boys. The records of work completed and carried out in 1864 show exactly how hard they did work, also the diversity of trades the convicts were taught. These included shoemaking, bookbinding and tailoring as well as more menial tasks such as washing, farming and oakum picking. The farm made a total of £2195.15s.10d. The roll of convicts on 1 January 1864 was 1060.

Some of the work completed in 1864 included the hard, back-breaking task of reclaiming the waste land. Penal cells were also constructed for No. 6 convict prison. The men in these penal cells were given tasks to complete within their rooms while sitting on a 12-inch round piece of wood about two-feet high, both ankles chained to posts concreted into the floor. There was no back rest. All this, along with poor food, meant that the penal cells were a place to be dreaded by even the hardest of convicts.

As a trades' officer, with six prisoners in his works' party, the author carried out refurbishments to the penal cells (now F-wing) in the 1970s. After removing the one inch of soft tar substance which covered the floor of the cell, the penal cell fittings were revealed, as shown in the sketches below:

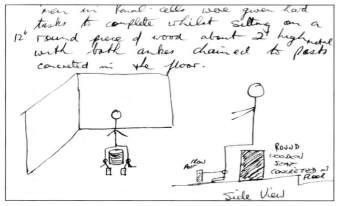

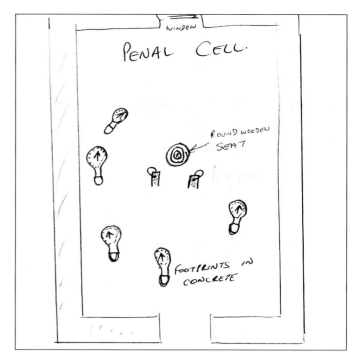

Above: *The author's rough sketch of a convict at labour in the penal cells, this usually entailed picking oakum.*
Right: *A sketch of the convict footprints in the concrete and the remains of the seat and leg-iron posts, found by the author during the renovations carried out by convicts in 1970.*

Beneath the tar finish we discovered several things. The seat concreted into the floor had been sawn off flush with the concrete and the two metal posts with the rings in them had been bent over to lie flat against the floor. There were also convicts' footprints embedded in the concrete which had obviously been wet when the cells were converted into penal cells. The prints had the broad arrow inset of boots worn by the men who made the cells in 1864, the same distinctive pattern used right up until the 1950s because it made escaping convicts so much easier to track in the soft ground of the moors. This broad arrow, or pheon, which was to become the distinctive mark of prison property, dates back to the reign of William and Mary when Henry Sidney, Earl of Romney, was appointed Master of Ordnance and was instructed to mark all government property. He chose the heraldic emblem of his coat of arms and shield, the pheon. The boots were studded as shown in the following sketch which was taken when I uncovered the prints in 1971.

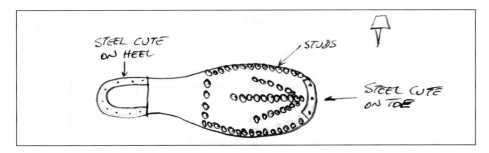

The author's sketch of a convict's footprint found in the penal cells, No. 6 convict hall (now F-wing). The concrete was laid during the conversion of No. 1 war prison to penal cells. The footprint was uncovered by the works' party during major refurbishment in the 1970s to provide better floors and plastered walls, modern decorations, lighting and heating.

During 1864 the reports on the good conduct of convicts were in excess of previous years, a matter attributed by the governor to increased vigilance by warders and severity of punishment.

When Governor Clifton arrived at Dartmoor, some new rules were brought into play. He considered that working in all weathers, snow, heavy rain, hailstorms, hot sun and gales, was a little too much for the invalid convicts. I have already emphasised how hard it would have been for these men, who were not physically strong, trying to battle in mud and rain high on the bleak moors. Clifton saw this unfairness. He also abolished evening prayer as it was not easy for the men to return from doing hard labour on the moors, march through the cold to the church and then sit through a service in a damp and mouldy uniform. This change was much appreciated by the convicts whose greatest desire after work was bed and rest.

In 1864 the state-of-buildings report declares that the buildings were now in fair repair. This statement does not carry the same connotations as the equivalent report would today for in the 1860s the buildings were still cold and damp. Indeed, many of them stayed this way until 1970 when refurbishment began in earnest. Even as recently as the late 1960s many of the cells had water running across the floors, and many cells could not be used at all.

The penal cells were completed by convict labour with artisan officers in charge. One of the works recommended to commence in 1864 was the construction of a visitors' waiting room. This is the building in the Agent's Square, just inside the outer arch on the right-hand side which provided shelter to visitors for the first time. Heat, however, was not on offer in the waiting room until 1970. Visitors were in any case few and far between in 1864. Women who were left at home by the inmates did not have money to travel all the way to such an inaccessible place as Dartmoor. Sentences were long and, as Dartmoor Prison was a 'lagging station', a term used to mean a prison holding only long-term prisoners; no lag ever served less than five years and usually double or treble that.

A second recommendation was a reception ward for new prisoners at Dartmoor. This enabled staff to assess a new prisoner on arrival with regard to his ability to perform labour and also his character to judge whether he would be an easy man to discipline.

Work on the farm was proceeding at a good pace in 1864 and there was no room for idleness. Indeed any laziness was severely punished. A report states that the crops that year were good and plentiful with 20 acres being cropped for the first time, eight acres of bog reclaimed and 1339 tons of peat cut and transported for fuel and gas.

Two new rules were imposed during 1864, the reduced rations of the New Diets scheme and the New Marks system. The former meant that convicts were worked as hard as before but with less sustenance to keep them going which in turn made it harder for the warders who had to make sure the men still made the same output. The second innovation meant that convicts were given marks for good behaviour. They would then earn release on licence but this would not be granted to any convict who had not been clear of being placed on report for six months.

Several days after the new scale of food rations was introduced 54 convicts were at work on the bogs. The men refused to work in protest at the savage conditions and were immediately marched back to the prison where they were placed on bread and water until they agreed to resume work. The majority of the men went back to their labouring after just a few days but ten of the 54 used threatening language and were put on further bread and water and placed in the penal cells.

On 24 October 1865 Governor Clifton left Dartmoor Prison after only one year of service and was replaced by Captain W.P. Stopford. Discipline under Governor Stopford was rigidly enforced, mainly because of three savage assaults on staff. A principal officer was knocked out in the peat bogs by a convict wielding a shovel and, but for the timely assistance of a warder, his life would surely have been sacrificed.

The new extension for the infirmary was, at this time, nearly ready for use and, in the adjoining barracks, wooden porches were to be fitted to the most exposed quarters. This was to prevent the fierce winds from penetrating the communal staircases and corridors.

The year 1866 saw a further 25 acres of moorland reclaimed and another 18 acres trenched. According to instructions issued by the governor, the day's timetable involved rising at 5am, prayers and moving to labour from 6.20–6.55am, the day spent labouring and eating a few meagre meals, reading, then bed at 8pm.

Additional clearance and drainage was carried out at No. 18 field, now called No. 19 field owing to the amalgamation of fields, and to Phillips Field where 'Old Cottage' repairs were carried out. Perhaps this old cottage was Rooks Cottage which was in that same area. A new shed was built by convicts at Baneck Meadow. Fields today have lost their identity to some extent thanks to the removal of walls to create larger fields, and often several changes of name as self-important farm bailiffs made their bid to establish themselves.

During this time, in 1866, there is the report of an accident at the quarry, something that happened at fairly regular intervals and was far from extraordinary:

There was a blast at the quarry and prisoners no. 7470 initials G.S. and 7073 initials J.W. received serious injuries due to a blast. 7470 G.S. died at the spot and 7073 J.W. an amputation of the right arm, a serious injury to the left arm and many other injuries. Dr Henry F. Askham.

The man with initials G.S. would have been taken to the prison church of St Michael and hurriedly buried in an unmarked grave, so any other record of him is lost for ever. The other convict, with barely adequate medical attention and the possibility of infection, would have been lucky to live.

Even in death, convicts' names were withheld; prisoners did not have names, just a number. There are cases where the terrible treatment went beyond atrocious. Men with only one arm were put into the harness of the carts so that the leather harness would wear away the skin and flesh on the amputated arm. These disabled men were expected to produce the same amount of work as their more able-bodied colleagues.

This event at the quarry was a common one owing to the use of black powder for blasting, a notoriously unstable explosive. The convicts would have to 'pick out' the explosives, as mentioned earlier, while the staff waited at a safe distance. It seems that the convicts at Dartmoor were treated as a disposable commodity by staff. Sixteen died in 1866 yet today there would be an outcry if there was one death alone.

In those days Princetown was a garrison town with the military in complete control of all the streets and the surrounding areas, including the prison estates. Even when the author first came to Dartmoor Prison in 1968 if a person from outside was seen on the prison roads – Burrator Avenue, Blackabrook Avenue, Heather Terrace, Moor Crescent (especially), Bellever Avenue, Woodville Avenue – all hell would break loose. We were trained to watch out for strange visitors at all times and would be out of the quarters like a shot to escort them off prison property, then the police would be notified.

Nobody came on to our prison roads and we always left our quarters unlocked. Many times when I was away visiting my home town of Bideford in North Devon it would be unnecessary to lock the house as all members of the staff would know you were not at home. It was a requirement to let the prison know where you were going to be on your off-duty days so that you could be recalled in case of emergency. The prison staff would watch over my house.

In the latter part of 1866, 15 cells were added to the penal cells for accommodating unruly prisoners. The farm also constructed two new clapper bridges on the prison estates which were absolutely necessary for staff supervision. The estates were criss-crossed by several water courses such as the Blackabrook river and the old Dock Leat (Devonport Leat) and open sewers to Tyrwhitt's land. The Dock Leat had to follow the contours of the land to enable it to flow so a substantial amount of it falls within prison land. There is also the prison leat which runs for about four miles on the prison estates.

The report for the year ending 10 January 1867 states that all juvenile convicts were to be removed from Dartmoor Prison. Twenty-seven were sent to Portland, one to Millbank and one to Woking. One wonders why only one went to Millbank and one to Woking but perhaps some compassion was shown and the boys were sent to these for family reasons; one can never tell, of course.

Granite steps and clapper bridges made by convicts enabled the easy movement of staff and convicts to their workplaces on the prison estates.

Also in 1867, eight prisoners were selected for prison work in Western Australia and were sent to Portland for embarkation, a practice usually carried out without consultation with the convict or his family. Indeed it would be strange to consult the convicts about anything at all. A letter would be sent to the family to inform them that their relative was in Australia. Imagine waking in the morning to be told, 'Hurry up and dress, you are going to Australia today.' Families would find out much later that their husband, father, son or brother was now thousands of miles away. The eight convicts selected for Western Australia were picked because, for many years, they had performed hard labour in the quarries and estates at Dartmoor. In reality they were treated like slaves.

A notable Dartmoor convict was a prisoner called John Boyle O'Reilly, who was transported to Australia in 1868 from Dartmoor Prison. He was sentenced to twenty years' transportation on 9 July 1866 for mutinous conduct whilst serving in the British Army in Dublin, and was sent to Dartmoor Prison.

Whilst in Dartmoor Prison it was said that he helped to reinter the bones of French and American prisoners of war who died there from 1809 to 1816 and had been buried in shallow graves. This is very possible because Captain Stopford, the governor of Dartmoor in 1865, had instructed the convicts to collect all those bones which had become exposed and then reinter them in two cemeteries, one for the French and one for the American prisoners.

This would have occurred for several years, and John Boyle O'Reilly would certainly have been at Dartmoor during that period. He was then sent to Western Australia and left London on 12 October 1867 on board the convict transport *Hougomont* (875 tons). This was the last ship to carry convicts to Western Australia. He was a staunch Republican and arrived in Perth on 9 January 1868 with 279 other convicts. One convict died during the voyage, near the coast of Africa, and was presumably buried at sea.

O'Reilly was still a prisoner in Australia and whilst in a road-making party near Bunbury, south of Perth, he managed to escape and stowed away on a ship which took him to America.

In later years (1876) he was involved in the planning of what is now known as the Catalpa Rescue, when a US whaler called the *Catalpa* landed in Australia on 27 March 1876. A pre-arranged jail break of six Fenians took place and these six prisoners were taken to the *Catalpa* lying offshore where they boarded her and escaped to the USA.

John Boyle O'Reilly became a famous author, publishing many titles in the USA, and was the owner of the *Boston Pilot*.

Chapter Five
CEMETERIES AND HARD LABOUR

During the governorship of Captain Stopford, from 1866 until 1868, the French and American cemeteries were established. The prisoners of war from 1809–16 saw nearly 1200 Frenchmen die and 271 Americans during the War of 1812.

Between 1809 and 1815 the bodies of these men were taken out of a gate near the infirmary (now the workshops) and deposited in a small building where the present prison stables now stand. This building was known as the 'dead house' and the bodies were stored there until buried at leisure by prisoners of war assigned to the task. The men were laid to rest in shallow graves in the field, known as Pig Field, adjoining the 'dead house'. Stories abound about the bodies being sent away for medical research but we have no solid evidence of this even though it was undoubtedly prevalent in those dark days.

The underlying granite on Dartmoor made deep graves an impossibility. The turf would be lifted off the surface and perhaps one-and-a-half feet of growan (decomposed granite) would be removed until solid granite was reached. The bodies would be put in the hole and covered with growan and turf. Over the years, especially between 1850 and 1860, pigs nuzzling the ground for roots would uncover French and American bones.

A Miss Rachael Evans who travelled widely in the 1860s noticed the bones shining in the sunlight, despite being some distance away, and reported the matter. Staff were already familiar with the situation having acted as guards to the convict parties all over the estates. Finally Captain Stopford ordered two areas of land close to the boundary wall to be enclosed by stone walls and made into French and American cemeteries. The bones of the dead were exhumed and the land dug up in the search for buried prisoners of war. It is a safe bet that many were missed and still lie today in the spot where they were buried by their fellow prisoners of war. The bones that were found were taken to the land set aside for the cemeteries and reburied in mass graves by the convicts. Two obelisks were cut and inscribed at the prison quarry, one for each of the nations. The inscriptions were the same on both, the only difference being the nationality on each:

> In memory of the American [French] prisoners of war who died between the years 1809 and 1814 and lie buried here. Dulce et decorum est pro patria mori. [It is sweet and glorious to die for one's country.]

Unfortunately the dates on the obelisk are incorrect and should, in fact, read 1813 and 1815. No American prisoners were held at Dartmoor until April 1813; the last Americans left around July 1815. The French obelisk should read 1809 and 1816. The cutting and installation of these obelisks was carried out by the convicts, a noble effort both by them and Governor Stopford. A field on the prison estate was named in honour of Captain Stopford. The marshes east of the prison boundary beside the Blackabrook river, the Devonport Leat and the Two Bridges road, which had been known as field No. 28, were now to be known as Stopford Marshes.

French obelisk in the French cemetery.

American obelisk in the American cemetery.

In 1987 the United States Daughters of 1812 visited the cemetery and handed over a bronze plaque which the author fitted to the obelisk. Bernard Sinclair, a member of my staff in the works' department, drilled the stone for the plaque to be attached.

On 15 April 1868 Captain Stopford moved on and was replaced by Mr W. Pitts Butts, who likewise did not stay long, and in 1869 moved to Chatham Prison, to be replaced by Major R.F. Hickey. Dartmoor Prison governors were often military men, at least 21 being army officers and several naval officers. Most of the subordinate staff had to be, by way of having the right experience, ex-military sergeants, WO1s and senior ranks in the navy. Even as late as 1924 an instruction was given to all governors to ensure that only ex-military men would be recruited as staff.

Circular distributed to all prisons giving priority to ex-servicemen to be employed as prison officers, 1924.

```
                              PRISON COMMISSION,
                                 HOME OFFICE,
                                 WHITEHALL, S.W.1.
No.1265.

(17491/141.FP.)                       11th February, 1924.


Circular to all Establishments.


     Governors are reminded of the Cabinet instruction that only
ex-Service men are to be employed as temporary officers, whether
regularly or casually.  Governors sometimes make representations
in favour of men who did some important civil work during the War
or who were exempted from Military Service.   These cases are
ineligible, as the definition of "ex-Service" is quite clear.  If
there is any difficulty in obtaining suitable men, application
should be addressed to the local Labour Exchange, who should be
asked to submit names after communication with the "Divisional
Selection Committee",   If it is found impossible to obtain
suitable men, non-ex-Service men can be employed, but the fact
should be reported to the Commissioners, with a statement of the
case, so that the Commissioners will be in a position to explain
the matter to the Joint Substitution Board.

     In order that the Commissioners may be aware of what non-
ex-service men are now being employed, Governors will be good
enough to submit the following particulars of each such case:-


     Name.

     Age.

     Date of first employment.

     Reason for employment.

     Reason for not employing an ex-Service man.



                              A.J.WALL.


                              Secretary.
```

Major Hickey arrived but brought little change in terms of the labour carried out by the convicts. The reclamation of land, tailoring, shoe-making, stone-cutting, building and farming carried on, with little rest for the convicts. In 1869 the livestock at the prison farm comprised 160 head of cattle, 31 calves reared and 14 horses. These horses were not used for ploughing as this was done by convicts. Small carts were pulled by the men, with a chain used to prevent unscheduled exits from the party. A break for freedom would always be followed by a rifle shot in the fleeing convict's direction and many convicts were shot in their attempts to escape. Staff who refused to fire at convicts would be summarily sacked and their family would be evicted from their government accommodation that same day.

There were 628 convicts in the prison on 1 January 1869, with many new arrivals during the year, including 179 from Millbank Prison and 87 from Pentonville. Six men were returned from Western Australia and on 31 December 1869 the total number of inmates was 997. The prison saw 121 men disposed during the year, a total of only seven deaths being surprisingly low.

It is interesting to look at the records for punishments at the prison. The director awarded 38 severe punishments in 1869 while the governor, who awarded such things as flogging, dietary punishment, loss of marks and the use of cross-irons and ankle-chains, subjected men to 1794 instances of punishment. The total was 1832 punishments, a frightening figure.

Punishments awarded, and the times of labour, 1869. Author's notes taken from original records.

In April 1870 Dr Askam, who had served at Dartmoor Prison for ten years, was transferred to the female prison at Woking. He was succeeded by Dr Power on promotion from Portsmouth. Captain Alexander who joined Dartmoor Prison as deputy governor was transferred to Portsmouth on 19 April 1870. His successor, Captain Bell, arrived on 23 April 1870. The chief warder, Mr Seeley, was nominated for superintendent Royal Gaol at Trinidad, his thirteen years' service at Dartmoor making him eminently suitable. Seeley had taken over the post at Dartmoor in 1862 having previously been superintendent of the Civil Guard for five-and-a-half years. He succeeded Chief Warder Lineham who had served in that position for eight years having been appointed in 1856, just six years after the opening of the prison. The post of chief warder was taken by Mr Courtman, described as an able and zealous officer. The chaplain in 1871 was James Francis.

Staff movements took place at regular intervals as conditions were difficult and the transferral system quite unfair. Subordinate movements during this time included 11 transferrals to other prisons and nine resignations, three men dismissed for misconduct and 11 discharged as unfit for service. The men who were transferred would have had no choice in the prison to which they were sent, this would have been at the whim of the governor. It was a take-it-or-leave-it situation. The nine men who resigned were probably escaping the difficult way of life on Dartmoor, working from 7am until 10pm with supervisors who were far from lenient. Or perhaps they had been on the receiving end of violence from the convicts.

Resignation was not to be considered lightly. A man who did so would be expected to leave his quarters that same day with all of his belongings and his family. If this was not done the furniture and the family would be moved into the street. Transport would have to be arranged, as well as somewhere new to live, a horse and cart being the most likely mode of relocation of possessions and relatives. There was no unemployment pay or Welfare State, to ease the transition. The men dismissed for misconduct, and those 11 dismissed as unfit faced these same problems of relocation and eviction.

In 1871 the farm report states that a drought had affected the land. Farm Bailiff Mr Ferguson died in the same year after a short illness. In his thirteen years in the job he had built the farm into a substantial enterprise so that it now covered a large area of named fields which included Old Flagstaff Field, Round Hill, Cemetery Field, Far Bog, Bairdown (Beardown) Field, Stopford Marsh, Bulls Field, Rundlestone, Barrack Meadows, Rooks Field and Rundlestone Newtake. Many of these carry the same names today, others have been changed over the years.

Staff are never mentioned in the prison reports so I feel that when a name is discovered it is worth noting. The building department carried out work on houses occupied by Warders Madden, Corney, Gamble and Oriel, also Principal Warder Wollway. These men would otherwise not have received a mention.

Nobody at the prison was ever unemployed and each day the convicts would be 'told off' for labour, even if it meant the digging and refilling of large holes. In 1872 work on eight fields was completed as well as work by masons on No. 5 prison, which was demolished in 1902. There were also alterations carried out to the governor's house with extensions being added to the south end. The farm bailiff received an office and there were alterations made to Rooks Cottage. A new gasworks was built, along with penal cells and a shed at the quarry. Repairs were made to Princetown School and the deputy governor's stables. C-ward at No. 3 prison and penal prisons 1, 2, 3 and 4 were recorded as having received work, as were the cook-house, bakehouse and wash-house, the prison chapel and RC chapel. The final item recorded for the year was work on the officers' mess room.

In 1872 the gasworks produced 2 678 737 cubic feet of gas. As ever, prisoners had to cut granite for road-making and building at the prison quarry, and again, seeing the amount of work carried out in a year, one realises just how hard these men were worked. Stone, both dressed and undressed, would have been produced in Herne Hole at the quarry by the stone-cutters.

In this year 13 convicts died, one of whom was killed, although it is unknown how. He might have been shot attempting an escape or killed by falling granite at the quarry, or an explosion. Sometimes three convicts a day were buried in unmarked graves at Princetown Church. In the same year of 1872, 79 officers were sent to the hospital either sick or injured, and it is also recorded that an incredible average of 30.7 officers were sick at home in the barracks.

Staff were rarely named so when they were, it provides a welcome opportunity to record some of their names from prison records.

The strength of the convicts was divided into three categories. This was used to determine the amount of work they could do each day picking oakum and 'cranking'. Cranking was the method by which the strength was built up as all the men were actually pumping was air. Category A meant that the convict must turn the crank 14 500 times and pick 11 ounces of oakum in a day. Category B was 12 500 turns of the crank and 8 ounces of oakum while C was 10 500 turns a day. These would all have a taken a tremendous amount of effort to complete and, if the criteria were not met, then a vindictive member of staff would punish the convict and tighten the braking system on the crank. As time progressed the convicts would become extremely fit which made the work somewhat easier. But as the number of turns rose, so the warders would merely tighten brakes further – it was a vicious circle.

Punishment for failing to reach targets ranged from dieting in the first instance to flogging with the cat-o'-nine-tails. The term 'screws' given to warders, which is a common term used today, is derived from this tightening of brake screws on the cranks.

In later years convicts were also used as 'pumpers', a similar idea to the crank but one that actually served a purpose. The convict was chained to a water pump connected to a spring below the prison quarry. The outlet from which the water arrived at the quarry was watched over by a supervising warder. If the water stopped or even slowed then a member of staff was despatched to the pump to wake up the convict! The photographs of the pump wheel illustrate how far from the quarry the convict was, so it would have been extremely hard work to force the water up to the quarry. The practice of pumping continued until fairly recent times, indeed, one man who worked at the prison prior to the 1932 mutiny can remember it well.

Tunnel under the road to prison quarry enabling convicts to get to the quarry without using public roads.

A convict would be chained to this pump and he would pump water continuously to the quarry from the spring below the quarry.

Below: *Letter written by senior foreman of works, Roy Duncan, to enquire about the prison pump (on page 48).*
Right and below right: *Details of pumps sent to Dartmoor Prison by the manufacturers.*

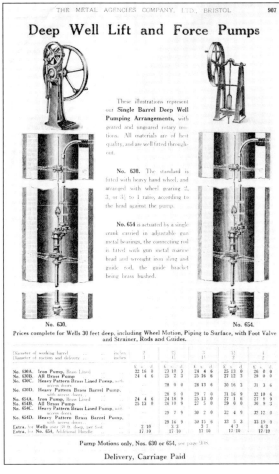

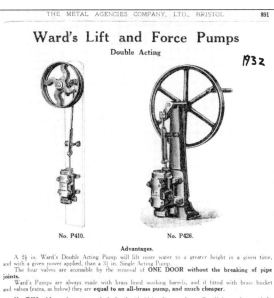

Home Office
H M PRISON
Dartmoor Princetown Yelverton Devon
Telephone 082-289 (Princetown) 261   ext

F. D. Outridge	Please reply to the Governor
Director	
British Pump Manufacturers Association	Your reference
37 Castle Street	
GUILDFORD	Our reference HRD
Surrey GU1 3UG	Date 9th April 1981

Dear Mr. Outridge,

Following our telephone conversation yesterday, I enclose for your perusaul the photographs which I have had taken from the open moor, in which the pump was situated. In fact this pump was situated on the prison farm estate and was apparently used to lift spring water from a natural water course to the prison quarry, some 300yds. away. The majority of the building stone for the prison having come from this quarry.

From local knowledge, it is known, that the pump, although still working, has not been in practical use for approximately 50 years. In fact one of our more ancient employees, who was born within a hundred yards of the pumps location, remembers it being in use 'when he was a boy'.

Whilst being grateful for any information which you may be able to furnish, the logical questions that occur to me are:-

(a)   What is the approximate age of the machine and the approximate period that it was available for purchase or manufactured.

(b)   Any knowledge of the manufacturers, Messrs Lambeth Brass and Iron Founders Co.

(c)   The lifting potential of such a pump.

(d)   The technical type and description.

(e)   Whilst my specific interest is in industrial artifacts, it would be interesting to know the approximate monetary value of the pump (if any).

(f)   Any general information which is gleanable from people in the pump buisness.

(g)   I would also be interested to know the likely colours industrially fashionable at the time of manufacture, or if it was practice to paint casts iron at that time.

The wheel is approximately 4' in diameter, the pump cylinder being 14" deep with a diameter of approximately 4". The cylinder being made from cast brass. The drive from the wheel to the cylinder being by crank mechanism. The whole thing presumably being reciprocating.

It is my intention to display the pump in a prominent place at the establishment and would like to be able to write an historical epitaph to this end, which is basically why I write.

The photographs that I have enclosed are copies and need not be returned to us. I would like to thankyou for your interest and look forward to your reply.

There has always been a strong link between Australia and Dartmoor Prison. There would have been hundreds of convicts transported there during early years and subsequently on public works' duty. The majority of these were sent to Western Australia, with some going to Van Diemen's Land (recorded in the 1872–73 DCP records).

The Western Australia depots at Albany, Vesse and Newcastle closed in March 1872, and Champion Bay closed a little later in August 1872. The latest date at which I have been able to trace convict movement from Australia is 1870 when it was recorded that 'six convicts received from Perth, Western Australia'. The last convicts from Dartmoor Prison were transported in 1868. When the above depots closed it put an end to transportation to Australia.

On 31 December 1872 the roll at Dartmoor Prison was 836 with the majority being sentenced to seven years. The minimum was five years, handed out to 11 of the men. There were 132 men sentenced to ten years, and six serving twenty years, with 11 sentenced to life imprisonment. This same year seven members of staff resigned, nine were transferred, four dismissed for misconduct and one discharged on medical grounds. There were three men superannuated and one death. The total number of subordinate staff changes was 25.

Above: *Author's notes of length of convicts' sentences at Dartmoor Prison in 1872.*

Right: *Notes of subordinate staff changes, together with the rainfall of 1872.*

During 1853 and 1854 there were only eight deaths at Dartmoor and two escapes, of which only one was successful. For the officer whose negligence was blamed it meant dismissal. No. 5 prison was declared ready for occupation, though it is now demolished and the base of it used for the gymnasium.

Staff quarters were under construction at this point. Thirty quarters were built in No. 1 block which was later known as E-block, then Devonshire House, before being demolished in the late 1960s. A convict hall was built and called No. 4 prison. Work was also carried out on the penal cells to fit the hard-labour cranks. This was an enormous amount of building and involved the cutting and dressing of vast quantities of granite which had to be carried from the quarry to the building sites. The amount of oakum picked during this period was 37cwts 3qts and 3 pounds, valued at £16.10s.10^{1}/$_{2}$d., which is a precise record.

Gas made between 1873 and 1874 was 3 381 985 cubic feet which was required to increase in following years with the ever-growing amount of cellular accommodation. No. 5 convict prison opened in 1873 with more than 300 cells. Dartmoor Prison cells always held one convict alone, unlike local prisons which often had three convicts to a cell. No. 5 prison was equipped with gas jets to light the cells and landings. One jet would be capable of lighting two cell tables with its valve being placed on the outside of the room for warders to operate at their convenience.

In 1873, 85 officers were sick with one, Warder Richards, being invalided out of service. There are also records showing that there were 11 deaths among the families of the officers in barracks, nine infants and two wives. The rainfall was extremely low at only 66.29 inches compared with 99.11 inches the previous year, which was around average.

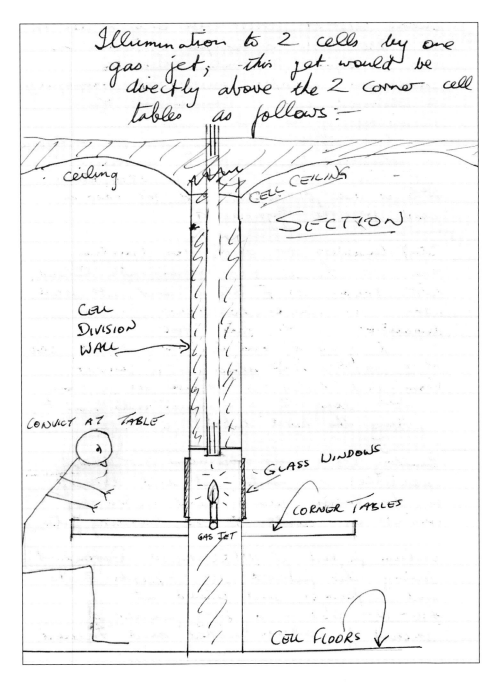

The author's sketch showing how to 'illuminate' two cells using just one gas jet; glass panels would prevent convicts getting to the flame. This gas jet would illuminate the corner table only and would not be on for long periods in the evenings.

Chapter Six
CONVICTS 1875–1900

The governor's report for 1874 records that five escapes were made, with one convict still at large in December 1874. The year 1874–75 reflected a year-on-year decline in convict deaths, with only seven being recorded. Rainfall continued to be remarkably low at only 80.46 inches, falling on 139 days. Prison life, however, changed little in terms of hard work and equally hard punishment. Severe punishment was meted out to 24 inmates from the director, while the governor ordered 1256! In total there were 1280 cases, with eight of these men being flogged by the dreaded cat-o'-nine-tails. This would have cut a man's back to shreds; the average number of lashes being 36, around 300 cuts to the back and shoulders would have resulted, along with myriad bruises. Any officer who has flogged prisoners agrees that it is a brutal punishment indeed.

Work during these years included banks of boundary hedges at North Hessary Tor and the trenching of waste land at Rundlestone. The Princetown and Rundlestone roads were coated with tar and work was carried out on the gasworks at the prison. There were 3 017 040 cubic feet of gas produced in the year ending 1874. There is also mention of work at a new area of the gasworks. The work begun in the previous report on prisons Nos 5 and 6 continued, and the prison also had a photographic studio built!

Work on the new quarters in No. 1 block was continued, as were the plans for Devonshire House which date from 22 November 1872 and are signed by E.F. Du Cane. The Princetown schools were the responsibility of the prison so the convicts were responsible for keeping them in shape. Work on the schools was completed in 1876 when the books show that 240 children were in attendance, all prison officers' children. Work was also completed on the churches, both the Church of England chapel and Princetown church.

The author came across a metal window in No. 4 prison, which is now the Church of England chapel, which enabled air to pass through but did not allow convicts in the penal cells to look out. A plumber called Rowe constructed these windows which were made up from curved pieces of interlocking metal.

Above: *A picture of a metal window which the author came across during refurbishment in No. 4 war prison cockloft (now Church of England chapel roofspace). This window allowed air in but prisoners could not look out.*
Right: *The author's sketch looking down on top of the window showing how it was made.*

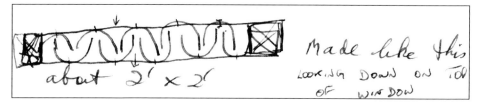

about 2' x 2'

Made like this looking down on top of window

A Civil Guard officer called Noster died in December 1874 and his funeral in Princetown was headed by the officers' band. Two officers were invalided out of the Convict Service. There were 24 changes of subordinate staff which included four men who made the difficult decision to resign while two were dismissed without choice. Ten men were transferred from Dartmoor, and five were discharged, either with notice or on medical grounds, and there were three officer deaths.

One of the dismissals was drink-related, the other was for trafficking, a most serious offence involving bringing in articles such as knives and tools in exchange for payment, an obvious danger to other officers' lives.

Seven convicts died in 1875–76, and there was one attempted escape which was foiled by the wife of an officer. The prison roll was at its highest with 972 convicts on 28 May and at its lowest with 914 on 11 January, a high roll year-round.

On the land, the convicts trenched, drained and fenced ten acres and the plantations were thriving well. The farm, growing yearly, now had 158 cows, 30 horses, 85 sheep and 18 pigs. In 1875 there were 216 days with rainfall and a significant amount of 4.15 inches on one day in January.

Assistant Warder Marshead was appointed to the quarry party which was a mark of praise. Men working at the quarry were constantly attempting to escape, injuring officers in the process, and only the best of the officers were sent there as a result. Incidentally, the last rifle to be fired at the prison was done so at the quarry in 1951 by an officer.

Prison leat (c.1806/9) showing water still flowing nicely when photographed in the 1980s.

Underneath the barracks there were badly constructed sewers, which had been built between 1806 and 1809 and over seventy years had deteriorated considerably. Corrosion had occurred through pressure of use and the fact that they were not constructed using sewerage pipes but instead with granite stones which trapped the sewage. There were also collapses in the system because of all the building going on in the prison and the heavy traffic passing overhead.

On 14 July 1877 Captain W.V.F. Harris became governor, taking over from F.H. Nooth. This year saw six deaths and two escapes while 234 men were discharged. On the staffing front there seemed to be problems. Resignation, as mentioned before, would not have been an easy decision, yet eight members of staff took the chance of finding new accommodation and new jobs, and resigned. Presumably something serious must have taken place to make eight men take this drastic step. Ten more officers were medically retired, with no reasons provided but it is fairly certain that some of them were injured – badly enough to prevent them from continuing with their duties.

During 1877 convicts trenched and drained 22 acres of the farm bogs, a formidable task. They also cut, conveyed and dried 300 tons of peat for use in the gasworks which had been expanded throughout the year. Amazingly, in view of the poor quality of the land, the farm produced 35 tons of swedes per acre. The convicts quarried huge amounts of stone, destined for a new piggery, the building of which entailed dressing the stone, hauling it to the site, then excavation and construction of the foundations, before finally building the piggery and fitting it out. Elsewhere, work on Devonshire House flats included the construction of five blocks of prison quarters which each contained six flats. This would have housed 30 families.

Prison piggery, built by the convicts and artisan warders.

Alongside all this, convicts cut and dressed 4700 feet of linear kerbing for Wormwood Scrubs Prison, plus work carried out on the prison officers' girls' and infants' school which was built in 1874.

On 28 May 1877 the prison held its maximum number of prisoners that year at 1003, the minimum of 938 being recorded on 17 January. The DCP made comparisons between convicts sentenced in 1877 and those forty-four years earlier in 1833, recorded in the DCP annual report:

1833 – 931 men sentenced to death out of a population of 14,328,477, i.e. 1 per 15,390.
1877 – 34 men sentenced to death out of a population of 23,904,108 i.e. 1 per 703,062.

1833 – 783 transported for life, i.e. 1 per 18,300.
1877 – 11 penal servitude for life, i.e. 1 per 2,173,100.

The above figures make one think about the differences between criminal treatment today and more than one-hundred years ago.

In 1877 there was a change in the position of deputy governor when Captain Arthur Hume was transferred to Portland, succeeded by Captain Frank Johnson. The Revd Frederick A. Gardiner was transferred to Woking Prison and the Revd Clifford Rickard took his place at Dartmoor on promotion from Portland Prison. The first-class schoolmaster Mr Brine was transferred as scriptures reader to Woking Male Prison.

In 1878 there were four staff resignations and six transfers. Nineteen men were discharged on medical grounds and three with notice, while two men died. It is easy to imagine the reaction today if 19 men were discharged on medical grounds. Conditions must have been appalling with work in all weather, poor food, poor pay and no suitable clothing. With rain usually falling on 200 days of the year there would have been little time to dry out clothing in the barracks with just one peat fire in a living room. It is not entirely surprising that so many men became ill.

The rainfall in 1878 was 106.81 inches with the highest measurement taken during January at 17.46 inches, the second highest month being November with 15.80 inches, and third highest August, at 11.91 inches.

Reinforcing the bad conditions suggested by the number of medical discharges in 1878 is the number of convict deaths in the same year, above average at 14. There were only two escapes and one was caught by a civilian near Plympton.

Plan showing how the inner gate at location 'A' was dismantled and then rebuilt at location 'B'. Walls were built enclosing the Civil Guard's dormitory and the day room for the Civil Guard and superintendent of the Civil Guard. The gate at location 'C' was formerly the outer gate, rebuilt in 1878. The movement of the gates from 'A' to 'B' also took place in 1878; this must have been an extremely traumatic time for the security staff.

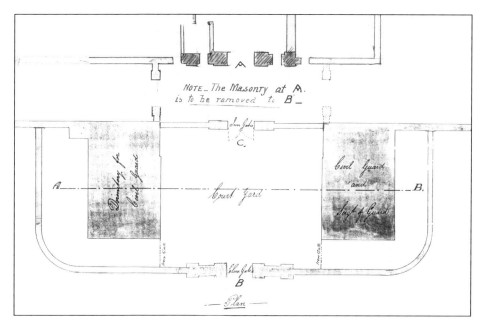

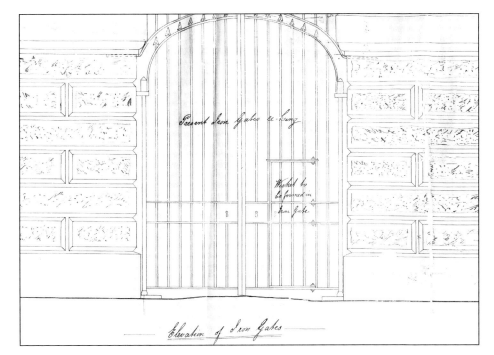

Left: *A sketch of the inner gate which, prior to 1878, was the outer gate.*
Above: *Photo of the now inner gate showing the 'VR AD1878' carved on the stonework, previously seen by the public when it was the outer gate but now unfortunately covered up.*

The plan of the prison courtyard (page 54) shows the project undertaken in 1878 to move masonry from different sites in the prison. The gate and all granite at position 'A', the main entrance to the prison, was demolished and the stone used to build a new gate and surrounding walls. A beautiful new granite gate was built at position 'C' and fixed with iron doors. The new main gate, position 'B', was fitted with wooden doors. The walls circling the diagram and joining position 'C' in the middle were new. Above the iron gate in the middle of the plan, convicts carved the date into the granite. This was a remarkable piece of work by the convicts who would have had to cut the stone in the quarry and convey it to the site, then heave each piece, weighing up to 15cwt a time, into place.

Other works recorded were workshops, the quarry, the farm, the deputy governor's house, prison leat walls, the old chaplain's house (note – not the vicarage), the south guardhouse, the No. 1 barracks reading room, Blackabrook House, the boundary walls, the officers' infirmary, the gashouses, the weighbridge, the walls on the Princetown roads, culverts to the Devonport Leat and playgrounds for the prison officers' schools. When listed like this the amount of work carried out in one year seems most impressive. Surprisingly in view of the amount of work carried out, there were no escapes and only ten convict deaths.

During 1879 a large amount of sand was screened at the prison quarry and used on the play areas of the prison officers' children's school which was built in 1876. This process was repeated for many years on a regular basis until sand and tar were used to stabilise the surface. Eventually tarmac replaced these. The roll at the prison officers' school was 122 boys, 150 girls and infants, one master, one mistress and nine pupil teachers.

An April epidemic of measles struck 150 staff, and 80 children were very ill in December as a result of the extreme cold. The winter was severe, causing many problems for the prison farm, building operations and the prison quarters in the barracks. Escapes during the year included eight at one time. All of the escapees were secured soon after and put into penal cells awaiting punishment. There were 13 deaths in 1879.

Owing to increasing pressure on convict places, work started on the extension of No. 4 prison to create an extra 161 cells and progressed extremely well with great effort from the quarry party who produced and dressed the stone. The convict building party had to lift the huge stones into place, with only wooden scaffold, ropes and pulleys available to help them move the granite into place. The artisan officers supervised the operations from start to finish. Many convicts were injured owing to ropes breaking and scaffold snapping which caused mayhem below.

During my apprenticeship in the 1940s we too used only wooden scaffold with ropes and pulleys but mercifully we were moving not huge granite rocks, but more manageable 45lb concrete blocks and lighter bricks and stones. The convict builders in the late 1870s were also kept busy building at the entrance courtyard to the prison, converting two blocks of officers' quarters into a stewards' and a foreman's works' offices.

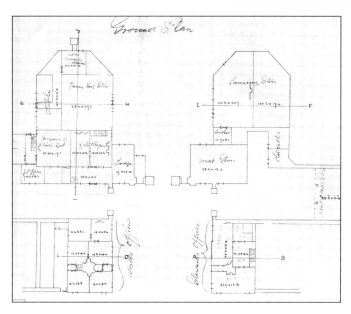
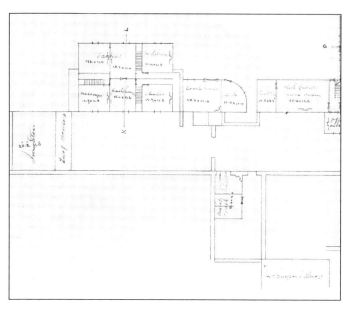

A very old plan showing just one main gate to the prison. This was located adjoining the lookout buildings of the old war prisons, with other gates at 90° from the lookout buildings to the now boundary wall, and inner walls of the old Civil Guard's buildings – marked Works' Offices on the left and Stewards' Offices on the right. This plan probably dates from around the time the prison opened in 1850.

An extension, since demolished, had also been built to No. 1 barrack block, the former officers' reading room. The oakum pickers were kept busy in their cells with around 54cwts produced. In No. 2 prison the corrugated iron cells required maintenance work.

The greatest roll during 1879 was on 29 May when 984 convicts were held, though this is far short of the greatest roll of convicts ever at about 1200. The smallest roll in 1879 was on 29 July when there were 951 inmates, all violent men.

There were five assaults made on staff during the year and on 12 November 1880 two convicts made a break from the quarry, refusing to stop on orders from the Civil Guard who duly opened fire. Both convicts were hit and dropped to the ground. One was seriously hurt but recovered from the gunshot wound, the second convict died from his injuries. A total of 17 inmates died during the year. Once again it was a very cold winter but the men had to go on working out on the land trenching and digging. Many civilian lives were also lost in the deep snow and drifts around the Princetown area.

The No. 4 prison was carried up to the second floor and work on extending prison No. 2 commenced, meaning that major projects were taking place simultaneously. The artisan warders and convict builders were becoming increasingly skilled, with the ability now to construct a cell block like today's B or D-blocks. To build such an enormous building out of granite, even today with modern steel scaffolding, hoists and air tools for the drilling, splitting and facing of granite, would be a tremendous achievement. To do it with only hammer, chisel and drifts to feather-and-tare the blocks was an example of utmost skill and devoted hard work.

In addition to the enormous cell blocks being built, No. 3 convict prison (now the old kitchen) was reconstructed with 136 cells on two floors, replacing the open-plan layout with hammocks that had been used by the French and American prisoners of war, from 1809 to 1815, when it was No. 6 war prison. Meanwhile, 1880 saw the penal cells of No. 6 prison being fitted with more cranks. The outside of the building was also fully repointed in an attempt to keep the worst of the weather out.

These illustrations were published in the Illustrated London News, *on 17 September 1910. They are as follows:* Top left: *The obelisk in the French cemetery.* Top centre: *The very old single main gate, as described on the previous page, and* (inset) *a spy hole through which prisoners in every cell could be observed.* Top right: *The building at Trena Bridge.* Middle: *The tailors shop.* Bottom left: *The old carpenters' shop.* Bottom right: *A convict on the 'pumps' i.e. the cranks, for hard labour.*

ILLUSTRATED LONDON NEWS

During this period work went on constantly on all existing buildings, Napoleonic and Victorian, in a bid to preserve them. The extreme weather conditions caused havoc to the granite buildings with water creeping between the granite blocks and soaking the centre of the walls. In winter the water would freeze and expand making the walls 'belly out'. The continuous freeze-thaw action, which is responsible for the appearance of Dartmoor's granite tors, had a devastating effect on the boundary wall. During the author's time at the prison, collapses were frequent as a result of the inner layers getting wet. The picture shows a hole nine-feet wide, six-feet high and two-feet deep. The fall of the stonework was attributed to frosts which occurred in the few days preceding. The joints in the stonework, consisting of sand and no trace of matrix, are totally permeable, allowing the water to sink deep before freezing and expanding. When a thaw occurs the loosened stonework falls away. This photograph was taken opposite D-wing, the shadow of which falls across the hole.

The freeze-thaw action on granite walls.

A catchwater ditch about six-feet deep was dug alongside the Dock Leat – now Devonport Leat – then lined with granite slabs. The first length of the ditch, built to protect Plymouth's water supply from sewage, was 1250 feet. During this time sewage was spread over the prison estate on the higher side of the Devonport Leat and the frequent rain would wash the effluent into it. The ditch was a tremendous achievement using only picks and shovels, with sledgehammers and gads to split the granite in order to gain a depth of six feet. While digging was carried out water would continue to flow into the ditch as it was below the water-table, so the convicts were working waist-deep in cold water much of the time.

The use of a hammer and gad in a water-filled trench must be one of the hardest tasks possible. The water softens the hands and the skin peels off while the abrasive action of the sledge soon makes blood run – excruciatingly painful. The same thing would have happened to the legs of the convicts as their rough fustian, or moleskin, trousers rubbed the surface of the skin off. The author can vouch for the accuracy of this from personal experience of time spent on the moors. The staff during this time at the prison were happier, however, than those watching over these convicts, Snider carbines at the ready to shoot any man who made an unexpected run for freedom.

While the ditch was being dug, work continued on other areas of the prison. No. 1 cottage, No. 5 barrack block, Nos 8 and 9 barracks, much of the boundary wall which had to be rebuilt, and the centre lodge which needed work, including replastering to separate cells. This was all part of the attempt to stem the deterioration of the walls. The superior staff would bully the subordinate staff who, in turn, would push the convicts harder and harder to complete these onerous and numerous tasks.

There were 17 cases of birching at Dartmoor around this time, 1881–82, and it is probable that these took place with the slightest excuse. Oliver Davies, a clerk at the prison, wrote a book called *Dartmoor Lyrics*, a collection of poems about the convicts. One was called 'The Assault' and included the line 'how old bloody moorland Jack's pretty pussy claws our backs'. A member of staff named Jack who lived on the nearby moors was responsible for the flogging of convicts with the cat-o'-nine-tails. The 'pretty pussy' was, of course, his cat-o'-nine-tails. It is a graphic reminder of the regularity with which 'the cat' was used during this time.

Four blacksmiths' forges were installed in sheds 170-feet long which are visible in the aerial photograph of the prison (see arrow, page 59). The blacksmiths would sharpen the tools used by the convicts to cut and shape granite for building Nos 2 and 4 halls. Two new gas-holders were also built to provide lighting for these new buildings, producing 4 315 800 cubic feet of gas which was piped to cells, village street lighting and prison staff quarters.

At the prison quarry 5000 tons of granite were cut and dressed by the quarry party for the use of the builders. But first, 650 cubic metres of earth and soft granite had to be removed from the quarry head to allow access to the good granite needed for the completion of the 136 cells in No. 3 prison. The quarry also produced 2200 feet of kerbstones for Wormwood Scrubs and 40 tons of shaped stone for Woking Prison. Farm irrigation works were also finished to prevent the sewage from entering the leat. The warders, after thirty years, were given a recreational hall.

During this time there were 100 convicts at the prison who were under twenty years old. It is noted in the records that a quiet and discreet warder supervising them was most beneficial to discipline. It also states in the records that there were only 11 convict deaths this year. One fell 40 feet from scaffolding while working on one of the halls. His registration number was E836, so that even in death he was not given the courtesy of having a name.

In January 1881 a blinding blizzard swept across Dartmoor and the prison and village were completely cut off for a long time. The governor ordered the farm animals to be killed, as required, in order to feed the prisoners and staff, as well as residents of the few villages nearby. Such gruelling conditions did not stop an experiment going ahead in the cells which involved painting the walls with luminous paint to save the lights. It failed dismally.

In 1882 the Princetown to Yelverton railway opened, mainly following the line of the old Tyrwhitt tramway. Prior to this the discharged convicts would have been marched to Ivybridge Station by experienced warders.

The records for 1882–83 show that the builders had completed the extension to No. 4 prison and the convicts had moved in. The extension to No. 2 prison, which would have 159 cells, had been taken up to the first floor. A recreation room and entrance building for the Civil Guard and gatekeeper were completed, and an additional room over a kitchen serving two quarters for staff was finished. This was in No. 3 barracks, now demolished. A block of quarters in the barracks and a block of quarters called North Guard were extensively remodelled and repaired, also both since demolished. Sixty earth closets were erected on the convict parade grounds (page 60).

Part of the old division wall between No. 2 prison and the infirmary was rebuilt and 12 new flushing cisterns and separate service to all water-closets were fixed. Three large windows were installed in the bakehouse, next to the boiler house, and the upright smokestacks for the heating apparatus and old underground flues were disconnected. The locks on No. 5 prison were remodelled and refixed.

Aerial view of the prison (in the prison archives, photographer unknown) taken before the 1932 mutiny, possibly 1920s. Note the gas storage tanks, upper left, and the blacksmiths' sheds.

A train stuck in the blizzard of 1881 – a famous photograph by Robert Burnard.

Plan of an earth closet. Convicts sat on a rounded wooden pole above a bucket partly filled with earth; after usage the buckets were taken out by the scavenging party and emptied on the prison estates.

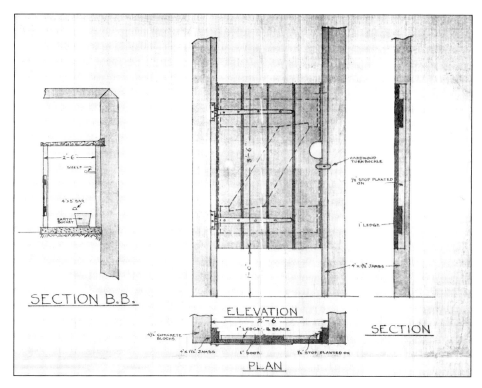

Plan of a few of these earth closets on A1 and A2 exercise yards, for use by convicts on these yards only.

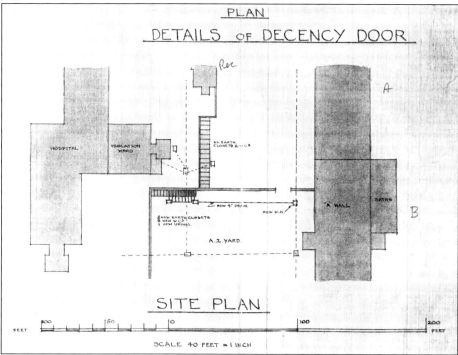

The quarry produced 20 tons of dressed granite for Portland Prison. Total granite produced for the year was about 4200 tons, all conveyed by handcart to the prison. A further 280 cubic metres of earth were excavated from the quarry head so that new granite could be exposed. During 1882 and 1883 the tailors, carpenters, blacksmiths, hammock-makers, shoemakers and all those involved with building, farm and land work, had a full programme and together completed a huge amount of work for the prison. In addition the walling party built a stone fence between West Rundlestone and the Far Bog Fields. These parties would also coat and repair the roads from Rundlestone to Princetown.

The prison gasworks produced 4 630 000 cubic feet of gas for cell, prison and street lighting. The year's supply of gas was not free of cost, however, and was in fact a huge expenditure for the prison. They had to pay the gas man £93 per year, the stoker £73.12s.0d. and the labourer £61. The total labour was thus £227.12s.0d. On top of this the cost of coal was £681.9s.1d. and lime for purifying was £17.11s.0d., while the materials for local maintenance cost £30.13s.1d. All of these expenses together meant that the prison spent £957.5s.1d. in one year, though this was offset by useful by-products. One year's gas-making produced just over 167 tons of coke for heating and 41 tons of breeze (cinders), which would be used on prison land and roads. Another by-product was tar of which 4916 gallons were produced to be used to waterproof buildings and to surface prison roads.

The chaplain's report for 1883 states that the roll for the prison was 1133 and his report on the prison officers' schools notes that discipline in the boys' school was very good. The girls' school discipline was also good but the lighting and ventilation were bad. The infants had been formed into a separate school and a new schoolmistress, Miss R. Hammett appointed.

Any services required at the school would be taken care of by the convicts. The scavenging party would be chained, in teams of six, to a cart escorted by guards armed with Snider carbines in case a convict did make a run for it. The party took kindling wood, coal and coke in the cart to each of the three schools where first they would remove the ash from the fireplaces and light new fires, then sweep and clean the classrooms before the children arrived in the mornings. Rubbish was taken to the prison dump beside the stables, and ash would be taken to Ashams where it would be spread on site. The dumping of rubbish by scavengers (later No. 3 party) during the author's time at the prison was continued until 1975 when the local authority introduced dustcarts to the area.

Scavenging parties 'servicing' the prison officers' infant, junior and senior schools. These schools were built in 1876 by convicts and the maintenance was carried out by the prison well into the twentieth century.

The hospital report for 1883 shows ten convict deaths, two recorded as accidents. The first man died from gunshot wounds a few minutes after arriving at the hospital. He had been shot out on the estates and it seems that it had taken some time to round up the party and march it back to the prison. The second man suffocated while cleaning out the bakehouse flues. He would have been sent up the large flues with brushes but obviously the fumes from the live fires proved too much for him. Again, one can imagine the outcry if two men died from such 'accidents' today.

There were six convicts with fractured limbs caused by stones falling from scaffolding. There were a number of injuries attributed to scaffold collapse and other building-site disasters. Staff were also injured. In 1883, 52 officers were on the sick-list; all of these were undoubtedly genuine as the doctor would have visited these men in their homes. Only four officers were invalided out of the Convict Service at Dartmoor, which meant they faced eviction in just as brutal a manner as those who had resigned. They would have had to vacate in one day leaving their homes available to any incoming members of staff. It was an unsavoury period in our history when a man who had served well at the prison for years was as good as thrown out.

On 9 January 1883 Warder Staddon was brutally assaulted by a convict, leaving him unable to return to duty until 10 March. An assault by convict A12 on Assistant Warder Bennett using a sharpened piece of hoop iron caused injuries to his face and temple. The hospital report also shows that there was a scarlet fever outbreak among the children of the warders which caused many problems. Total hospital admissions amounted to 727 throughout the year, with one fatality to convict RF258 who choked to death after bolting his food.

In 1884 there were 46 officers on the sick-list and five officers invalided out of the service. One of these men was a plumber named Rowe who had been a faithful employee for many years. Rowe lived in the old gatehouse with his family but they would all have been evicted to make way for his successor.

There were four serious assaults on officers during the period 1884 to 1885. Warder Mays was badly injured with a violent blow from an iron jumper on 22 September 1884 during building works. An iron jumper was a chisel used to make holes in the granite. Feathers would then be inserted into the hole and a tare used to force the feathers apart and split the granite. Mays was in hospital for a long time.

The author's sketch of a hole cut in a granite block using a hammer and a jumper. Pieces of metal, called feathers, were then placed in the hole and a tare was placed between the two feathers and hammered home. A large granite block required several holes to be cut along its length, and then the tares were hammered home progressively.

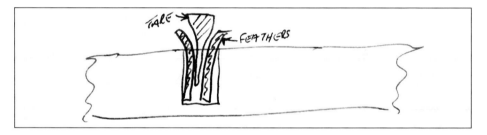

On 22 July 1884 prisoner A1940 escaped from his work party during dense fog. Despite being immediately pursued by staff he made good his escape and remained at large until 28 July 1884 when he was recaptured and handed over to the police. He was subsequently tried at Exeter and given an extra five years.

The extension to No. 2 hall was completed and the building ready for occupation. This was a massive job involving the cutting and trimming of granite at the quarry, transportation to the site, the building of a five-storey cell block and then the allocation of convicts to cells. The whole job was carried out by convicts and overseen by artisan warders. The extension to the prison officers' schools was also completed and a new classroom for the girls' school and one for the infants' school finished.

During 1884 and 1885 the chaplain's Bible class averaged 48 convicts per night. This was an excellent turnout bearing in mind the work carried out through the day. This year also saw 502 convicts moved to other prisons. The educational standards of convicts were recorded as follows:

Those who could read and write well	*217*
Those who could read and write fairly well	*192*
Those who could read and write a little	*76*
Those who could read a little only	*12*
Those who could write a little only	*6*
Those who could neither read nor write	*5*

MONEY EARNED/SAVED

Works

Convicts worked 311 days per year we start with 365 and deduct 52 sundays which leaves 313 days then deduct Xmas day and Good Friday — this leaves a working year of 311 days labour per year.

Value of Labour of convicts for the year ending 31-3- 1885, as follows:-

WORK	DAILY AVERAGE	NO OF DAYS	DAILY RATE	VALUE
PRISON BUILDINGS	282 $\frac{281}{311}$	87,983	2s 0½d	£9008/4
MANUFACTURING	169 $\frac{25}{311}$	52,584	1s 7d	£4195/10/4
FARM	262 $\frac{117}{311}$	81,599	0s 10½d	£3569/6/5
PRISON EMPLOYMENT	178 $\frac{196}{311}$	55,554	1s 8d	£4635/19/6
TOTALS.	892 $\frac{308}{311}$	277,720	AVERAGE 1s 8½d	£21,406/7/5

None effectives (unemployed convicts)

	CONVICT DAILY AVERAGE	NO OF DAYS
Sick	48 $\frac{141}{311}$	15069
PUNISHMENTS	9 $\frac{142}{311}$	2941
NOT TOLD OFF TO PARTIES }	4 $\frac{270}{311}$	1514
LOST TIME RAIN/SNOW ETC }	98 $\frac{72}{311}$	30550

a tremedos amount of time lost to the extremly bad weather at Dartmoor in 1885 of 30,550 days

The author's notes taken from a prison document recording how much convict time was spent on the four main areas of the prison. A convict was required to work 311 days per year; 365 days less 52 Sundays is 313 days, less Christmas Day and Easter Day, leaving a full year of 311 working days. Time was recorded as years and fractions of. Looking at the centre line of Totals, it states 892 years and a fraction of 308 days, that is 892 x 311 plus 308 which equals 277 720 days worked in the year ending 31 March 1885. Below it gives the ineffective time of convicts during the year as a total of 50 550 working days lost due to various reasons, mainly bad weather. In 1885 a vast amount of building work was taking place, and large granite walls cannot be built in wet weather. These figures are useful in determining the number of convicts employed – the 277 720 days worked divided by 311 gives a total of 893 convicts. The total of 50 074 ineffective days means 50 074 divided by 311 giving a total of 161 convicts not working, add to this the 893 convicts which gives the Prison Roll of 1054 for 1885.

The following medical report illustrates what the medical staff thought of the convicts. The report begins by saying 'there were few events calling for special remarks, however...' and this follows:

1. *Diarrhoea amongst prisoners reduced due to spring water to be used for drinking instead of bog line* (this was the Mis Tor line).
2. *Two deaths during year, prisoner H335 died a week after a stone fell on him.*
3. *Prisoner J910 died, in the opinion of the medical officer, 'of injuries received from a feigned suicide attempt'.* [One wonders what would have happened if it had not been a feigned suicide attempt.]
4. *In January 1885 an explosion of dynamite on the works caused more or less serious injuries to five convicts, four have returned to labour after treatments to their injuries, one is still progressing in hospital.*
5. *The medical officer died in 1884 after a short illness.*
6. *Forty-six officers sick during year, four were invalided out of the service.*

It seems strange that the report begins by saying that these events are of little importance, when they appear to be quite the opposite.

The year ending 31 March 1886 shows incredibly low numbers of staff in comparison to today. Yet these men had to be on the alert and vigilant at all times, mindful of the convicts who were constantly trying to injure them and their own superiors who were seen as sadistic in their efforts to try and catch out junior officers and, of course, catch the governor's eye.

Staff employed were as follows:

2 governors (1 deputy)
2 medical officers (1 deputy)
1 steward
6 clerks
6 teachers
1 chief warder
1 foreman of works
1 farm bailiff
10 principal officers
35 warders
59 assistant warders
15 cooks/bakers
1 engineer
1 gas man
1 stoker
5 labs/cow men
27 Civil Guards
176 total

In 1992 there were about 300 members of staff who had the benefit of modern equipment such as radios, security lights, better clothing and, of course, inmates who were relatively harmless.

The works' list for 1885 and 1886 was very long. This year it was reported that one officer fell from scaffolding and was seriously injured. Thirty-two officers received medical attention at the hospital, two died and nine were invalided out of the service. The year ending 31 March 1887 saw the completion and opening of the large bath-house alongside new 2C, though there was no heating and indeed no hot water for the bath!

Blackabrook House, five blocks of six quarters, was under construction for staff. The twine-spinning shed was erected around 1886 and survived until 1945; it is now the site of the main store.

A total of 23 officers were on the sick-list, probably due to hard work, lack of heating and cramped conditions, with so many large families all crammed in together. Convict G53 stabbed Assistant Warder Horne with a pair of scissors and the wound was recorded as slight though it would be a nasty injury by today's standards.

At the end of 1888 a block of 30 flats in Blackabrook House was completed, and the plans for this major building make interesting reading. For each six flats (two per floor on three floors) there were only six water-closets and the same number of wash-troughs. Six families, often with six members in each, would have been sharing these troughs for washing clothes. There were only two boilers for heating water so on wash-day all the families would get together and light the peat-boiler fires. They would then dip out the warm water to the six troughs. There were only two communal benches for the six complete families.

The 1888 report on the prison officers' schools states that in the boys' school handwriting, slatework and paperwork was good. The girls' school reported the same except that spelling was not as good in the 4th grade. The roll showed 101 boys, 72 girls and 76 infants, a total of 249 officers' children.

In 1890 there were four serious assaults on officers with an average convict roll of 887. The greatest number held was 1187. There were 105 convicts found guilty of violence and two attempts at escape, 66 convicts were guilty of idleness and there were 832 breaches of regulations. Three convicts were restrained by leg-irons and two were flogged, while 660 were sentenced to dietary punishments. Many convicts served the whole of their sentence without being placed on report, but in 1890, 710 men lost their privileges.

The following letter, sent to a local newspaper by an ex-warder, concerns the shooting of convicts in 1890:

Sir,
In your issue of today I see strong language is used as to whether the circumstances of the case should not be tried before a court of assize respecting warders shooting and killing runaway convicts.
During my experience as warder, when a warder had charge of a party of convicts he was responsible to the governor to bring them to the prison dead or alive, as his situation was at stake, and the governor was liable to a fine of £50 should a prisoner get away.
If this were not the case a great many warders would, no doubt, be very careless with convicts. Goodwin whilst at large was a wolf in Mr Balkwell's clothing. Whilst we consider the evidence of the guard we must not lose sight of the fact that the excitement was great. The warder did not know but there might have been 23 or more going to run off. When the ranks are broken it affords a much better chance for others. I have known both warders and Civil Guard dismissed from the service for not stopping them in days gone by. It was always recognised that the Guard was armed for the purpose of preventing escapes while flanking in and out, and the warders who are in immediate charge of the convicts are armed to protect themselves as best they can when attacked, which is not a strange occurrence.
On one occasion a convict got away from his party and while I was in pursuit of him I fired over his head and frightened him, so he dropped in front of me and exclaimed, 'I am shot'.
I took him back and I was told that I ought to lose my situation for not shooting him. If I had lost my situation I should have been afraid that I could not get another after completing twenty-five years.
I felt that I would rather be free from such a service as it is dangerous, because one's life is in the hands of the greatest criminals of the land – I hope that in future our warders and Guards will be well schooled and drilled for these duties.

This warder had probably been retired for some years and it is likely he had been in the service in 1850–75, having served twenty-five years.

During 1890 a Black convict called Denny, who had been extremely troublesome over the years, was discharged from Dartmoor and taken to the train. He was sent off and forgotten. On 17 August 1890 an alarm was sounded in the guardroom (now the gatehouse). The alarm had been triggered by someone walking into an alarm wire on the wall somewhere between the semaphore station (now the CIT builders' yard) and the gate. A fast search ensued and convict Denny was found hiding in the clocktower gate (at the bottom of the drive). Questioning established that he had broken into the prison with the intention of killing the chief officer and setting fire to the buildings. At the assizes he received a substantial sentence and eventually died in prison.

At the barrack quarters they were fighting a losing battle against the elements in a waterlogged building 1550 feet above sea level, with an annual rainfall of 100 inches per year. Work continued on the prison officers' schools with a new porch being built on to the infants' school and a partition constructed to divide the schoolroom. A new skylight and Buchan ventilator were fitted to get rid of foul air in the classrooms. Within the prison the storekeepers' No. 1 store had its roof stripped and reslated. The quarry continued to provide all the granite needed for building work. In addition 20 tons of spur-stones, runners and sills were dressed for Holloway Prison. Wormwood Scrubs was sent 12.5 tons of

Convicts returning from labour at the bottom of the main drive, on their way back to cells; armed Guards were always in attendance.

kerbstones and new keysafes were made at the blacksmiths for Gloucester and Swansea prisons.

There were 12 convict deaths this year. An intake of 500 was received during the year 1892–93 and the roll was 1008. There were also 47 officers under medical treatment. On 1 March 1893 there were 275 prisoners still listed to be sent to Western Australia for public works, though this was many years after transportation had ended and these men would never actually be sent.

In 1894–95 a very wet summer followed a long, cold winter. Ten consecutive weeks of frost interfered with building works and farming. In the enclosed workshops, however, production was moving along at a tremendous pace as many articles were manufactured. The building programme included the No. 2 barrack quarter being reconstructed. A new reservoir filter and a beautiful arched underwater storage tank for drinking-water were installed. The tank held 90 000 gallons of treated water. The gasworks had a new gas-holder fixed and a five-inch gas main leading to the centre of the prison installed. In the storekeepers' office a new boiler was fitted and circulating pipes were laid for warming. Ironically, the central heating system in the prison was far superior to anything in quarters. During the author's ten years in prison officers' quarters in Princetown (Burrator Avenue) there was never any heating system except for an open coal fire. Central heating was finally installed as a requirement to relinquishing the lease. Today the council-house tenants at Burrator Avenue have warm insulated homes. This was denied to all the prison officers who occupied the houses for almost a century.

The years 1894 and 1895 saw some rebuilding on the boundary wall. There were 17 new buttresses built to try to hold together the collapsing wall, and 164 linear feet of concrete coping was laid on top of the wall to try to prevent water from soaking it. New drains were laid in the kitchen, and the new extension to the wash-house (laundry) and passage to the Church of England chapel were both completed. The footpath from the prison to the prison officers' schools, previously coated in spread stone, were relaid with tar concrete. The footpath from the old cottages at Government Row to the church was similarly treated, a tremendous improvement. The schoolyards were also paved.

The year saw 475 receptions and 506 discharges at the prison. Several self-contained quarters at Burrator Avenue were occupied, 58 officers were on the sick-list and 11 were later invalided out. One man died. The Bishop of Exeter visited and held a confirmation in the prison chapel when 22 candidates were presented. There were heavy snowfalls in the year 1894–95 and 2386 convict days of labour were spent on this alone.

Convicts preparing sheep for the various shows entered c.1900.

Convicts with horses and the prison bull, c.1900. The author was told by an old prison officer, c.1927, that the bull would only allow one convict to touch him, the convict would hum a tune to the bull and all was peace and quiet.

Convicts on the hard-labour harrowing party on the prison estates; horses were not used for this or other farm tasks. The photograph dates from around 1900.

This was a terrible year for the families living in prison quarters without heating or water supply. Small quarters and large families made life particularly frenetic, and superiors were less than helpful, making the task of prison officers more difficult during this bitter period. The threat of assault was always present as vicious supervisors felt the need to put those below them 'in their place'.

The year 1895–96 saw six quarters for warders and four quarters for principal officers completed as C-block on Garcia Avenue. This was in addition to eight new quarters for principal warders and ten for warders being started. These would be B-block and part of D-block in Burrator Avenue. The recently built filter beds and underground water tank were ready for use pending analysis. Eight new gas pumps were fitted and 1760 feet of two-inch pipe laid to feed the lamps along the main road from the prison to the schools. The prison supplied gas for all the lights in Princetown village including the Jubilee Lamp in the square and the other roads, from Tavistock Road to A-block, for example.

Above: *The Jubilee Lamp was lit by gas from the prison.*
Right: *Convicts on the hard-labour party clearing granite from the prison fields c.1900.*

The go-ahead was given for the construction of 61 new separate cells for E-hall and a site was cleared on top of the old bathing pond. A new 12-inch pipe was laid to convey the old French Leat away from this site. This has had many repercussions over the years during periods of heavy rainfall as the diameter of the pipes proved insufficient, causing the basement of the new block to flood many times. Eventually, in 1988 the author undertook the building of four-feet high walls around the sump in the basement floor which were sufficient to prevent floodwater from entering.

On Christmas Eve 1896 three convicts named Carter, Martin and Ralph Goodwin made a break for it from an outside working party. Carter, who was undergoing a sentence of twelve years' penal solitude, was shot dead as he ran. The second man, a notorious convict called Martin, was struck down by warders' staves and taken. Ralph Goodwin eluded the gun guards and ran away. It was later discovered that he had broken into a house at Postbridge where he stole enough food for three or four days. It seems incredible that he then made his way to Tavistock and committed another burglary, collecting further supplies of food. Goodwin must have come close to Princetown in his journey from Postbridge to Tavistock. He then made his way to Devonport and broke into yet another house. After three days' liberty he was arrested by a policeman named Priestwood, aided by a sailor called Thorne from Devonport Naval Base.

Devonport Watch Committee presented Thorne with a guinea. The inhabitants of Devonport were to recognise Priestwood's action. One can imagine Goodwin's thoughts on seeing one of his escape party shot down and the other struck to the ground, then his mad dash across the relentless moors pursued by police and warders with Snider carbines, then back across the moors where armed warders were searching for him, all the way to Tavistock and finally Devonport, where he was arrested and sent back to Dartmoor. He would have received punishments and extended penal servitude.

Housing for warders was moving along at a great pace with 13 warders' and eight principal warders' quarters completed – B and D-blocks on Garcia Avenue (now Burrator). The granite for these houses was split at the quarry and carted to the site by the prisoners. In 1897 the prison walls were again causing trouble and 25 additional buttresses were built. Another 1167 feet of coping were added to the wall to keep it dry internally.

The Church of England chapel was installed with a hot-water boiler and circulating pipes built for warmth during services. Sheds were built on the prison yards for the large gang of convicts engaged in stone-cutting to try to keep them from being exposed to the severest of weather conditions. This was more to ensure that cutting was not interrupted than as a sign of kindness to the convicts. A new shed was built on the artisans' yard to house the engine, saw and mortar mills. This would be essential to house the stocks of timber needed by the huge convict labour party of carpenters for making roofs, floors and doors. The twine shop, a most important building, also had a new boiler-room fitted and a new roof put on. Ventilation was improved so that the twine shop could carry out essential work for other prisons.

A new cell block was planned which would become the punishment block and called E-wing (this was still the segregation unit in 2000). Excavating the foundations on the site, the area of the old bathing pool for French and American prisoners of war, involved digging 15-feet deep to remove the top peat. Then decomposed granite would have to be removed so that the foundations could be built on solid granite. The project took two to three years to complete.

By now the prison schoolmaster had five separate schools set up in various halls. There were 480 convict discharges and only 358 receptions. The farm stock in 1897 included 84 horses and ponies, 140 cattle, 541 sheep, 42 pigs and 30 fowl. There were four acres of land reclaimed and 13 acres dug over and reclaimed for the planting of 18 840 trees.

In 1897–98 there were 313 prisoners discharged and medical receptions amounted to 275. There were only five deaths, which was the best on record since 1867–68, despite a flu epidemic with 98 cases. Some of the old barracks were demolished and other improvements were carried out at the Civil Guards' blocks. Along with 96 officers on the sick-list, there were two deaths and 11 men invalided out of the service, a traumatic period indeed.

It is recorded that Civil Guard officers were paid £60 per year; the form on page 71 shows the employment terms for Portland Convict Prison which would have been the same at Dartmoor at the turn of the century. The £60 per year would have been worth a lot less in real terms because of fines for even the most trivial offence. It would be impossible in those days even to go one month without incurring many fines, as was explained to me by an old Dartmoor warder, Cyril Penny, who worked there at the time of the 1932 riot.

Officer Cyril Penny joined in 1928, serving at Durham, Dartmoor and Exeter. Officer Penny's father, Gilbert, joined the Convict Service in 1888, serving at Shepton Mallet, Wandsworth, Bristol, Leicester and Exeter, retiring in 1921 with thirty-three years' service. Officer Penny's brother Charles, who joined

Officer Gilbert Penny, who joined the Convict Service in 1888. He was the father of Cyril Penny, also a Dartmoor Prison officer, who joined in 1928.

in 1921, served at Manchester, Plymouth, Leeds, Chelmsford, Birmingham, Parkhurst and retired in 1951 with thirty years' service. Officer Penny's eldest brother, also called Gilbert, declined to join the Convict Service despite strong encouragement from the Prison Commissioners. He joined the army in 1915 as a private and finished up as a lieutenant colonel on the staff of Field Marshal Montgomery in the Second World War, after an extremely long military career.

Officer Penny and the author had many conversations sharing information about the early Convict Service which he had gleaned from long talks with his father.

In 1898 and 1899 new quarters were built for the chief officer, the foreman of works and the farm bailiff. The parsonage in Princetown also had six storm-sash windows made out and fitted, and in 1899 the church was enlarged.

More of the illustrious Penny family. Top: Officer Charles Penny, brother of Dartmoor Officer Cyril Penny. Officer Charles Penny served in many prisons including the old Plymouth Prison.
Right: Officer Cyril Penny, fourth from left at Exeter Prison.

Officer Cyril Penny at Wakefield Training School, 1928, extreme right.

Employment Daily average of Prisoners in 1898

Manufactures

Basket makers	36
Carps – Smiths – Tinners	3
Knitters	2
Mail bags	13
Oakum Pickers	18
Sack makers	2
Shoe makers	24
Tailors	59
Tent maker	1
Twine makers	23
Daily average	181

Farm

Breaking stones and bones	25
Crofting	62
Gardening	22
Haymaking	10
Manuring	4
Reclaiming Land	35
Walling party	9
Sundries	43
Daily average	210

Buildings (average no of Daily Prisoners)

Building	19
Carps	13
Excavators	15
Labourers	98
Plasterers	1
Plumbers	1
Quarrymen	35
Wood Sawyers	1
Slaters	2
Smiths & Fitters	24
Stone Cutters	46
Daily average	262

Prison

Baking for Prisoners	8
Cooking " "	13
Cleaning + Jobbing	53
Gas Making	5
Nursing + attending Prisoners	47
Repairs to clothing etc	13
" " Shoes	6
" Prison utensils	5
Books	2
Stoking Prison Furnaces	13
Washing	
Daily averages	166
Non effectives Sick	45 (aver
Punishments	9
Not Told off	4
Daily average	58

Grand Total ie Roll

Man.	181
Farm	210
Buildings	262
Prison	166
Non effective	58
	877

Roll of Prison 1897/98

(M)

PRISON COMMISSION,

HOME OFFICE, WHITEHALL, S.W.

16th December 1899.

In reference to your application, dated *13th October 1899* you are informed that you have been appointed *a Civil Guard* in the Prison Service, on probation, and you are requested to report yourself to the Governor of *Portland* Prison, for duty as soon as possible.

You are required to join the Prison at your own expense, and to undergo an examination by a Medical Officer of the Establishment Should you not then be considered medically fit for the Service, your appointment may be cancelled.

Your commencing rate of salary will be £ *60* per annum, with other emoluments, as under :—

(a) Uniform.
(b) Quarters, rent free, or, subject to certain conditions, an allowance of £9. 2s. per annum in lieu.
(c) Medical attendance (by the Medical Officer or his approved substitute only) and medicines for yourself, and, in certain circumstances, for your family also.

There are no other allowances of any kind, nor will you be permitted to receive any gratuity or perquisite whatever.

The salary and allowances of your office will not begin until you have actually commenced your duties ; nor will you be entitled to uniform until the confirmation of your appointment after the period of probation.

You will be liable to deductions from your salary, by way of fine, for neglect of duty or misconduct.

You will continue on probation until your appointment is confirmed or your engagement terminated. Your engagement will be terminated if, from observation of your general abilities and attention to duty, you are not considered likely to become a satisfactory Prison Officer ; or if, for medical reasons, you are not considered fit for the office to which you have been appointed on probation.

You will not be permitted to take any other occupation or employment, or to hold without special permission any other public office ; and it will be part of your engagement to give such instruction or assistance in any trade with which you may be acquainted, as may be directed.

You will be required to act in strict conformity with the existing Orders and Regulations, and with such as may from time to time be established.

On joining the Prison you will be required, if married, to produce your Certificate of Marriage.

To *Mr. W. A. Abbott*

(B) *You are requested to communicate at once with the Governor of the Prison to which you have been posted stating the date on which you propose to join for duty. If you do not communicate within a week, your appointment is liable to be cancelled.*

Above: *An official form, dated 1899, confirming the appointment of a Civil Guard at Portland Prison. A similar form would have been in use at Dartmoor.*

Left top, middle and bottom: *Taken from official records, the author's hand-written notes show the average number of convicts employed in building new halls, working on prison duties, as cleaners and in the hospital, manufacturing and on the farm in 1898.*

Chapter Seven
CONVICTS 1900–1931

On 3 May of the new century Governor W.H.O. Russell joined Dartmoor Prison, replacing Captain Johnson who had been in office since 1890; a long term indeed.

That year, a serious attempt at mutiny took place on the peat bogs. The convicts working there were subjected to appalling conditions with insufficient food and totally inappropriate clothing even though they had to work in water which could, at times, be waist high. The men would have to march from the prison to commence work then back to the prison for lunch, following which they would again march out to the bogs and then back again in the evening. The mutiny was quickly quelled and the three ringleaders were punished severely. No mention was made in DCP records as to their punishment but presumably it was most severe, as a warning to others.

Owing to this tiring march to and from the prison twice a day, the convicts would arrive to work on the bogs already exhausted. In order to combat this it was proposed that work on the far bogs should cease and a light railway should be laid on the track of the peat railway in order to convey prisoners to their labour. The labouring party, meanwhile, was to be distributed to other areas such as the quarry, stone-cutting, excavating and building. The principle laid down was that 'all labour men to the building party and quarries, second-class and light labour to the industrial parties'.

This indicates that unfit second-class and light-labour convicts (invalids) previously had been put on the excruciatingly hard labour on the far bogs. These men must have been relieved to be relocated to the industrial party in the warm workshops. The full-labour men sent to the quarry and building parties must also have been glad not to march out to the bogs.

At this time two convicts ran away from two different farm parties. One ran off in broad daylight and the other in fog but both were captured speedily. A third convict broke out of his cell at night but was detected at once and locked up again. This was a particularly futile bid as warders patrolled the prison blocks and the man would have been punished by having his sentence extended.

In 1900 monks from Buckfast Abbey visited the prison and were well received. On 28 February 1900 the chaplain, the Revd Clifford Rickards, retired due to ill health after twenty-seven years as a prison chaplain, the last twenty-one of them at Dartmoor. Thousands of men must have attended his services over the years.

Under the Prison Act of 1898 a Board of Visitors was formed, and is still with us today. There were 11 members on the board and, as from 1 May 1899, the powers of the Directors of Convict Prisons to award corporal punishment passed to these boards. Failing them, the power would be passed to a stipendiary magistrate. There were to be two classes for which a flogging could be awarded; one was mutiny or the incitement to mutiny, the other gross personal violence to an officer of the prison.

Some convict parties c.1900.
Top left: *The gardens party.*
Left: *The basket shop.*
Above: *Outside the blacksmiths' shop, with an armed sentry and lookout post in the background. This lookout would be able to see signalling posts from the estates in the event of trouble.*

Prisoners at work in the twine shop c.1900.

The author talked to very old prison officers who had served at Dartmoor in the 1930s and who would, of course, have been under the control of older officers who served at the turn of the century. They told me that gross personal violence was whatever an officer wanted it to be. The knocking off of a prison officer's hat was an act of gross personal violence, for which a prisoner would be flogged. At this period, under the new rules, the privilege of being able to talk on Sundays was awarded to fourth-stage and special-stage prisoners.

The prisoner's 'stage' was marked by a symbol worn on the right arm of convict dress:

First stage – Awarded after a minimum of six months' good behaviour and marks; this was distinguished by a green horizontal bar about an inch long and a quarter of an inch wide.

Second stage – After another six months' good behaviour a second bar would be added.

Third stage – Again after a suitable period and the gaining of sufficient marks a third bar was added.

Fourth stage – A green triangle was worn on the outer clothing when suitable marks had been attained. These awards could be put back if so-called bad behaviour took place.

Special stage – A single green bar was added beneath the triangle and thus the maximum was reached. On reaching the special stage, a convict was transferred to the special wing, known in my early years as D2 specials.

These special-stage men had privileges which included the right to eat outside their cell in association with other prisoners, play cards, darts and even snooker. There was a limited number of cells so men would not be granted special stage until a vacancy arose. The staff in DII specials were older, experienced officers, as a normal officer from another wing might cause problems by enforcing too much discipline. This wing ran excellently. The men had a lot to lose so behaved impeccably, making the life of the staff easy.

In 1900 the south side of the Protestant chapel roof was reboarded, felted and slated and the side windows glazed with lighter-coloured glass. The shoemaker's shop had improvements made to the gas lighting by removing overhead arrangements and fixing pillar lights to the floor. Guard bars were made and fitted to the three windows of the officers' mess kitchen. Four pale-blue sentry boxes were made and sited on the prison parades, one of which can be seen in the photograph of General Booth leaving the prison in 1911.

General Booth of the Salvation Army leaving the prison after performing a long service for the convicts in the Church of England chapel. He was a fairly frequent visitor to Dartmoor Prison and in a local newspaper, dated 31 January 1906, a good account is given of the service in the chapel. He visited again and gave a sermon on 25 January 1911.

The boundary wall had again been causing problems and 18 buttresses were built in an attempt to stave off total collapse. A run of cement 572-feet long was put on to try and prevent water seeping through. To prevent prisoners from attempting to climb up downpipes on the prison buildings, cement was used to fill in the gaps behind each pipe so that it was flush with the wall. The convicts would be unable to get any grip on the pipe and thus there would be no route this way.

The dressing of granite for the aqueduct to convey the 12-inch sewer pipes across a low portion of prison land to the sewage works was completed. The aqueduct was 275-feet long and comprised 11 arches. Each arch has a 20-feet span and ten piers. The excavation of trenches for the 12-inch and 9-inch drain-pipes was completed and 4000 feet of pipes laid. Eight manholes were built, seven lamp-holes formed and the whole lot back-filled.

Above: *The rebuilding of the boundary wall in the 1970s. This wall gave the prison many problems during this period.* Left: *The 11-arch aqueduct on the prison estates which carries the main prison sewage across a low depression to the sewer works.*

During the year ending 31 March 1902 the conduct of officers had been good, with the exception of two. On 11 September 1901 five convicts were tried for mutinous conduct on the bogs and for inciting others to misbehave. The ring-leaders were flogged and others involved sentenced to long terms of dietary punishment and forfeit of prison marks. There were six assaults on officers and five convict deaths during the year. Three cases of corporal punishment were noted, two using the cat-o'-nine-tails and one using the birch. The Board of Visitors held monthly meetings throughout. Sir Massey Lopes resigned as chairman of the Board of Visitors on account of ill health but remained a member.

In his annual report the governor noted the end of another era:

> I *regret to report the retirement of Mr John Hodge chief warder of the prison after a continuous service of upwards of forty-three years. He has been an excellent officer and his courage in dealing with some of the worst criminals in times of great difficulty has been most praiseworthy.*

Chief Warder Hodge was an exceptional officer of the prison as the report overleaf illustrates. This was taken from the *Prison Officers' Magazine* dated January 1913.

In 1902 an extension to No. 6 prison was underway. Concrete foundations were put in and the footing walls of 12 cells built. Convicts at the prison quarry completed the granite dressing of the stones for the basements. The work was relentless. Drawings were supplied to the stone-cutter and dressers at the quarry, to the builders in the prison, the works' department supervisor and head office. Frantic work would take place at the quarry to be sure that the stone-cutters party was ahead of the building. The builders would specify which stones were to be cut first and the date on which they would be required. So, regardless of labour

Chief Warder, John Hodge, a truly remarkable officer whose story was told in the Prison Officers' Magazine *January 1913.*

Article taken from the Prison Officers'
Magazine *ref. Chief Warder John
Hodge.*

THE PRISON OFFICERS' MAGAZINE. January 1913. 5

DARTMOOR PRISON LIFE.

THE career of Mr. John Hodge, ex-Chief Warder of Dartmoor Prison, whose funeral took place at Princetown on Saturday, November 30th, will no doubt be interesting to many Officers who have visited Dartmoor on Escort.

For more than 43 years the ex-Chief Warder has had no inconsiderable share in moulding the discipline of the Convict establishment on the Moor. A fine specimen of manhood, about six feet in height, Mr. Hodge began his career as an Officer in the Boys' Reformatory at Exeter in 1856. He was specially recommended by the late Earl of Iddesleigh (then Sir Stafford Northcote) for employment in the Convict Department which he entered in 1858 as an Assistant Warder. Possessing great tact and perfect control over those men placed in his charge, his promotion was rapid. With the exception of one year as Chief Warder of Parkhurst Prison, his whole time has been spent at Dartmoor, under twelve Governors and fourteen successive Deputy Governors. The years 1858–64 were known as the "dark days," and Convict Prisons were perfect pandemoniums.

To Prison Officers those years under the old system represented a "reign of terror." The convicts were well fed, in fact, over-fed, and their doings caused public opinion to call out for a new method of dealing with them. Colonel Anderson succeeded Colonel Jebb, and the system was completely altered, and the Dietary Scale was reduced to two-thirds. Bread and cheese and beer were regularly supplied on Sundays. In each hall and ward large baskets are placed for the waste bread. This was given to the pigs. Convicts working in the bogs took their luncheon with them. This consisted of an ample supply of bread, meat, and pudding, and where they crossed the Tavistock road the Moor children came with aprons and baskets. As each man passed he put in all the food he could spare until the baskets could hold no more. With such good living the convicts became strong, impudent, and lazy. Scarcely a week passed without a mutiny, and assaults on Officers were of daily occurence. When formed up on parade it was customary for the convicts to have a stone tied up in their handkerchiefs. On one occasion six Officers (including the Deputy Governor) were borne off to the infirmary, having been "floored" by the convicts with stones. Of course, such doings could not long be tolerated, and the advent of Colonel Anderson marked the change. The cartoons of *Punch* at this period exactly expressed the niceties of the situation. But the introduction of firmer discipline caused at first a lot of trouble both on the works and in the gaol; whole parties mutinied, and once every man in a particular hall refused to leave chapel to go to his cell.

Twenty of the ringleaders were put under restraint and flogged—nine from one party—and a few were sent to other Prisons. At night the convicts were lodged in Association Wards. Four of these wards contained 80 men each, another held 120, divided into bays with six men in a bay. They lay in hammocks side by side with only one Officer in charge of the ward. He was locked in with the men, and did Night Duty for a month at a time. Howlings, screams, and yells uttered night after night continuously for the especial benefit of young Officers, served their purpose, for several had to leave the Service. The present system of convict location is too well known to be described here. On one occasion Mr. Hodge was in charge of a night ward when the gas suddenly went out. One man with a hard sweeping-broom struck him a terrible blow on the head. He staggered, but was able to close with his assailant, and held on to him until relief came. Frequently, when "relief" came round the whole of the men in the ward would "howl" the Officer out. On several occasions Mr. Hodge was assaulted. When a Warder, he was in charge of a stone-picking party; two men in the party standing near a stone heap commenced pelting him with stones. He so vigorously replied with stones from another heap that he conquered them both and they were glad to desist and allow themselves to be handcuffed. Another time a powerful convict nearly garroted him, but sinking suddenly on one knee, the man lost his hitch, and was himself captured, taken before the Director, and severely punished. Once, when Principal Warder, in charge of a party at Rundlestone, a dense fog arose; when the party assembled, and the word "to march in" was given; three men attempted to escape—one from front, one in the centre, and the other from the rear. They were all shot; two were lamed, but the third managed to get as far as Mis Tor. At another time, whilst the parties were at work, a terrific hailstorm came on. Two men bolted through the chain of sentries and made for Rundlestone. Mr. Hodge pursued them, and caught up both within a mile, and brought them back handcuffed. The railway from Plymouth to Tavistock was not then in existence, and discharged convicts and Officers on leave had to tramp across the Moors to Ivybridge. Convicts for Dartmoor were brought to Plymouth, and from thence taken to Princetown in wagonettes. Formerly on discharge each man was supplied with a prayer-book and hymn book. These were generally thrown away on getting clear of the village. Many notable prisoners have been under the immediate charge of Mr. Hodge, including the Bidwells, the great bank forgers, one of whom was in the Prison Infirmary for nearly three years as an assumed cripple. He was also

in charge of the first batch of Fenians, and was specially selected (with five other Officers) to take the "famous seven" to Portland, where they safely handed them over.

Mr. Hodge attributes his great success in dealing with convicts "By using tact and affable firmness, and not continually nagging or barking at the men." As the Chief Warder, one must be the head, centre, and eyes of a Prison. He has to be continually amongst his 1,000 men, to advise them and try to keep them right. He has more to think of than arrangements for the discipline of the Prison. Day or night, he must be ever ready to answer questions. A curt reply from him does no good, but leaves a sting behind. His profession is never learned, the last week or last day even bringing some new point of duty into prominence. An old ex-Prison Officer relates the following, as shewing

the quality of Mr. Hodge's iron nerves : "Whilst in charge of the Shoemakers' Shop at Dartmoor, a rising had been planned among the very lawless set of convicts then engaged on that work. The signal was to be given by a particular convict making a rush at his Officer, and stabbing him with a shoemaker's knife. At an apparently favourable opportunity the attack was made, but Mr. Hodge, turning quickly, saw the man's intention and, calmly putting one foot on a stool, faced him, and leaning forward said : ' Don't be a fool. Stop that, you can't do much. Go on with your work.' The situation was saved ; no rising took place."

A very serious outbreak occurred on a dark day in November, 1864. About 300 men were at work in Round Hill field, about a mile and a half from the Prison. Signs of disaffection had been visible throughout the morning. Suddenly

a couple of leaders of the movement stepped out in front of the others with their spades, and called out : "Three cheers! Come on, boys ; don't be cowards. Now's your time!" Of course, there was great uproar and confusion, and 13 men responded to the call, armed with picks and shovels. These formed together and marched to where Mr. Hodge (then an Assistant Warder) and another sentry were posted. When within six paces the former called : "Halt! no further. Another step, and we fire!" The gang halted. They were next ordered to fall in. This they did, and then were immediately disarmed by the two Officers, one presenting his rifle while the other took the tools away from them. Assistance then came, and the men were marched back to the Prison. Each of the ringleaders received a flogging, and the two

Officers got credit and promotion for their pluck.

To very few Officers has such a reference as the following appeared in orders :—" The Governor is very sorry to have to notify the retirement from the Service of Chief Warder Hodge, who is about to be superannuated under the Age Clause after a continuous service of upwards of 43 years. He is sure that all Officers equally with himself will receive the intelligence with great regret. Chief Warder Hodge has rendered excellent service, and has discharged the onerous and responsible duties of his office with great zeal, tact, and fidelity, and in a most efficient and satisfactory manner. The Governor begs to thank him sincerely for the great help and assistance he has afforded him in all matters during the time he has been Governor of Dartmoor."

availability, or the terrible weather, the stones had to be ready and transported to the building site, altogether a mammoth task. At the same time there would be many other building works going on at the prison, also requiring stone.

Meanwhile new stables were being constructed outside the prison walls and these, too, exhibit the sheer expertise of the labourers. They were true craftsmen and the buildings were of excellent quality. I do not think that enough emphasis has been placed on the work put in by the men who constructed the impressive buildings at Dartmoor – a tremendous feat.

During the 1971 refurbishment of G-wing, the author examined the building work that was carried out between 1901 and 1904 and found the levels to be exact and the quality of building superb. The governor's report, which stated that building had 'commenced' on No. 6 prison, also contained details of another project. The Princetown 1901 drainage scheme was nearing completion with 6560 feet of drains excavated. Sometimes, in solid granite, the drains were laid and back-filled. Seventeen separate manholes were built and 13 lamp-holes were formed. During the progress of this monumental task, considerable amounts of granite were encountered during excavation. In order to have the correct falls the drains were sometimes excavated to a depth of 13 feet. It is easy to imagine the effort it would have taken to dig trenches to this depth. These drains are still used by the prison today and have since had all the drains for Princetown added to the system.

It was reported at one point in 1901 that 4300 tons of granite were quarried and 2900 tons split into various sizes, dressed and carted to the prison for additional dressing and incorporating into the building. To gain further access to granite at the quarry about 900 cubic yards of earth and surface rock were excavated from the quarry-head and wheeled-back 60 yards. At the same time a new boiler-room for the bath-house was completed and a circulating boiler added. Cylinders were installed and all the necessary hot and cold pipes laid on to this new building. Astonishingly, all that this hard work merited in the governor's report was, 'new boiler-room for bath-house built and all equipment installed'.

A 1300-gallon-capacity tank for gas-water (contaminated water resulting from the cooling process) was installed which required a large excavation to be made, as well as the preparation of yet more granite. The necessary pumping equipment and pipework was installed to allow for the gas-water to be spread over and mixed with earth. This would then be carted away and spread to allow the gas-water to soak into the ground again. The governor recorded the operation succinctly as, 'gas-water tank built and pump installed'.

The Chapel of St John Vianney was built in 1914 at the end of Woodville Estate, but is now a private house. Before this, Roman Catholics used Hisworthy House at the top of Burrator Avenue, the home of the priest, which had its own self-contained chapel. The plan shows a few additions to this house for the benefit of the Roman Catholic priest.

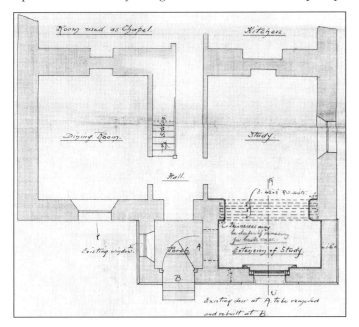

Structural alterations were made to the Roman Catholic priest's house to allow room for a bigger study. Again the quarry produced all the basic building materials before the house was painted and papered throughout.

Improvements made to the prison's heating system were a major undertaking. Two boiler houses had to be built and the boilers installed, from which four-inch circulatory pipework had to pass through hundreds of walls, reaching all parts of the complex before returning to the boilers. Once up and running, the boilers had to be continually maintained and fed fuel which had to be delivered and could never be allowed to fall short even in the worst of weather. Much of the pipework carried out on this job was still in operation in 1971 when new heating coils were provided.

Alterations were made to the chaplain's house and new drainage was installed and connected up to the new Princetown drainage scheme. Buchan ventilators were made and fitted to the roof of the Civil Guards' day and night-rooms. A new bell-cote was made and fitted to the gatekeeper's lodge on the left-hand side.

Improvements were made to No. 4 convict prison (now D-wing) by the intro-duction of four gurney stoves. Fourteen tons of special granite were quarried and dressed, and sent to Portland for use as paving. In 2C, 4C and No. 5 prison, guard bars made by the blacksmith were fixed to the clerestory windows. In addition, opening gear was made and fixed to the windows. To cope with all the granite being cut and dressed, a new 120-feet long stone-cutting shed was built. The blacksmiths also had plenty of work, necessitat-ing an extension on their shops. Walls were built to a height of 15 feet and the roof prepared prior to fixing.

The stone-breakers (as opposed to cutters and dressers) broke up 1200 cubic yards of granite just prior to the governor's report, all the work done by hand. It was used for building work, making concrete and laying road surface all over the estate. Along with the building of D1 block (now G-wing) the new special cells (now E-wing) were being constructed at quite a pace. The cells, at the time of the report, were waiting to be certified by an inspector as fit for occupation before the prisoners of penal cells No. 6 were transferred.

The building of separate cells was a marvellous achievement for the artisan staff and convicts. Little if any credit was given to those involved, least of all to the prisoners who were building their own prison.

E-wing, the punishment block known to staff as chokey block. Many of the older convicts called it the 'Tea Garden' and if a convict was placed on report and was sent to E-wing, they would always say 'I've had a letter to go to the Tea Garden' – a place to be avoided at all costs.

Between October 1901 and the time at which the report was made, terrible weather had struck the prison, impeding the progress of building works on separate cells and block D1. Fog and heavy rain in the early part of winter meant the convicts were working with damp granite, and the lime mortar used to build the structure would cause severe burns to hands, necks and ankles. The author, too, suffered from these conditions during his time in the works' department. It was hoped that D1, once completed, would house those prisoners living in the small, wet, corrugated-iron cells in 2A and 2B. These iron cells could then be demolished and work taken up on expanding Block 2.

The extension to Block 2 (now B-wing) is of a remarkable size and would possibly have been the most impressive task ever taken on by convicts in such a short time. The quarrying of so much granite today with pneumatic drills, jackhammers, electric hoists and scaffolding would still be a hard task even with the help of all this equipment.

The year 1902–03 was a good one for the prison farm. The horses were a particular success with the cart stallion Holcombe Conqueror, purchased for £105 in 1896, selling for £205. During Holcombe Conqueror's time at the prison he was exhibited at local and county shows and won seven first prizes and one second – a truly remarkable animal.

In 1902 and 1903 the transference of well-behaved and trained prisoners to Borstal and the reception of badly-behaved men at Dartmoor caused the number of reports made by staff to swell. This has been noted all through convict history; even in 1994 staff at the prison complained that Dartmoor was a dumping ground for rubbish convicts from all the prisons in the country. In 1902–03 there were 12 serious escapees from Dartmoor all of whom were recaptured by the vigilance of the staff.

This year saw the completion of the separate cells and their certification as fit for convict occupation. A lot of thought was given to the staffing of this new area as well as to the supply of beds, bedding and equipment, the provision of fuel for boilers to heat the area, the supply of water and gas and the disposal of sewage. Every effort was also taken to push on with the extension to No. 6 prison. This was delayed by bad weather and the new building had reached a height of only five feet above ground level by the end of the year. But a large amount of work had been completed below ground level including excavations through granite and the building of foundation walls ten-feet deep. All the heating ducts and separate vents were installed for each cell. The governor's report makes no mention of all this activity, although the Princetown drainage system was now finished and the last eight manholes built. A further 1200 feet of 12-inch drain was completed.

On the farm a new stallion was purchased, Royal Sovereign IV by Markeaton Royal Harold, to replace Holcombe Conqueror.

Employment at the prison now included 295 men in manufacturing, 169 on the farm and 350 in building. There were 104 involved in prison services and 61 non-effective. The total roll at the prison was 979 men. The chaplain reported that three lectures had taken place and there were also three schoolmasters in attendance for the benefit of the education of the prisoners.

Drainage to one part of the prison was connected to a newly-built septic tank. The food was reportedly good during this time as new dietary scales came into force in September 1902 meeting the needs of all the convicts. This was in the opinion of the governor so one wonders if the convicts would have agreed. There were three convict deaths in 1902–03.

The initiation of a separate class of juvenile convict under the age of twenty-one was instituted on 31 March 1902 with 12 young convicts in No. 6 prison refitted for their accommodation. The extension to No. 6 prison had continued throughout the year with much time being spent on the actual convict accommodation. A stable extension nearer the prison was also worked on during the year. A telephone line was installed between the prison and the quarry to increase security. Six earth-closets and lean-to sheds were built for the working party assigned to breaking animal bones for fertilizer. There were also earth-closets built for the juvenile offenders' party in No. 6 prison (now F-wing).

To provide work for the juveniles, 16 carpenters' double-benches were installed. These would be used by juveniles and adults. The ventilation of the bath-house next door was also improved. The yards at the back of C-tenement were divided and separate back entrances made for them. The author lived in 17 Burrator Avenue as a prison officer for ten years and these divisions are still there and very useful. The walls are seven-feet high which gives an amazing sense of privacy as well as providing shelter from the high winds. During 1903–04 the governor reported that the conduct of the officers had been satisfactory, with only three dismissals. This seems a bit of a contradiction in terms but, due to strict discipline, staff would be dismissed for sometimes trivial offences. A difference with an officer of higher rank could result in an immediate sacking.

A tremendous change took place in July 1903 regarding the prevention of talking between prisoners. Prisoners were to be treated according to their employment so opportunities for clandestine talks were diminished. The prison was broken into six units – A, B, C, D1, D2 and E – and each unit was to parade on different grounds. This would mean that some men would seldom spend any time together. The largest parties were moved into the largest prisons so that the men in the workshops would be in the bigger buildings and those working on open land, in the smaller. More than 700 convicts changed cells in one day without a hitch. All the effects of this move were deemed positive and discipline heightened. Previously, even under the most stringent discipline, there were opportunities for illicit talking whilst marching to labour. Now that the prisoners only circulated with those men they worked with it was much easier for officers to keep an eye on the talking that went on between men.

Sketch of prisoners' headgear made by the author following a conversation with a prison officer who had served in the 1920s. Convicts attending chapel would wear these hats to prevent recognition by other convicts, which would make solitary confinement very solitary. At the bottom is a leather label which was attached to the front of the jacket. It gives no name, only the hall number and the number of the cell. The prisoner who wore this label was held in A-hall cell No. 57; this is how he would be addressed by staff, never by name.

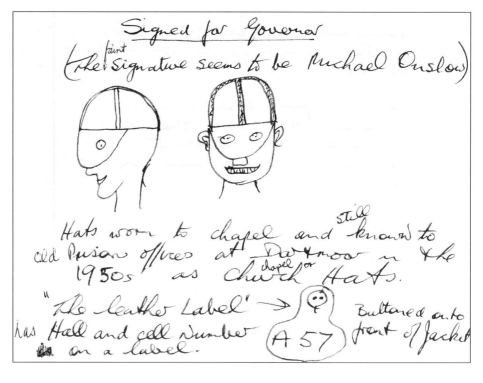

Small economies were made by substituting horse-drawn vehicles for carts pulled by convicts, thus increasing the available convict labour. The lookout station at the quarry was connected to the prison by telephone erected by the

Post Office, a useful arrangement in the event of a disturbance or escape. The field telephone system which connected parties working on the land to the prison was also extended. Underground cables were laid connecting to posts with telephone points at various locations on the prison lands so that a warder could plug in his telephone, wind the handle, and be connected to the gate-lodge area of the prison. The system, which extended in three directions over the estates for a distance of four miles, was opened and tested early in 1904. During the only attempted escape of the year, it duly prevented the prisoner from passing the prison boundaries, proving its worth!

In 1903–04 mounted patrols were also established to assist the maintenance of security and the checking of escapes. The patrols were highly praised and continued for seventy years until 5.30pm on Christmas Eve, 1974. The last officer to ride on patrol was Officer Dave Bone whom the author has talked to about his experience. More of this later.

Good progress was made on the building of new cell block extensions to No. 6 prison but it would be some time before prisoners were housed in modern cells. In the meantime convicts would languish in old iron cells.

On 22 July 1904 the Prince and Princess of Wales visited the prison and inspected all parts whilst the convicts were working. The satisfaction of the officers by the honour conveyed on them was shared by the convicts.

Heavy rain fell on 220 days during the year and amounted to 101.87 inches. Owing to very wet fields, crops were poor, making it necessary to buy fodder for the coming winter. It was considered better policy to sell more stock at the prison autumn sale and buy in the spring when fodder was cheaper thus reducing the amount of food necessary in the winter. Grain crops were heavy but badly damaged by heavy rain.

The chaplain reported that the new chapel organ was dedicated on Christmas Day by A. Amherst Webber Esq., Oxford. The hospital medical officer reported that four deaths of prisoners occurred in 1904. The officers' quarters were hardly free of infection either, with many problems arising from the close, confined quarters. The drainage from the prison was reported to be satisfactory while in Princetown some houses were without connection to the sewers, and those that were had no flushing mechanisms in the water-closet.

Sixteen 'weak-minded' prisoners were transferred to Parkhurst Prison. The juvenile roll was up to 81 at Dartmoor. The Swedish Drill excercise regime had been instituted since 1905, and Dr Dyer had taken over as the medical officer. In works, the drainage system reconstruction was almost complete, making it far more hygienic. With gas being in ever greater demand from the new quarters and convict halls, a new gas-holder was erected for storage.

Pipes were laid to convey the Mis Tor Leat through the plantations, taking water to the leats in the fields, a system still working as late as 1993. A dining hall for prisoners was erected but was discontinued, probably during the First World War. The bakehouse was given an extension which is surprising considering the amount of work being committed to the bigger buildings. The Roman Catholic church was enlarged, with space below utilised as a fire-engine shed and the priest's office above. The fire engine still used the same premises in 1998.

Despite all the building work going on inside and outside the prison, the foundations for ten new officers' cottages were laid. Prison officers used these cottages until they were altered by the Duchy/Housing Trust and let, I believe, in 1994. They were named Heather Terrace in later years but at the time of the building in 1905–06, and up until the 1940s, they were known as F-block Nos 1–10.

During the year 1907–08 eight floggings took place. Two escapes were made from juvenile quarters by young men who ran off from their horse and cart in fog. Both were recaptured two days later on the moors not far from Princetown. The average number of juvenile-adult prisoners this year was 90. The additional quarters for staff were being pushed forward as rapidly as possible in the hope that six of these would be occupied by July 1908. A new hall of 160 cells was also completed and the corrugated iron cells demolished. The only iron cells left were 4A and 4B (now A-wing).

The following list shows how many cells there were in each of the prison buildings, as well as the present and past name of the buildings, the total being 1213:

Old No. 6, now F-wing	*64*
New No. 6, now G-wing	*180*
No. 5, C before demolition	*265*
Separate cells, now E-hall	*61*
Old No. 4 bunks, now	
* demolished with B-hall on site*	*124*
New No. 4, now D-hall	*168*
New No. 2, now B-wing	*157*
Hospital	*57*
Miscellaneous	*10*

By 28 May 1908, staff quarters were recorded thus:

[Superior officers' quarters.]
1. *Governor to the right of the prison gate.*
2. *Storekeeper behind the governor.*
3. *Deputy governor in what is now the front of the works' block.*
4. *Deputy medical officer at the rear of the works' block nearest the prison wall.*
5. *Chaplain on the left adjoining the church which is now a private house.*
6. *The Roman Catholic priest lived in what is now Hisworthy House.*
7. *The medical officer lived in Amos House which is now a private house.*
8. *Schoolmasters lived in what is now ISCA prison house.*
9. *Chief officer 1, the farm bailiff and foreman of works lived in New Villas which are private houses today.*

In 1908 there were 18 principal warders at the prison, with 46 warders and 138 assistant warders, plus two other officers, making a total of 204. There were 16 bachelors living in quarters above the office in the main drive and 18 in what is now the old works' block, plus 34 men who did not live in outside quarters. Altogether there were 157 homes for warders and their families, as well as bachelor quarters inside the prison for a large number of single officers who would not be allowed to live in official quarters until married.

When the author joined Dartmoor Prison from Exeter Prison in 1968, a large number of staff members lived out. They were paid an allowance to do so and would travel to work from Plymouth, Tavistock and other towns. Most of the accommodation was occupied and the author had to wait eleven weeks for a single vacancy to arise. Total staff housing in 1968 was 241 which included 30 rooms for staff at the Duchy Hotel.

Quarters available for staff in 1968:

Duchy Hotel [for single officers]	*30*
Governor's house	*1*
Assistant governor's	*1*
Basic grade officer [adjoining]	*1*
Tor View	*6*
New Villas	*3*
Isca	*1*
Hisworthy	*1*
Amos House [a medical officer's house]	*1*

Burrator Avenue	*31*
Woodville Avenue	*42*
Oratory of St John Vianney (RC priest)	*1*
Chaplain's house	*1*
Heather Terrace	*10*
Hessary Terrace	*18*
Moor Crescent	*13*
Grosvenor House	*4*
Dart Cottage	*1*
Reading room (later Ladies' Club)	*nil*
Blackabrook Avenue	*30*
Bellever Close	*44*
Total	*241*

In 1909–10 it was hoped that the last of the old war prisons would disappear by the year 1911–12. The average roll for the year was 1169, with five floggings taking place for serious assaults on officers. Two of these assaults were of murderous intent with officers being cut down with spades, one of whom had to be invalided out of the service. There was one escape and two unsuccessful attempts. The one escapee ran from his party but was captured by a Civil Guard officer in just a few minutes. The two unsuccessful escapees tried to get out of their cells by filing the cell window.

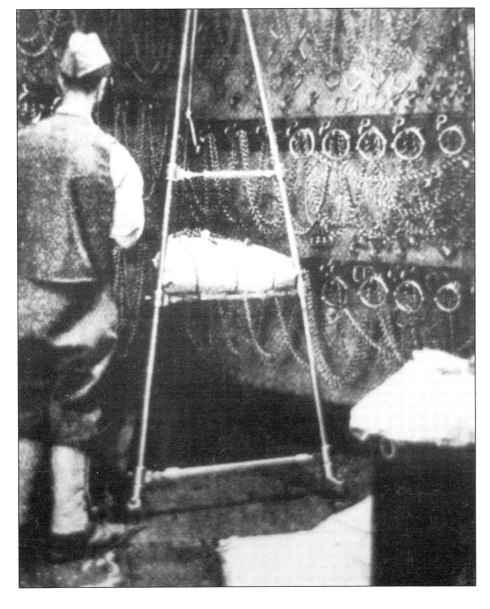

The Chain Room, located adjacent to the old No. 3 convict prison, now the old kitchen. It shows chains which were used at Dartmoor. Some were used to chain convicts together when they pulled their carts around the estates, to prevent escapes. Others were closeting chains which allowed a convict to go to the toilet with the officer outside, others were personal chains for close control. The 'A' frame is the flogging frame which was bolted to the floor and the leather pillow was used to prevent injury to certain areas of the prisoner's back.

Twenty-four houses had been occupied, taking the place of the cold, wet barracks which were pulled down. Meanwhile 13 additional houses, H-block (Moor Crescent), were being built. There were many bachelor officers waiting for quarters so that they could get married. Foundations were laid for the prison hospital extension. Enlarging the gasworks became a priority at this point and construction was begun on a workshop for juvenile-adult prisoners. At the farm there was sad news when two of the cart mares died whilst foaling.

The labourers of the prison now included 382 in manufacturing, 322 on the farm, 380 on building works and 113 on prison works. There were 72 men who were non-effective in labour, making the average roll 1169.

Right: *A convict with a horse and cart on the top of Cemetery Hill, adjacent to the French cemetery.*
Below: *Convicts loading mangel-wurzels at a place known to staff as 'Ashams' at the bottom of Cemetery Hill; snow is on the ground.*

The chaplain reported that the Lord Bishop of Crediton had confirmed 32 men on 5 April 1909, and 22 men on 23 March 1910. The medical officer reported five convict deaths, with six attempted suicides, none successful. There were eight 'weak-minded' and 16 invalid prisoners transferred to Parkhurst from the invalid prison, which is now the lower classrooms. A few cases of chicken pox were reported in quarters.

The year ending 31 March 1911 showed an average roll of 1093. There was one case of corporal punishment reported and three attempted suicides, none of which were successful. There were no escapes and only one attempt thanks to good control by the staff. The juvenile-adult prisoners' roll averaged 68 during the year.

Despite a great deal of wet weather over the year, crops were good in the run-up to the farm sale which was due on 5 September 1910. The works included quarters for 13 officers and their families well under construction, along with provision of a mess for bachelor officers within the prison. The hospital extension was developing quickly and at this point was up to full height, with the new workshop for juvenile-adults being completed.

In 1912–13 the daily average of convicts was 1040. There was one case of corporal punishment and one failed suicide attempt. The Preventive Building opened in March and 19 prisoners transferred there. The conduct of the staff was very good and it was reported that they performed their most arduous duties very well. The weather conditions, the treatment by superior staff and convicts, and the housing conditions these warders were subjected to should not be forgotten.

Continuous wet weather was recorded 'since October' (1911) and the governor reported that it had been very trying for the cattle. Presumably it would have been much more 'trying' for staff working in heavy rain and snow on the bogs! If one small step was taken outside the iron rules of discipline, then punishment of warders by superior staff would have been instantaneous. This would have affected the warder's family as badly, with children being forced to change school and move house. It was a precarious lifestyle.

The fire engines were tested monthly and a new fire escape was purchased which was reported to be 'a great improvement in that department'.

The farm produced 195 lambs out of a total of 130 ewes. As ever, wet weather made it difficult for the farm, though at the annual sale of stock on 6 September 1912, conditions were fine and attendance high, attracting buyers from all over the country. The following sales totals were achieved:

Horses and ponies	*£179.16s.3d.*
Cattle	*£620.15s.0d.*
Sheep	*£348.1s.3d.*
Pigs	*£219.15s.6d.*
Wool	*£139.16s.3d.*
A total of	*£1508.4s.3d.*

In works it was hoped that 13 new quarters would be completed by August 1913, these being those at Moor Crescent, as mentioned in the report from the year before. The new mess rooms and bunks, converted from the old works' block inside the prison for the bachelor officers, were near completion and in full occupation. In 1993 the old works' block was modernised and was now the administrative block. The old works' block is where the author joined the service in 1968 and a building that holds particularly happy memories.

The new extensions and the reconstruction carried out on the hospital were in full progress. Today the date 1912 is still visible above the front entrance. The quality of the stone-cutting and masonry is, of course, very high. The refitting of cook-house equipment was completed, as well as the provision of a hot closet for food warming. The floor tiling was almost finished this year. The gaswork plans, as mentioned in the previous report, were finished and ladders provided to gain access to the top of the gas-holders making maintenance easier. The new bath-house was fitted with 27 baths and the entire system was completed.

The medical officer reported no deaths this year and 26 'weak-minded' and 13 invalid prisoners transferred to Parkhurst. One case of diphtheria occurred in quarters and a few cases of whooping cough and chicken pox also developed.

In 1913–14 the average roll was lower than previous years at 989 convicts. There was one case of corporal punishment and two attempts at suicide. Three escape attempts were made from the farm and quarry, all of which were foiled and the convicts captured within a few minutes, showing how foolish such attempts were. The average juvenile-adult roll was 56. These prisoners had used the new workshops to fit new buildings with windows and doors.

The Sherwood Foresters Regimental Band gave two concerts at the prison and there were two lectures, reported to have been much appreciated by the convicts. Things were not so rosy on the farm thanks to relentless wet weather. Despite this the sheep did very well at the West of England Fat Show held at Plymouth. Two pens of fat wethers were exhibited, one taking first prize and a special prize, and the second pen taking third place.

The 13 terraced houses on Moor Crescent known as H-block were completed and fully occupied. When the author was a junior prison officer in 1968, he was told that he could never apply for any of these houses if they became vacant as they were for superior staff only. The houses overlook the playing field and are in a prime position, hence being designated for higher ranking staff.

There were considerable excavations carried as part of an experiment for a new and better water supply involving the screening of water through settling beds. These existed up to the 1980s when a contract was let to upgrade the water supply. The settling tanks were filled in, which proved to be a disastrous move as the water was peat-laden and caused a number of problems until the South West Water Authority brought mains up to Princetown in 1994. If the old system had been left in place it would have been far superior to any modern system. Having worked in Princetown for twenty-four years, the author can vouch for the excellence of the cold water supply founded in 1913.

The new hospital wing was making good progress and when completed would provide much-needed accommodation. The many years of building work took full advantage of the skilled labour of the convicts while it was available. Of late this skilled labour appears to be getting scarcer each year. All the buildings constructed by convicts have proved to be of superb and lasting quality, as has the general upkeep, for which credit must be given to the artisan warders and the convicts.

The hospital medical officer reported one death from cancer and two convicts were released on medical grounds, one on account of a serious injury received at work, the other on account of cancer. During this dramatic, hard, vicious time in Dartmoor Prison history there were seven attempts at suicide. Twenty-two 'weak-minded' and nine invalids were sent to Parkhurst. Over the years many unsuitable convicts were sent to Dartmoor Prison thus reducing the number of fit convicts. The medical officer reported that there had been an unusual amount of sickness amongst officers' families owing to a severe epidemic of measles and one, less severe, of whooping cough, as well as scarlet fever and diphtheria.

The report noted hopes that by the end of this year two bright and airy wards in the new wing at the hospital would be ready for accepting patients.

The construction of the new cell block was going well at this point and again both of these major works were built entirely by convicts. This feat lead to three photographs taken at Dartmoor Prison being sent to the Ghent International Exhibition where they attracted great interest in the prison section. The first picture showed convicts carting stone from the quarry for use in the building. The second was of the farmyard and the third showed the prison flock of sheep. Sadly these photographs are missing, nearly ninety years on.

The rainfall in 1913 was 112 inches. At the farm sale held in September 1914 eight horses were sold, along with 33 cattle, 46 pigs, 177 sheep and 3000lbs of wool. The prison roll averaged 989 and the number of cells remained at 1097. But changes were in the offing with the outbreak of the First World War, many prison staff being sent for military service in France. Work on the last of the cell blocks under the reconstruction scheme was retarded as completion of the new hospital block was deemed more urgent.

In 1917–18 the unprecedented fall in prison population made it possible to surrender Dartmoor Prison, along with Warwick and Wakefield, to a Home Office scheme to find employment for conscientious objectors. The remaining 365 prisoners were to be distributed among other prisons, with the governor and some staff staying in situ.

Conscientious objectors going to labour during the First World War. Conchies' Field on the prison estates was turned up using garden spades and the Conchies' Road is close to the railway in Princetown.

Dartmoor's conscientious objectors numbered a daily average of 211 and carried out land reclamation, dairy work and farm work, valued at £11 577.

Personnel released from the prison service for war service included 91 superior officers, 56 clerks and 827 subordinate officers, many of them from Dartmoor. Decorations awarded to prison officers on active service in France during the First World War included:

1	*Companion of the Order of St Michael and St George.*
3	*DSOs.*
2	*OBEs.*
2	*Chevaliers of Legion of Honour.*
14	*Mentioned in Despatches.*
6	*DCMs.*
8	*MMs.*
5	*Croix de Guerre.*
1	*Italian Croca di Guerra.*
7	*Meritorious Service Medals.*

For 26 subordinate officers there was promotion to commissioned rank in the armed services on the battlefields. Prison populations remained low with so many ex-convicts having been released to serve in the forces against Germany.

These men also showed great valour and won decorations for their time spent on the battlefields of France.

With the roll so reduced because of the war, no new prison officers were appointed after early in 1915. This continued until 1919 when the conscientious objectors left and the convicts returned. The estates were soon ringing with the sounds of convicts working again. The wages for staff in 1920 were as follows:

Warder	£1.9s.0d.
Principal warder	£2.5s.0d.
Chief II	£2.17s.0d.
Chief I	£3.13s.0d.

On the works' department pay was as follows:

Artisan warder	£1.9s.0d.
Eng II	£2.13s.0d.
Eng I	£2.19s.0d.
Foreman of works	£3.5s.0d.

In 1921 the Geddes axe fell and no more individual reports were made. This was a great pity as these gave a lively picture of daily, weekly and yearly happenings in the prison and estates. We know how many convicts were employed in each area, the amount of work done, the spending and the value of everything. Life progressed through the 1920s in much the same way. Dartmoor Prison was the last prison to have the broad arrow on the prison clothing and the arrow-marked soles on their boots because hundreds of convicts were working outside and many escapes were attempted. This distinctive clothing would pay off when any escapes were made.

A diagram showing field names on the prison estates, and the route taken by the Devonport Leat.

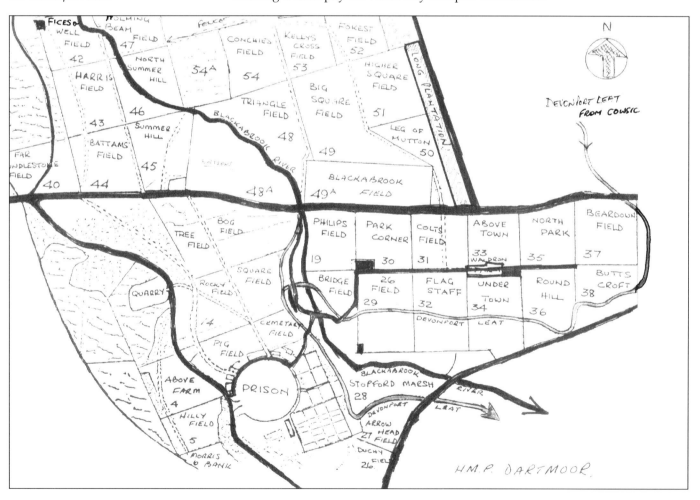

Above: *Christmas card sent from Dartmoor Prison by a conscientious objector, dated 1917.*
Left: *The same location from which the prisoner drew the card is outside what is now F-wing, on a foggy day.*

Chapter Eight
THE MUTINY OF 1932

Discipline at the prison between 1920 and 1930 was increasing in severity and convicts were on tenterhooks as they could be sent down to the punishment block for little or no reason. They felt that they were overworked, poorly fed and inadequately clothed. After a day's labour in the bogs they still had nowhere to dry their clothes. It was a powder-keg scenario.

Staff too were under enormous pressure to perform as the threat of being sacked and evicted for even the smallest of misdemeanours hung over them constantly. The staff became hard and cold, giving the convicts no leeway whatsoever. This attitude caused trouble among the convicts whom staff would then be forced to send to the punishment block. Superiors would accuse lower members of staff of not carrying out their duties if they did not send men to be punished.

By late 1931, tension was building up to boiling point at Dartmoor. Coshes that had been made by the convicts were found by the officers, even hacksaw blades were found in the prison. It was suspected that these were brought in from outside by some members of staff, perhaps for money. Some of the convicts had been sent 'under suspicion' from other prisons to Dartmoor so that the tough routine at Dartmoor would straighten them out. It was expected that these men would always be under supervision and a close watch kept but that in itself was an impossible task.

Just before Christmas in 1931 it was discovered that four convicts who were being watched by staff had drawn up plans to escape. Steps were taken to keep them apart and not allow them to mix so that they could not plan anything with others. There must have been a feeling in the air. The author has, in later years, sensed such an atmosphere. There is a strange silence among the convicts and the staff. It is a sure sign that things are about to happen.

On Friday 22 January 1932 the breakfast porridge was not properly cooked. The food at the prison was one of the key topics of conversation between the convicts, and the quality of it was their particular concern. On this occasion excess water had been added to the tank of porridge, perhaps by a convict working in the kitchen, so that it was described later as water with grains floating in it.

Governor Roberts recognised that the meal was not of its normal thickness and authorised the issue of an extra ration of bread, potatoes and margarine in lieu of the bad porridge. Possibly this action sowed the seeds of revolution. If the convicts think that they can get anything they want by making a small amount of fuss they get the idea that they have control. On this day they would have said 'we have won'. It seems that they were being led from a position where they would not even have blinked without asking permission to one where they could openly complain without redress.

Staff, even in the author's time, would say that if you give a convict even one thousandth of an inch then you have lost; it appears that Governor Roberts thought different. Things at Dartmoor were certainly coming to a head. On Friday afternoon Officer Birch, the man in charge of the twine shed, gave his party the order to fall out. Immediately convict 341 Thomas Davis ran towards Officer Birch and jumped on to his back, then slashed both sides of the officer's face with a razor blade attached to a piece of wood. The blade was fixed lengthways against the wood with a nail, creating a blade with a handle. This was a commonly used form of chiv (convict parlance for a knife). No convict went to the aid of Officer Birch and Davis was immediately taken to E-wing (separate cells) which was also known as the chokey block.

Tension increased visibly in the prison. The 'weak-minded' convict who made the attack was well liked by other convicts and they were convinced that undue violence would be used against Davis in the punishment block. It would take the slightest spark to ignite everything into a major conflagration.

Later it would be seen that the mutineers' aims were to release the prisoner in the punishment block and cause a disturbance on either Saturday 23 or Sunday 24 January. On Saturday 23 January 1932 Governor Roberts decided that he would visit the kitchen early in the morning to ensure that the food would be fit for breakfast. He wanted no further complaints from the convicts. The author checked the gate occurrence book for that day and noted that he came into the prison at five minutes past midnight and left at eighteen minutes past. He inspected the porridge and noted that it was thick and appeared quite good. He returned to the prison at 8.15am and again visited the kitchen. He again looked at the porridge and found it to be watery and thin. Somebody must have added more water to it.

Who can tell how? Perhaps somebody visited the kitchen in the early hours. The circumstances were very suspicious. Governor Roberts again bowed to the convicts and gave them four ounces of corned beef in lieu of the porridge. The convicts must have felt like it was Christmas with all the additional food being issued. It certainly gave them the wrong impression and was definitely a big mistake.

At first the convicts were fairly quiet but later became noisy. They had been forbidden to talk for years and had never opened their mouths; now they complained and received treats. Governor Roberts' soft treatment had made them realise that if they applied enough pressure they would have their way. As a great deal of effort went into taking away that which the convicts already had, a major and irreversible change had taken place.

It was difficult to work out who the ringleaders of the convict uprising were because convicts had learned to communicate without moving their lips. They were thus able to hide their plans from the officers and warders. On Saturdays the convicts would be taken to the Church of England chapel. Here the news of the preceding week would be read out to them, censored of course. The roll at this time was 440. Without those being punished, the sick or the men on duty, the total going to the chapel would have been about 400. There was plenty of room as 800 men had been in the chapel at other times, but experienced officers had warned their superiors that it was the height of folly to gather 400 convicts in one place at this troublesome time, with revolt in the air.

Even in exercise the convicts were kept in small groups on the principle of 'divide and conquer'. The groups were divided into AI, AII, B, C and D. They would then exercise on the yard or parade according to their designated group with their group name.

On 23 January, however, 400 convicts were being assembled in the chapel, their chance to associate with other prisoners in a way impossible elsewhere. Here the men could plan and conspire to their hearts' content and one experienced officer noted the danger of this at the time, saying, 'the holding of this meeting at this time is the most foolish thing that has ever been done'.

The author's rough sketch of the different parade grounds used by the halls in 1932, now known as exercise yards.

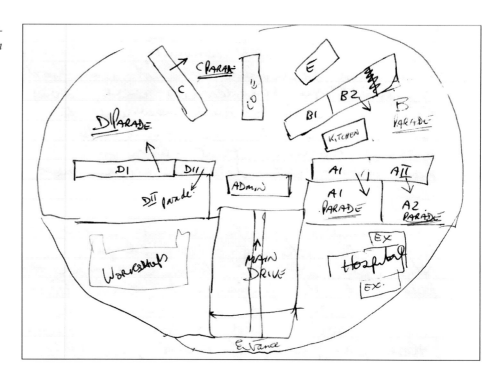

Governor Roberts thought otherwise. He attended the meeting and addressed the convicts from the pulpit:

I want to just talk to you this morning…

Immediately the convicts started shouting and banging, in normal situations the heavy gang would be sent in to put a stop to this noise. Governor Roberts went on:

Surely you are going to give me a hearing, I am sorry the porridge yesterday was not up to standard, and today again it is not quite as it should be, yesterday I issued you with bread, potatoes and margarine, and today I have issued you with corned beef.
Tonight I have arranged for the master cook [principal officer] to come into the prison and cook the porridge himself to find out what the trouble is, I hope this will satisfy you. I am anxious that you get fair play and we shall have no further trouble with the porridge after tonight.

In the author's view this statement was a recipe for disaster as the convicts now realised that they could beat the governor whenever they wanted; they had frightened him. Deputy Governor Richards later stated that 'immediately the governor entered the pulpit two men started shouting and many others took it up, I tried to identify the two convicts who started the shouting but couldn't.'

Governor Roberts got a hearing in the end and there was a distinct effort of applause from one part but this was drowned out by the vociferous minority. After this he left the chapel and the Church Army chaplain Captain Ball came out to the front to the pulpit. He gave out the number of the hymn to be sung and the choir stood up plus about a third of the convicts. The rowdy element shouted them down and Captain Ball sang the hymn alone which was very courageous. He then read a prayer and left the pulpit.

The convicts were boiling. Later, as they were leaving the chapel one of them, close to Deputy Governor Richards, was heard to say, 'now we will start on parade', but unfortunately he failed to attach any importance to this comment.

Captain Ball returned to the pulpit and started to read the usual weekly news which, apart from one small item, was well received. The atmosphere was still electric. He later explained that there was a small interruption during a piece of news about an aeroplane flight, because the convicts wanted to hear about a football match. Results were desperately sought after in the prison, mainly for the purpose of gambling which was rife, then and now. The gambling barons would take a lot of tobacco bets on the result, making them a powerful force to be reckoned with.

Sunday 24 January 1932 is now a day of infamy for Dartmoor Prison. The governor again entered the prison at 5am according to the gate-book. He checked the two boiling vats of porridge and found that one was perfectly satisfactory but one had again failed. The suggestion was that it had again been tampered with.

Because of the tense atmosphere in the prison all available staff were called in. The number of staff at the time of the mutiny was one chief officer 1, eight principal officers and 69 officers, a total of 78 men only, though many men were held in reserve. Two principal officers and ten officers were posted at the main gate and one principal officer and ten officers were posted to No. 3 prison (now the old kitchen). These men, until the author's time as a discipline officer, were known as the 'heavy gang', namely a group of officers who stand by in case of trouble. Sadly they are no longer made available.

These additional staff would have been noticed by the convicts who would be thinking 'we have them scared'. After breakfast on 24 January there was a good deal of shouting in the cells and the convicts were getting very worked up. In B2 hall it was decided that some of the most vociferous prisoners would be moved to the separate cells. Divide and rule – it was a decision of common sense. In the separate cells the men would await adjudication and punishment. This was a perfectly normal routine carried out during the author's time; usually four other officers were present to put the offender down.

On this Sunday a convict, whom we shall call X, and another, Y, were in adjoining cells in B2 hall. Y had a reputation among the prisoners for being simple-minded and he was amongst those taken to the block for shouting. While he was being removed to the block he mildly protested his innocence but did not cause even the slightest problem as he was taken quietly to the separate cells.

A member of staff called Officer Udy then received an order to remove X to the prisoner block. On entering the cell he placed a hand on the convict's shoulder. As he did so prisoner X struck out at him with a piece of wood to which was attached a razor blade, the same device with which Officer Birch had been injured. Officer Udy quite rightly jumped back, closed the cell door and called for assistance in removing the dangerous prisoner to the punishment block – perfectly normal procedure.

Once again Officer Udy and his back-up entered the cell and again he was threatened with the chiv whereupon an accompanying officer struck X on the head with his baton and stunned him. The chiv was taken away. While he was unconscious, prisoner X was taken to the prison hospital with a head wound. At this time in Dartmoor's turbulent history, whenever a convict was taken down to the punishment block, the remainder of the prisoners would be locked in their cells, allowing plenty of staff to be on hand to assist if there was any trouble. They would 'line the route' to the punishment block while the convict would shout and scream at the staff for the benefit of the locked up prisoners to prove how tough he was.

The commotion caused by removing convict X from his cell, and the blow to his head, would have been heard by the convicts locked up on the same landing. They immediately imagined that the simple-minded Y had been viciously attacked and bludgeoned without cause, another factor in the ever-building tension.

Only too aware of it, the experienced officers felt strongly that mass exercise and chapel on a day like this should be cancelled but Governor Roberts consulted

Colonel Turner and it was decided that they should attend, to the dismay of the officers who would have to deal with the mutinous inmates. On exercise the convicts would be in the open and thus harder to control. This was a curious decision on the governor's part, with all of his officers prepared for trouble.

Deputy Governor Richards was also opposed to the prisoners being removed from their cells and allowed to exercise en masse. Prisoners would never be allowed to stay in their cells indefinitely but a controlled exercise regime throughout the day would have kept more staff on hand and released some of the convict tension.

Unfortunately the order was given to unlock and proceed with exercise as normal. Officer Udy, a senior basic-grade officer, was in charge of B2 parade exercise yard. B2 parade was between A and B-halls (now B and D) at the back of what is now the old kitchen. At about 9.30am there were approximately 90 convicts at exercise with only six officers monitoring. Following their exercise the convicts were given the order to 'form up', and then to 'fall out' to the water-closets. Some of the 90 prisoners obeyed but others shouted 'Stand still you bastards! Obey and draw your sticks!' The order to draw sticks can be explained by the fact that a lot of the convicts had secreted coshes about the person in readiness for this pre-planned revolt.

The convicts shouted that Officer Udy ought to be kicked to death for knocking out the simple-minded prisoner the day before. Officer Udy bravely stood his ground and told the 90 mutineers that 500 members of staff would be arriving in a matter of minutes to put a stop to this nonsense. He then reasoned with the angry prisoners and appealed to their common sense not to do anything that they would regret later.

The ringleaders shouted to the convicts to go to the other parade grounds, A, C and D, and join the convicts there, demanding that the governor be brought out. About 40 or 50 of the 90 rioting men ran off in search of the other revolting convicts who would obviously have heard the noise and joined in. The convicts who remained on the exercise yard were formed up and marched back to B2 hall where they were 'put away'. All of the staff from B2 were now available to help with the trouble.

The B2 mutiny had reached C-hall parade and Officer Kelly on duty there reported that, just after 9.15am, he heard tremendous shouts coming from the direction of the bath-house. Suddenly several convicts came on to the enormous exercise yard shouting and bawling. Kelly reported that these convicts then incited his men to join the rampage.

Gate Officer Dowse, seeing and hearing how serious things were, phoned Plymouth shortly after 9.30am. He also asked that Devon County Constabulary be notified. He then rang Crownhill Barracks where the Eighth Infantry Brigade, which included the 1st Battalion Worcester Regiment, were stationed. These soldiers were put on standby.

Convicts rushed the main gate where staff with Snider carbines were positioned. The staff were instructed not to take their rifles into the prison but to make sure that the convicts could not leave, by firing if necessary, which of course happened. Convicts broke into the prison officers' block just inside the gate and stole cigarettes and other possessions. The rioters then travelled down the main drive to the administration block where they broke windows to gain access then set fire to the block housing the records office. Some of the convicts tried to extinguish the fire but many others had iron bars, pickaxe handles and axes stolen from the fire station. The fire was by now out of control and eventually the administration department was burnt to the ground. Staff fired at the rioters, hitting one convict in the neck. He was badly enough injured to be taken later to Plymouth Hospital. Another man who was in the boiler-house trying to wreck the boilers was hit when staff fired into the building.

At 10.45am about 38 police officers, including a chief constable, entered the prison. A charge was made by the police and stones were thrown at them by the convicts. The mutiny was finally ended using the necessary force. The fire brigade arrived to put out the fire that had destroyed the administration block and finally extinguished it at 9pm.

The administration building and record offices on fire during the 1932 mutiny, the loss of the record office is, of course, a great disappointment to all historians.

The burnt-out shell of the administration block and record office prior to its demolition.

There are two main facts to consider when looking at this mutiny: 1. Owing to the professionalism of the warders not a single prisoner escaped from the prison. 2. Only one of the convicts was seriously injured.

Ten convicts were sent to the hospital and 13 kept in the halls with baton wounds. Four convicts were in hospital and three in the halls with shot wounds. Officer Birch was slashed across the face three days before the mutiny and 20 officers were injured during it but returned to their duties immediately. Four of the officers were incapacitated. Two convicts were hospitalised for injuries inflicted by other convicts, and a number of other men were hurt but were afraid to come forward and instead suffered in silence in their cells.

I searched the gatekeeper's occurrence book which is known by the staff as 'the bible'. Unfortunately the book does not record subordinate staff movements to and from duty. All staff called in on special duty would be recorded, along with all administration staff, gatekeepers and doctors.

The lists in the book for Saturday 23 and Sunday 24 January show that the police were called in on Sunday from 10.45am until 9pm, a long day indeed for them. The soldiers from 1st Battalion Worcester Regiment were in the prison on Monday 25 January from 9am until 6.30am on Tuesday, a total of thirty-three-and-a-half hours, though much of the time would be spent on standby.

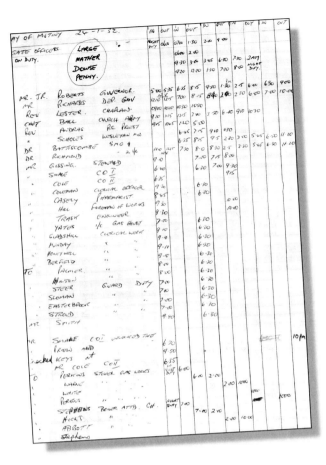

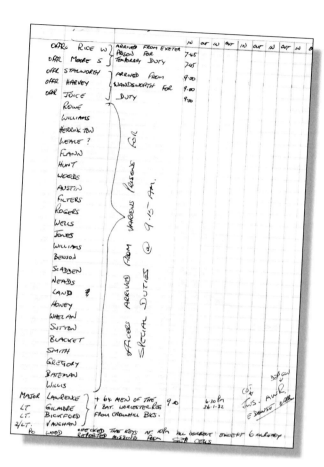

Some notes taken from the gate-book. Staff on scheduled duties were not entered but staff on annual leave, sick leave or special duties were entered. The page on the far right shows some prison officers from other prisons who were sent to Dartmoor, with the military at the bottom of the page. The photograph (below) shows the police leaving the prison, with the usual group of photographers outside the prison gate in the days following the mutiny.

The prisoners involved in the mutiny were sent to the Duchy Hall (now demolished) on a regular basis, transported in lorries escorted by the police. The trips to the special assize court at the Duchy Hall went on for sixteen days after which Mr Justice Finlay passed sentence on the rioters. Friday 13 May 1932 was an unlucky day indeed for the men, but especially for prisoner 341 Davis who received twelve years consecutive. All sentences would commence at the completion of the present sentence. The top sentence, given for slashing Officer Birch's face, meant that Davis was sent straight to Parkhurst Prison on the Isle of Wight.

This series of photographs portray the scenes in Princetown in the weeks following the mutiny. Convicts and their police escort were taken to the Duchy Hall (seen bottom left, *but now demolished), for their trial. In the photograph* (bottom right) *can be seen the judge and his entourage entering St Michael's Church, Princetown for a service.*

With one exception, all the convicted prisoners were transferred to other prisons; this action by the prison authorities aimed at weeding out the troublemakers. The accused were brought into the dock at Duchy Hall from which all the seats had been removed and as soon as sentence was passed, immediately removed from the dock and put into a car with prison-officer escorts. They were driven straight to other prisons to prevent the formation of a group of rioters such as those present on the day of the mutiny.

One man named Gardiner pleaded guilty at the special assize on Wednesday 27 April 1932 and did not attend until the day the sentences were given. He received six months consecutive and was sent back to Dartmoor to complete his sentence.

The author's handwritten notes on sentences received by the 32 convicts on mutiny charges, taken from the gatebook, officially known as the Gatekeepers' Daily Occurrence Book dated Friday, 13 May 1932, a truly unlucky 'Friday the 13th' for the mutineers.

all Sentences consecutive to to commence when current sentences are completed

1	BEADLES	Discharged
2	Thomas Bullows	8 years
3	Harry Burgess	3 years
4	— Carter	Discharged
5	Joseph Canning	10 years
6	Patrick Cosgrove	20 months
7	James Del Mar	18 months
8	Thomas G Dewhurst	3 years
9	— Greenhow	Discharged
10	William Gardiner	6 months
11	George Garton	3 years
12	Hardy	Discharged
13	— Hart	Discharged
14	— Hill	Discharged
15	James Horn	21 months
16	James Ibbesson	10 years
17	John Jackson	6 years
18	Edward James	18 months
19	Patrick Kavanagh	15 months
20	— Kendall	Discharged
21	William Mason	8 years
22	Walter E Moore	3 years
23	Alexander Muir	3 years
24	Mullins	Discharged
25	Frederick Roberts	3 years
26	— Sexton	Discharged
27	Frederick Smith	8 years
28	Charles J. Sparks	4 years
29	Harry Stoddart	4 years
30	Sidney Tappenden	6 months
31	Joseph Taylor	3 years
32	341 — Davis	12 years for wounding Officer Birch

Of the 32 convicts sent to trial for the mutiny of 1932, nine were discharged and sent back to Dartmoor to finish their existing sentences, while 23 were sentenced to consecutive time and immediately transferred elsewhere. In addition, David Brown was found not guilty of trying to injure Officer Udy in his cell.

With the mutiny and subsequent trials over, Dartmoor Prison resumed normal duties with increased discipline imposed on both staff and convicts. The convicts in particular were treated with the utmost severity. The author has had long, informative talks with previous members of staff from HMP Dartmoor over the years, especially with those who worked there between 1927 and 1939. They provided first-hand accounts of the days' happenings during this difficult period. These men include Officers Tim Easterbrook, Penny, Chilli Frampton, Principal Officer Stan Mutton and many more.

Prison life continued along the same lines until the Second World War when men were sent to the armed forces and were responsible for bringing fresh honour to the prison service. The list of the names of the men can be seen in the Roman Catholic church porch at Dartmoor Prison. Two humanitarian concessions were made for convicts at the prison in 1937, one being the payment of allowances for the purchase of small luxuries, along with the extension of permission to smoke in the cells. Men were now paid on a scale relating to the length of their incarceration and the type of work carried out. The maximum payment for a week of hard labour was 1s.7d. per week. With this money the convicts would be able to purchase items such as cigarettes and tobacco, confectionery and preserves from the canteen, but little could be afforded with their scant payments.

The prison roll in 1937 was a meagre 300, one of the lowest on record. During the Second World War some of the prisons and buildings were used for the storage of materials. Blackabrook House was full of stores, and Nissen huts were erected to hold more.

Princetown was supposed to be outside the bombing area, but all prison quarters were provided with Anderson shelters. These are still to be found in Burrator Avenue and are grand garden sheds! During the author's occupation of a quarter in Burrator Avenue, convicts from the Long Plantation forestry party would bring logs and store them in the Anderson shelter.

During the war, members of the Irish Republican Army (IRA) were sent to Dartmoor. There is a code of conduct among prisoners that all convicts are equal and that convicts must never judge other convicts. But the IRA prisoners were hated by the other convicts at Dartmoor. The IRA were hated for their injuring of, and violence towards, innocent civilians. At one point the IRA prisoners took two officers hostage and locked them in the cells with their own keys, then set fire to D-wing. An ex-officer informed the author that the insurrection was ended by the necessary amount of force.

In No. 4 war prison roof cockloft, now known as the Church of England roof space, the burn marks are from French and American prisoners of war. Irish Republican prisoners were put to work in this building, they left their mark by hammering nails into one of the old beams.

It seems that part of the problem at Dartmoor Prison in the days of the mutiny was that it had been deliberately run down by old convicts and new staff who simply were not up to the strict discipline and conditions of the prison. Major Charles Pannal MC DSO (called Charlie behind his back), was a man whom all the officers respected for his firm attitude toward the convicts. He was sent to Dartmoor in January 1932 in order to sort the prison out following the unrest and was able to get a firm grip on the situation and steer a good strong disciplined course.

I have spoken to three ex-officers who served under Major Pannal and all three spoke in glowing terms of his strength of character and fierce control of staff and convicts. If you exert a strict control over staff it is only natural that they in turn will exert greater control over the prisoners. Major Pannal was assaulted and injured by convicts several times but he never faltered or wavered in his firm actions.

Looking at the punishment book for the early part of the war, the following strict action was taken towards the convicts during this troublesome time:

15-08-40	*Convict M*	*12 strokes cat-o'-nine-tails*
20-09-40	*Convict S*	*12 strokes birch*
02-12-40	*Convict F*	*12 strokes birch*
10-03-41	*Convict J*	*18 strokes cat-o'-nine-tails*
10-03-41	*Convict M*	*12 strokes birch*
18-10-41	*Convict K*	*18 strokes cat-o'-nine-tails*

These were some of the cruellest punishments awarded, and there were many hundreds of lesser punishments handed out, so that gradually a firm grip was gained on the convicts.

During the Second World War a lot of staff left Dartmoor to serve in the armed forces. Many were decorated for bravery and several basic-grade prison officers were commissioned as officers. They had tremendous experience in the handling of awkward men so it was only natural for them to become senior non-commissioned officers.

Convicts from prisons in areas subject to bombing areas were transferred to Dartmoor Prison for their own safety so the population grew from around 350 to 500. Conditions at that time were relaxed in comparison to the strict pre-war discipline. New convicts always thought that it was an easy prison to be kept in and many took advantage of the situation.

And what of today? In the author's experience, if you give a prisoner everything, they still want the moon! As a discipline officer in the 1960s I invariably kept all of my party below the maximum wage to give them a target to aim at through hard work. I would only give a convict a pay rise if he had worked hard enough to earn it; if he asked for it I would alter the form by deducting the amount that he had requested from his present wages. He would then double his efforts for a week or two and I would increase the wages to the previous level again. I always explained that increases were a result of hard work and in my experience a convict who had been awarded an increase through his hard labour would very rarely go back to his former ways.

In 1947 the conditions for staff at the prison were eased slightly when the standard seven years of service, which had to be spent prior to gaining a transfer, was reduced to five years. The Dartmoor allowance was also increased marginally to compensate for the terrible living conditions experienced on Dartmoor. This payment was enough for staff to visit Plymouth or Tavistock on a shopping trip. The sum was small but greatly appreciated of course. In the author's time it was £2.50 a week, and in 1947 would have been much less.

Few members of staff owned cars in 1947 and staff were compelled to live in prison quarters. If they had a day's leave they had to notify the prison in case their presence was immediately required. On a week's annual leave the holiday address would be given to the prison in case of 'call back'.

The staff accommodation post-war was damp and cold. Blackabrook House was a large building of 30 flats at the bottom of Burrator Avenue (Piano Street) and was used for storage by the Royal Navy during the Second World War. It was a dark, cold building and a nasty place to live in the cold winters. The house was demolished soon after the war to allow 30 Cornish Units to be built on the site. These are still staff houses, called Blackabrook Avenue, and in comparison to the old house they are palatial. With good wages and the many hours of compulsory overtime the standard of living for staff improved dramatically.

For a short period the Dartmoor convict halls held military prisoners who had deserted or contravened King's Regulations. They were sentenced by Courts Martial and taken to Dartmoor. A very puzzling decision was made at this time to house Borstal boys at Dartmoor. The Home Office issued the following statement:

The Home Secretary and the prison commissioners are conscious that the name of Dartmoor is associated in the public mind with a tradition very different from those ideas of borstal training, and it is only in the light of the unprecedented situation that they have all felt able to consider the step.
They are equally convinced that the evil of youths spending long waiting months in prison must be ended, and that the periods of waiting for admission to the institutions, to which they were committed, must be substantially reduced, with the hope of eventually abolishing them.
In the present circumstances the use of the buildings at Dartmoor is the only practical solution.
In view of the great shortages of houses it is not to be contemplated that labour and materials should be set aside for the building of a new institution at the present time.

So began another episode in the long history of Dartmoor Prison. Borstal boys were an extremely different group to handle. The author had first-hand experience of this while serving as a prison officer at Portland Borstal. A Borstal 'boy' could be six-feet, six-inches tall and married with three children. He could be the most violent of prisoners. It was the only prison in the country where a prison officer had been killed on duty, though subsequently an officer was killed in Norwich.

The new intake wreaked havoc at Dartmoor, and the number of escapes and attempted escapes rose dramatically. There were 12 attempted escapes in the first eighteen days alone, and though most of the perpetrators were recaptured on prison grounds some got as far as London.

Convicts serving long sentences at Dartmoor were in time trained by the intense discipline and conditioned to the type of behaviour accepted by staff. The Borstal boys, who were only in for a short period and had nothing to lose, acted with due wrecklessness, as when they set fire to the roof of the D1 hall.

Staff braved missiles of slates and granite stones to climb the rafters and enter the burning roof space above the cells. As the roof space was 70 feet above a granite-slabbed floor, the men were courageous in their work. They subdued the prisoners one by one and soon the fire brigade had controlled the blaze. The prison officers stated that the prison was 50 per cent under-staffed and insisted that the disciplinary powers over Borstal boys must be increased to a similar position as those with normal convicts. It was also stated that Dartmoor Prison was not a suitable place for them to be held.

After some of the most notorious boys were removed to other locations conditions improved slightly, but the military prisoners in other halls then began to show unrest. Some of them were sentenced to ten years' penal servitude, or hard labour, and eventually a strike by 40 soldiers took place. They were sentenced to bread and water and after a couple of days 15 of them gave in and resumed labour. The remaining men continued the strike for four more days before they too gave in. It was then agreed that the Borstal experiment was a disaster and the boys were slowly removed to other prisons. By the middle of April 1947 the last of them had left for good. Of course in later years many were to return as convicts.

With their departure ordinary convicts were sent to replace them and Dartmoor resumed its tightly-controlled existence. The 250 military prisoners were then removed to make room for more convicts.

This photograph (opposite) *purports to have been taken at Portland Convict Prison c.1900. In reality these convicts were photographed leaving Dartmoor Prison, the officer at the back is standing in the shadow of the Dartmoor Prison Arch, see photo below.*

Chapter Nine
PERSONAL RECOLLECTIONS

I arrived at Dartmoor Prison in 1968 having previously been employed at Exeter Gaol. I reported to the gate officer at 6.45am for a 7am start. When I rang the bell the gate was opened by a surly prison officer who told me to come in, shut up and stand still. Then I was told to wait beside the gate-keeper's hut and that somebody would be coming to meet me. I was in civvies of course.

After an endlessly long wait a principal officer (training) came over to me and said, 'Today is the day you will wake up for all time, this is Dartmoor Prison and Dartmoor Prison will never let you forget it... you can take an officer from Dartmoor but you cannot take Dartmoor from the officer.' This, I guarantee, was his exact speech. They were just words at the time and I did not fully realise what the officer meant but over the last thirty years I have discovered exactly how true they were.

I was taken to the first chief officer who welcomed me and told me to 'get a grip on those b_____ from day one'. He then gave me quite a talk and some good advice. I did not appreciate it all at the time but certainly have since. I have subsequently trained new works' staff on induction courses and have passed on those words given to me.

I was taken to the stores to draw my uniform. The uniform was heavy black serge with braces and no belt. The material was extremely hard-wearing which kept you warm in the winter but was suffocating in the summer, especially on hot sticky nights in my hall, B2, with 120 convicts in association. We wore blue separate collars, fixed to the shirt with two studs which, when new, would cut into your throat and leave purple bruises. Nobody told me that you should wash them a couple of times before wearing them to soften the starched edges of the collar.

I was then taken to the administration office and introduced to the staff there. Finally I was given a tour of the prison by another member of the POUTs (Prison Officer Under Training) training team. He elaborated on how to deal with 'the b_____s' and introduced me to the security require-ments at Dartmoor. My induction course was very thorough and lasted for three days. I was detailed to a wing which turned out to be B2 hall which was dubbed 'super B2' by the staff at the prison because of the very high standards of discipline demanded by the principal officer in B2 (now D-wing).

I was taken to the principal officer's office on B3 landing and introduced to him. He was a tall formidable man, weatherbeaten by many years on the moor, with a fierce attitude towards everything. He hated convicts and if anything was not absolutely correct he would explode and swear for five minutes without repeating himself once! The principal officer gave me his orders to forget all the other halls which I would see at certain times, and to concentrate on B-hall. He told me everything that he would require me to do and he defi-nitely expected me to comply at high speed.

One of his first instructions to me was that he would never be happy until all of the convicts were locked in their cells, the bolts put on, a final check made and the cell flaps put up, followed by the patrolling of the landing in complete and utter control and silence. That was his idea of how a landing should be run. A favourite comment was 'give them nothing and then take that away'. I soon learnt how to lock and unlock the cells very quickly.

There were usually three officers on each landing, sometimes two, depending on whether men were sick or detailed elsewhere. A rookie landing officer, such as me, would always have an experienced officer with him. All officers kept an eye on each other in case of trouble. We would arrive in the hall at 6.55am for a 7am unlock. At exactly 7am the principal officer would come out of his office and bellow 'unlock'. All of the officers would run to unlock as fast as we could, keeping one eye on each other for safety. The third officer would supervise the recess where the contents of the chamber pots were emptied.

Unlocking was the most dangerous time of the day. The convicts were extremely grumpy and usually without 'snout' (cigarettes) which made them irritable. The officer supervising the recess was surrounded by 40 convicts crowded into a small area. This meant that we could not see him at times which was unnerving. The convicts would take this opportunity at the recess to settle differences such as the non-payment of debts, a common practice that often resulted in slashings.

Being in debt to the tobacco barons was a dangerous situation for anyone to get into. For officers it made the speed of unlocking important so that everyone could concentrate on supervising all of the convicts on the landing. Sometimes I would see a prisoner entering another man's cell on the landing. I would then run to that cell as fast as possible and spring the lock on the door so that it could not slam shut with me inside. Why was the prisoner in somebody else's cell? Was he going to injure the prisoner occupying the cell? Was he going to steal something from a weaker prisoner? With so many other prisoners on the landing left unsupervised, was this merely a ploy to get me out of sight so that something could take place outside? All of these questions had to be kept in mind at such a moment. It was not an option to make a mistake; I had to be on the top line at all times.

When opening the cells at unlock time, a metal jug or the contents of a chamber pot could be thrown at your head. It happens to most officers at one time or another and is not a pleasant experience. These things are often not provoked by the officers but come as a result of the convict being wound up by the tobacco barons, or brooding through the night over a Dear John letter or a death in his family. The officer, likewise might be stressed over a problem at home. The result is usually an almighty clash. The officer has a lot to do with unlocking, slopping out and then returning the convicts to the cells, and he is already stressed. All of this time the convicts are asking constant questions, most of which you do not know the answer to. This all has to be coped with under the eye of the principal officer.

When finally all of the men were sorted and back in their cells the call 'nines' went out. This meant that it was time for your landing to go down three flights of stairs to collect their breakfast. Again, at the speed of light, you had to unlock the cells and get the convicts down to the hot plate on the ground floor. Then they must all be returned to the cells. Strong words might be exchanged with convicts who stopped to talk to their mates on the threes, fives or sevens landing.

The men were then issued with a razor blade so that they could shave. On return from breakfast these blades were collected. The prisoner was alone in his cell to shave so there was no danger of harm being caused to others. Razor blades were changed twice per week and any convict upsetting staff would have the same blade for a whole week. No comment from the

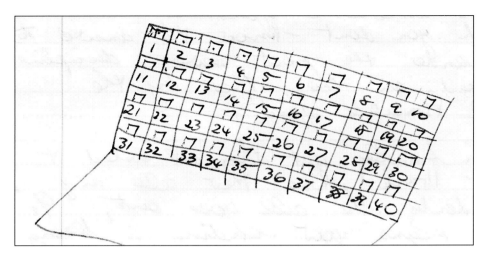

The author's rough sketch of the razor-blade holder. Blades were issued to convicts in their cells in the mornings enabling them to shave, the blades were then collected before convicts were unlocked for exercise. The blade holder was numbered so convicts received the same blade each day and blades were changed twice a week.

prisoner was tolerated at any time. The blades were stored in a folder for the landing with the cell number on the pocket so that the convict would always receive the right blade.

The prisoners would collect their breakfast, and all other meals, on a metal tray divided into sections, with a metal bowl for soup. As the convicts made their way back to their cells to eat – there was no dining room at Dartmoor Prison – the stronger convicts would sometimes try to steal choice items from the trays of the weaker men. The officers would have to keep a lookout for this as the convicts made their way back up the stairs. As soon as all the prisoners were 'away' I would shout my landing roll to the principal officer, for example, 'nines 36 sir, nines 35 in cell one working on the farm party', or whatever the state of the roll was.

Following this procedure I would make my way to the ground floor to sign a book and a certificate stating your roll. Needless to say the more senior officers would be on the ground-floor landing in B-hall which was the 'threes'. The next most senior officers would be on the next landing which was the 'fives' and so on to the most junior officers on the top landing, the 'nines'. Woe betide a junior officer who was 'out of position'.

I was asked by the principal officer who greeted me on arrival where I was planning to sleep the night. I informed him that I had booked a room in the Duchy Hotel which was known to staff as Heartbreak Hotel or Bleak House, depending on their mood! I was to remain there until I was allocated a prison quarter twelve weeks later.

After our own quick breakfast the order was given to 'unlock for exercise' and again the high-speed opening of cells would commence. We had to hold our prisoners on the landing despite their being keen to get out on to the exercise yard. A new officer had to be very careful as the old convicts would know he was green and take advantage. Sometimes an old lag would creep down to the next landing to cadge a snout off his mates. Invariably an old officer would spot him and a loud bellow would be heard. The convict would immediately return to his landing and the officer would lecture him in no uncertain terms that if he repeated this action he would be 'nicked'. This meant that he would be placed on report. The older convicts used to say he was 'getting a telegram to go to the Tea Garden' which was E-hall. The convict would in this case be taken by four officers to the chokey block, E-hall, to await punishment.

Usually a good firm telling off would be enough, with a severe warning of the trouble to come if the convict ever repeated the action. The hall principal officer would, in the meantime, take notice and later call the officer to somewhere the convicts could not hear. The officer would then get a good telling off for allowing the event to happen and be given a warning to keep his eyes open in future.

The landing would then be called down to exercise. The men had to be formed up in two ranks at the foot of the stairs. The other officer would make sure each cell was vacated and locked up so that the hall cleaners could not steal anything. Then away to the exercise yard.

A junior officer invariably got the worst position on the yard which was where the large D-hall almost met the boundary wall. A small road passed between them and the breakaway fence had not yet been fitted. Gale-force winds would be channelled through the gap and scream past the junior officer. In mid-winter this was purgatory! On a calm day the winds were quite strong and on a windy day it was difficult to stand upright. This famous spot for officers was called 'pneumonia corner'. The more senior basic-grade officers were always allocated sheltered, often sunny, spaces on the exercise yard, while the top-grade basic officers were with the exercise principal officer.

We would watch the convicts, who were generally in pairs, walk around and around and make sure we knew the number of convicts on the yard. The exercise officer would try to catch out the juniors by asking them how many men were exercising. His method of asking would be to bellow the word 'roll?' The junior was expected to give the answer immediately and, if he did not know, he would be told to find out and sent to the chief officer. He would then have to tell chief officer that he had not known the number of convicts on the exercise yard. The chief officer always knew the roll all over the prison for the hall, landing, farm, shop and the exercise yards. A lot of trouble could take place on the yards so utmost vigilance was paramount.

A 'Tally stone' set flush with ground on the exercise yard. On the call 'Form up' the prisoners would line up on their respective party stones. 19 party was a farm party and there was a corresponding stone for each of the many parties.

After thirty minutes of purgatory in the bitter Dartmoor winds, sometimes with snow in the air, the exercise principal officer would bellow 'form up' and the various parties would congregate alongside a tally stone, a slab with the number of the party cut into it. It was laid flush with the exercise yard. My my own party fell in alongside the No. 9 stone.

As soon as the tally principal officer was satisfied with the party numbers he would give the order to 'march off to labour'. One party at a time would comply until all parties had exited the yard. The party marched off with the senior party officer at the rear of the column where he could easily watch the men. The junior officer would be at the head of the column and the second senior office would be checking that the workshops were ready to receive the party. The second senior officer would check that the alarms and recesses were working and that the lights were good. He would then check for any planted items like coshes and blades. When satisfied he would go to the entrance of the shop to admit the party which I (the junior) would have brought to a halt.

The second officer opened the door and counted, with me, the numbers of convicts entering the shop. This number would be recorded in the daily occurrence book which was held by the senior basic officer in charge of No. 9 party. Any convict collected from No. 9-party shop for visits, haircuts, bathing or hospital would be entered in the book. It was absolutely critical that the book was accurate otherwise nobody would know if a man escaped.

There were two boxes where staff sat to supervise convicts, each with an alarm in case of trouble – this would alert the heavy gang who would arrive to sort out the problem. The senior and second officer always took these boxes with the senior officer at the entrance to keep his roll up to date. The junior officer was the patrol officer and I was detailed to patrol the whole shop supervising around 80 convicts (120 in the mailbag shop), all of whom had sharp implements in their hands.

I vividly remember my first day in the No. 9-party shop as the convicts were making pointed stakes out of three-quarter-inch diameter rod. They were about six-feet long and looked like spears, indeed they were being made for the military. The convict would put a rod into the roaring forges, operate the bellows and get about nine inches of the rod red-hot, then put it on an anvil and hammer it to a sharp point. This meant several trips from the forge to the anvils and back again and each time the convict would size up the officer as he passed him.

It was a disturbing experience for me as the brand new discipline officer. Every time a convict passed me he would hold the rod in the attack position and stare at me, making the threat obvious. I would then go right up to him, look him straight in the eye and order him to get on with his work, emphasising that if he continued to malinger he would be hearing from me again. He would look me up and down then smile and get on with his task. The convict would be satisfied that I could not be frightened. If only they knew that on this chilly November day I had a sweat on. I had been well trained by the fierce training principal officer and owe my most grateful thanks to him. One officer was run through the shoulder with a red hot spear by a mentally-ill convict.

Soon an officer relief would come into the blacksmiths' shop and replace the two senior officers on the boxes so that they could go to the tea boat for a break. At first they would take quite a time to go and come back, leaving me, as the junior, without any tea-break at all. As time went on and the two officers got to know and trust me, their breaks would speed up and I would have a short time in the tea boat as well. I was now accepted by the other officers in the blacksmiths' shop.

It was soon time to finish work and the senior officer would shout 'cease labour'. All of the tools would be checked and handed in and each of the prisoners searched as they left the shop. The prisoners 'formed up' into two ranks outside and I would be responsible for keeping the men in line. As soon as the officers returned to the party the order to 'march off' was given by the senior officer who would, again, be at the rear of the column. I would lead the party down the main drive trying to maintain a sensible speed. The convicts heading the team would do their best to speed up, leaving those at the back with a job to catch up.

The convicts would be marching in pairs at all times and, when we reached the tally officer, I would give the order to halt. As soon as the party had all caught up and lined themselves up in pairs the tally officer would give the order to 'march off'. I would lead the party into B-hall and up to the landings. Here I would await the arrival of the remaining two party officers. The tally principal officer would have counted the party past him and roll would be agreed with the senior officer at the rear of the party.

Each prisoner had been trained, sometimes for more than fifteen years, to stand in the doorway to their cell without talking or moving. This was a tricky point during the day when men would be tempted to talk and wander. It was my job to keep them standing there until other officers arrived. As soon as they did we would unlock all the cells at speed and put all of the convicts in before locking and bolting the doors. The bolt sliding across indicated that a convict was in so the senior officer would march quickly around the landing checking that the bolts were across. He would then report to the hall principal officer 'B nine, 39 sir', or whatever the state of the landing.

Any mail for the prisoners would then be brought up and delivered to the correct cell. Some of the men did not receive a single letter for years on end; some never had a single visitor.

All this brought the time to 11.30am and I would be completely drained. The senior staff on the landing would not seem tired and it took some years before I reached the same state as the old sweats. This was only half the day's work completed. If you were scheduled on evening duty this would have been the equivalent of much less than half a day's work. The same procedure took place in the afternoon and then I would be away for tea.

The evening duty staff would take control at this point and the prisoners would be unlocked for classes, games and association until 9pm. Convicts taking part in classes outside the hall would have to be marched there under close control as it would now be dark outside. Two officers would escort the party as it snaked its way up corridors and around corners. This meant that the party was sometimes out of sight of the officer which allowed dirty deeds to be carried out by one convict to another, perhaps associated with debts or failure of a convict to recognise the leader of a convict pack.

The classes and association at an end, all convicts returned to their hall. On each hall a junior officer would be on duty on the gate. He would have first booked out the parties on to a board which indicated the number leaving the wing to go to respective classes. The class principal officer would check the board and go to the classes to check the roll was correct – something that was done many times throughout the day. The junior officer would check the returning party to ensure that numbers were correct and then apply a special lock to the door once the officer in charge of the party had entered the hall. This lock was on the outside so that if the prisoners snatched keys from men inside the hall they still would not be able to leave it.

The party would go up to their landing and were given ten minutes in which to collect water in metal jugs from the taps in the recess. They could also go to the toilet under strict control. Then the shout of 'all away' would come from the hall principal officer on the ground floor. The officers would meticulously check each cell, lock the door and put the cell flap up. If the convict wanted medical assistance in the night, and that only, he could push a button in his cell. This would push a bar through the cell wall causing the flap to drop. An officer coming up to the landing would be able to see which cell need attention. He would not be able to unlock the cell as no staff carried keys at night but could call an orderly if assistance or access to the cell was required.

A main evening duty shift was from 6.30pm, when I would leave the Duchy Hotel until 9.45pm when I would finally get back to my room – an unforget-table experience in itself. There would be no breakfast available when I got up at 5.45am and no supper when I returned at 9.45pm. The convicts who worked at the Duchy would have been marched back to the prison at 5pm and would not arrive in the morning until 8am. I soon learned that the best thing was to buy a kettle and a supply of food from Bolt's Store opposite. There was no heating in the hotel and no floor covering. Everything would freeze up in the winter, including glasses of water on the bedside table. Nobody ever men-tioned anything about the Duchy Hotel to new officers as it was a case of letting them find out and get a grip on things for themselves. The first week in 'Bleak House' in December was quite an experience but I can honestly say I would not have missed it for the world.

The first week of my service at Dartmoor was certainly traumatic. Many staff members would not tell you what to do or how to do it. Sometimes they would not even answer you properly, the only comment from a few officers was, 'nobody told me either but I learnt OK, you do the same'. Some of the officers would not talk to a junior even if it was only two of you on one particular job, at least until he got to know and trust you. I accepted this as normal but swore that when I became a senior officer I would never act the same way as these men towards a junior officer.

The working week was supposed to be five days with two rest days off. That was purely theoretical as we were detailed three main shifts plus two main shifts with evening duty. In addition we were guaranteed a call-in on at least one of the rest days or, if staff was short owing to sickness or annual leave, then it might be on both rest days. This would mean seven days a week of very hard work. All of this was good training for young officers who were taught to be self-sufficient and reliable. They must also be disciplined and loyal to fellow officers. You would never let a fellow officer out of your sight while on duty.

The years 1969 and 1970 saw major changes to inmate conditions at Dartmoor. Previously, cells had rough, bare granite walls with limewash applied to the granite. This was called bug-blinding as the limewash killed off a lot of the insect infestation of the granite. Sometimes, if the wash had been applied for many years, layer over layer, it would be very thick. The works' department trades' officers were discipline officers who trained and worked with a gang of convicts who carried out the ongoing maintenance work on the prison. Thus the prisoners learned building techniques such as plastering, painting, electrical work and plumbing, many doing well for themselves after their release by setting up their own firms.

The water system was diabolical with the main water supply to the bath-house, slop sinks for slopping out, and all water-closets being from the bog water supply. This water had collected on the moor and was completely untreated. Because of the quantity of peat in suspension it looked like Guinness and would stain cups a deep brown. The drinking-water supply was called Mis Tor Line. That is exactly what it was. The natural spring water was collected on the prison estate in an underground chamber with ladders down into it. Here it was collected in a six-inch cast-iron pipe and taken all the way to the water treatment works above the North Hessary Tor side of the prison estates.

A water treatment worker would clean the water to a high standard which was tested daily by the government chemist. A supply was piped to the prison halls with a tap in each recess for drinking only. Of course water was also piped to all of the staff quarters, and inadvertently to some private accommodation in Princetown where pipes were connected to the Mis Tor prison supply by mistake, instead of to South West Water Authority pipes. Theirs, incidentally came from the same source above Wheel Lucky.

Once a week convicts would be collected from the workshops by the bathing officer and taken to the bath-house. The baths were filled halfway by a convict known as the bath-house orderly. It would be impossible to see the bottom of the bath because of the colour of the water. When drained out the peat would stain the bathtub a mahogany colour and the metal residues would leave red streaks on the bath which were nigh on impossible to remove, so few people bothered to try. The general feeling at Dartmoor Prison was that if you did not like it, you should not have come.

The old bath-house prior to its demolition. A new bath-house was built in the 1960s; the water came straight from the Bog Line on the moors and therefore was untreated and a dark brown colour.

HENRY AND THE PRISON POND

The prison pond outside the hospital has a small fountain in its centre which kept the pond topped up, the overflow going into an old prison leat, which took it away to the Blackabrook river. But the most important function of the fountain was to indicate the pressure of the bog water supply. We set the fountain-water height by means of an adjacent valve, to about 18 inches high.

The principal officer responsible for water supplies (we had three) would check the height of the water on his rounds. If lower than 18 inches, it meant the pressure was reduced, sometimes due to heavy usage. When all the halls stopped using water at lock-up, the pressure would come up and the fountain would resume its normal height. Thus it was a useful visual sign that all was well. In our bog water (untreated, unmetered) supply we would often get small trout which found their way into the roof tanks, causing blockages in the pipeworks around the prison.

A famous fish was a huge trout, called Henry by the red-band convict who was responsible, among other things, for taking care of this pond and its plants. He had found this small fish in the bog supply in the halls, kept it in a jar and fed it. When it grew too large for the jar, he put it in the pond and fed it with boiled egg and other morsels he had saved from his own meals. On my regular checks around the prison I would see the convict attending to the pond and would ask, 'How is Henry, today?'

He always told me with some pride that his fish was fine. In due course Henry died, which caused much anguish to the old convict. He managed to bury it in one of the prison gardens, only he knows where.

Above: *Beautiful gardens at the bottom of the main drive, possibly where Henry, the trout, was buried by the old convict who took such good care of him.*
Above right: *Henry's pond outside the hospital entrance.*

FAREWELL TO ARMS

The works' department, of which I was now a member, did extremely well in maintaining all of the prison buildings. I have already spoken of the convicts who would quarry and dress the granite before transporting it to the prison where it was used to construct the impressive buildings. This work was watched over by the artisan warders, in other words the works' department. A1, A2, B1, B2, C, D1 and D2 specials halls were all constructed by these men, and during the work many of the convicts lost their lives through accident. The buildings remain as the only lasting tribute to these men who worked so hard. The tradition of the artisan warder and his team of workers has continued up to the present day and has proved the works' department to be a splendid organisation which has saved the prison enormous sums of money over one-hundred-and-fifty years.

Deaths at the quarry were, unfortunately, fairly regular. In 1887 two warders and one convict were injured and another convict died when dynamite exploded prematurely. It was a tremendous explosion which dislodged huge lumps of granite, about six-feet cubed. One convict was crushed by a stone and a crane was hurried to the scene to lift the huge boulder. The man was removed but only lived for half an hour as a result of serious internal injuries. The two warders and one convict received minor injuries from flying pieces of rock.

Guns were used at Dartmoor Prison from its opening in 1809 until they were withdrawn in 1953, one-hundred-and-forty-four years later. Firstly old muskets were used which were followed by Snider carbines. These fired large balls of lead which measured .577 inch. Because of the number of serious injuries inflicted on escaping convicts the carbines were bored smooth from about 1897 in order to reduce the range. Buckshot was also introduced to make the area of spread greater and reduce the loss of life.

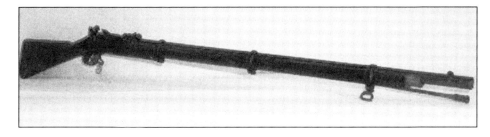

Buckshot consisted of twelve balls of lead per charge, each ball being more than a quarter-inch in diameter, so it was still lethal. With the reduced power of the charge and the replacement of balls with buckshot, the chance of hitting convicts increased while the chance of killing them decreased. This was the intention, to halt the men but not to kill them. The last officer to fire a carbine at an escaping convict at Dartmoor was Charlie Elcombe.

One Friday in early October 1951 Charlie was out with No. 23 farm party, comprising C. Dunkley, the officer in charge, Charlie as the gun guard, and Pedlar Palmer on pony patrol, along with about a dozen convicts. Two convicts called Cook and Smith made a dash for freedom, jumping over the farm gate and running at great speed towards some woodland. Charlie called for them to stop, to no avail, so he fired the gun. He missed both of them and they got away, perhaps because they were out of range.

The two men were at large for three days before being recaptured. It was later discovered that they had reached the Mary Tavy area before one of them fell into a flooded quarry. The other convict jumped in to help him out. This was confirmed in evidence at the subsequent adjudication. Gun guards continued to carry carbines until 1953 when Governor Major Harvey called Charlie to his office and informed him that he had acceded to a request from Head Office that the incident in 1951 would be the last time a firearm would be used at Dartmoor. Charlie would be entered in the annals of Dartmoor Prison as the last man to fire at convicts. The carbines were withdrawn, along with the pistols carried by the pony and night patrols.

Snider carbines issued to all outside gun guards and to the sentries at the main gate.

After the Second World War three German officers attacked a fellow country-man in a prisoner-of-war camp because they suspected him of being a 'grass' or informer. The three prisoners were sentenced to five years' imprisonment. One of the men, Herman Wurdermann, was finally sent to Dartmoor in December 1947. He took notes throughout his imprisonment and eventually used them to compile a book about his experiences, called *Schwere Jahre als Soldat an Ost- und Westfront und als Sträfling in Dartmoor*.

Herr Wurdermann's book gives a good idea of how staff and convicts acted in 1947, and checks with prison officers of the day confirm that it is indeed a very accurate document.

Wurdermann was released from Dartmoor on 1 October 1948 having spent the final part of his sentence working in the prison officers' mess at the Duchy Hotel, now the Dartmoor High Moorland Centre. In 1978 Wurdermann asked permission to visit Dartmoor Prison. This was granted and Governor Colin Heald, and Chief Officer Denis Sutton, escorted him down to his old cell. It was a fruitful visit for him as he was treated as a VIP and given a full tour of the prison. Little could he have known during his incarceration at the dreaded prison that thirty years later he would return as an honoured guest.

Dartmoor Prison's four gates, c.1890s. No. 1 is the outer arch with the armed sentry, and the principal officer is armed with a sabre. No. 2 is the main wooden gates left open for the photographer. No. 3 gates are the iron double gates with two staff in attendance. No. 4 gates are at the entrance into the administration building at the bottom of the main drive. When the author joined Dartmoor there was an additional sliding door between the outer wooden gates and the inner iron gates, now removed.

Chapter Ten
MEMORABLE MEN

A DYMOND CHARACTER

On 28 February 1873 William Dymond arrived at Dartmoor Prison as an assistant warder. His service at Dartmoor would lead to many great things for Dymond, including being governor of a prison in Australia. He was born on 6 June 1848, and on 29 October 1869 he joined the Devon Constabulary at Exeter. His police number was 337L and he served at C Division, Thorverton, Devon, for just over three years.

Dymond resigned on 30 November 1872 to join the convict prison services. He was sent to Millbrook Prison in London for three months of convict prison training. His three years' experience in policing stood him in good stead. He was then transferred to Dartmoor.

Dartmoor Prison in the late 1800s was not a pleasant working environment. I have already spoken of the back-breaking work, the savage weather and the violence of convicts towards the staff. This included the convicts striking the staff with shovels and axes, crowbars, spades and granite rocks, all being easily come by on the farm, in the quarry and in the workshops. Many warders had to be invalided out of the service after such assaults.

William Dymond served for more than five years at Dartmoor under this serious threat of injury, as well as the strict rule of his superior officers, before leaving on 20 September 1878.

In February 1879 Dymond sailed to Sydney, Australia where he joined the New South Wales Prison Service on 1 March 1879. Dymond was then rapidly promoted due to his experience as a policeman and his five years of experience on Dartmoor. He served as a chief warder at Darlinghurst, Goulburn, Berrima and Trials Bay gaols. In 1888 the Forbes police lock-up was upgraded to a gaol and William Dymond became its first governor. He was positioned there from 15 November 1888 until 30 June 1894 when he was forced to resign due to ill health after an attack by a prisoner.

Above: *William Dymond was a police officer at Thorverton, Devon, and a warder in Australia.*
Left: *The Trials Bay gaol where Dymond was the chief warder.*

Top: *Laggers Point built by transported convicts.* Above: *Lookout post at Laggers Point.* Above right: *Trials Bay gaol cells.*

On 16 July 1894, after fifteen years away, William Dymond sailed from Sydney to Plymouth aboard the SS *Ophir* with his family, arriving back in England on 29 August 1894. Perhaps he went up to Dartmoor Prison to see the changes that had taken place, mindful of the saying, 'you can take the man from Dartmoor but you cannot take Dartmoor from the man'.

William purchased a farm in West Hatch, Somerset, in 1895 and farmed there until 23 March 1903. One of the main reasons for the family's return to England was so that his two sons, thirteen-year-old Arthur George and eleven-year-old Basil Claude could receive an English education. They were sent to St John's Hospital School, Exeter, where they remained until May 1903, a total of eight years.

Dymond then sold the farm in Somerset and returned to Sydney with his family, sailing on the SS *Salamis* on 25 May 1903. Later that year Dymond bought a 150-acre farm in Bargo and farmed there until the death of his second wife in June 1920. He then married his third wife, Emma Shields, in Mittagong on 10 May 1923 at seventy-five years old. He retired to Auburn with Emma and lived happily there for twelve years. He died aged eighty-seven on 20 August 1935. Later a street in Bargo was named after him. This seems quite a life for a Dartmoor Prison warder, to seek new horizons and never give up, and to work hard at everything until success was achieved. He was certainly a credit to Dartmoor Prison.

During my service there I met many other unforgettable people, both staff and convicts. Here I will share some of my memories about these men.

THE BIRD-MAN OF DARTMOOR PRISON

Paddy W was a convict at Dartmoor who, early in his sentence, found a baby jackdaw on the ground. The bird had fallen out of its nest and was really too young to survive on its own. Paddy smuggled the bird into his cell and fed it, firstly on spittle, to try to recover its strength. Under his care the jackdaw soon grew into a strong bird and believed Paddy to be one of its parents! Paddy would put the bird on to his window ledge and feed it throughout the day. On one occasion Paddy opened the sliding pane of his cell window and let the bird outside. Paddy would call him and the bird would return.

One day he let the bird out and it flew away. I was on the works' party and had the men lined up so that they could be distributed for labouring by the works' officer. Paddy suddenly called out. Prisoners in ranks were not allowed to talk and Paddy was told to shut up or he would be sent to see the governor in the morning. The bird, meanwhile, had recognised Paddy's call and flown down to sit on his shoulder, so Paddy immediately secreted it inside his coat. I noticed him do so but took no action.

Many times when Paddy was working in the open air he would call the jackdaw and it would fly down to see him. He nearly always had titbits hidden in his pocket which he would feed to his beloved bird. On returning to the hall at cease labour Paddy would release the bird to allow it to fly onto the hall roof. Once back in his cell, he would open the window and call the bird which would fly down to join him in the hall. Here the jackdaw would be fed and would remain all night. In the morning he would again be released through the window prior to Paddy leaving for labour, only to be reunited elsewhere in the prison during the day. This routine went on for about a year when, after being released at breakfast time, the bird was never seen again by Paddy.

He told me this with tears running down his cheeks and dripping from his chin. Paddy was a well-built convict, six-feet tall and hard as nails, but a real softy at heart. This escapade with the jackdaw had remained with me for ever. Wherever you are Paddy may you live a long time and never set foot inside a prison again! You are far too much a gentleman to be a convict.

It is a strongly believed tradition of the old Dartmoor convicts that when one dies he will return to haunt the prison in the form of a jackdaw. This poem, a conversation between a convict and a jackdaw he has seen on the roof of the prison wing, is by Oliver Davies, a former clerk there, from his book of *Dartmoor Prison Lyrics*:

Transmigration

Convict	*'Jackdaw, Jackdaw, why do you croak* *High on your old rooftree?'*
Jackdaw	*'Once I was a four-letter bloke.* *And I again may be.'*
Convict	*'Jackdaw, Jackdaw, what was the name* *Of him whose soul you bear?'*
Jackdaw	*'William Jones inhabits my frame* *Though he was laid elsewhere.'*
Convict	*'Jackdaw, Jackdaw, pity my groans* *Was it the truth you spoke?'*
Jackdaw	*'Yes, I surely was William Jones* *When a four-letter bloke.'*
Convict	*'Jackdaw, Jackdaw, down from your tree,* *William Jones was my Sire* *You shall come home when I am free* *And sit beside my fire.'*

Every convict wears a badge on his arm and cap, which tells staff how many sentences he has served, the years in which he received them, and the length of his current sentence. So a four-letter bloke is a convict whose badge denotes that he has spent most of his life in prison.

TAFFY'S BALL AND CHAIN BALLYHOO

A second convict I remember very well was a man who worked with me whom we shall call Taffy Horsfall. One day we were working at the Duchy Hotel prison officers' mess repairing some water-closets and, having finished, took our rubbish to the Duchy secure yard. Unknown to me Taffy had found a short piece of chain and a ballcock from a lavatory cistern at the dump and managed to tie them to look like a ball and chain around his ankle.

As we came out of the Duchy there was, as usual, a large crowd of visitors who had come to see the prisoners at Dartmoor. Taff let out a cry, 'Don't hit me no more boss, I will work harder in future!' The crowd stood staring like polecats while I took hold of Taff and ordered him to remove the ball and chain. I told him that he was 'nicked' (placed on report) and we headed back to the prison. Much later I saw the funny side and gave Taff a serious lecture on behaviour outside the prison. I told him that he had let me down badly and that he was risking being transferred to the dreaded mailbag party (No. 4). I never did put Taff on report and the subject was never mentioned again.

On another occasion I was working on the Mis Tor water supply, a long way out on the prison estates when I heard somebody calling out loudly. I immediately stopped Taffy from working and we hurried towards the sound. We were on prison property where there should have been nobody else around. On running round a corner of the prison leat we saw a horse and rider in the leat struggling desperately to get out but sinking slowly.

The rider was a young girl who had gone for a ride across the moors and mistakenly strayed on to prison property. Seeing the leat ahead, she had picked up speed to jump over it but the horse had slipped and they had both tumbled in. In several places at the bottom of a leat there are springs which bubble up from way below and the sand is very soft so a person or animal can sink rapidly. The struggling horse was getting deeper and deeper as the girl tried to hold its head above the water.

We reached the scene and I realised that we would need a rope. I ordered Taff to run a mile back to the leat hut on his own to fetch one. As he did so, I jumped into the water to try to keep the girl from sinking. I was sinking into the springs myself so told the girl to get out and leave the horse but naturally she refused and did manage to calm the horse quite a bit. After a while Taffy, whom I had forgotten all about in the heat of the moment, returned. Holding the rope, he jumped into the leat, took a deep breath and vanished under the water. He reappeared then dived again, swam to the other side of the horse and again resurfaced holding the end of the rope, having managed to get the rope underneath the horse and up the other side.

Together we all pulled on the rope and the horse finally managed to stagger from the leat and lay on the grass shaking. Eventually it recovered enough to be led away by the young girl, after she had received a lecture about going into the leat and indeed being on prison property in the first place. Taffy was also shaking like a leaf. It was extremely cold on the estates, he had taken several kicks from the horse and was bleeding from scratches and small wounds.

I immediately took Taffy back to the prison. As we passed his office, the deputy governor appeared and said, 'What has happened? Come in and tell me.' We went upstairs to the governor's office to explain the situation and he was most impressed. He later arranged for Taffy's sentence to be shortened. Taffy, although a convict, was a true gentleman who never took liberties with anyone.

It is surprising to outsiders to hear that bonds exist between the hated screws and the convicts. Out of my respect for Taffy's hard work and his never causing trouble, and because I never abused him by overwork or placed him on report for trivial things, we got on well together. Inside the prison he received the same treatment as the other convicts and told me once that he would never want it any other way.

THE GALLOPING MAJOR

Another time I was working on the manholes leading down to the take-off point on the prison leat with two convicts. One of the patrol officers on horseback approached. Their duty was security and he was heading my way at some speed to check up on things. I was horrified to see that he intended to jump the very wide leat. The horse slipped and unshipped the officer straight into the leat, then followed him in, but managed to scramble out immediately. Memories of the young girl flooded back but the officer climbed out unscathed, remounted, checked that I was OK, and rode off.

The two convicts were holding their faces with both hands trying their utmost not to laugh out loud. I turned a blind eye to this and told them to get on with their work and avoid getting into trouble. The officer was known ever after as the 'Galloping Major'. I am not quite sure how the news got back to the prison.

FATHER FAMINE

There was an officer cook and baker at the prison who was known as Father Famine due to the very small meals often served by him. He was very touchy about the name and all hell would be let loose if it was let slip by convicts or by the staff. One day, when I was on duty as a discipline officer in charge of security, the officer decided to do a special recipe which he called the Dartmoor fishcake. The 30-strong convict staff would muck in to help him with food preparation.

The prisoners piled an enormous amount of unknown ingredients on to the mixing table. A well was made in the middle of the mound and water was added, much like the concrete making I used to do in my building days. Too much water was added in my opinion but it was one of the convicts who spoke up and said to Father Famine, 'There is too much water, sir.' With this Father Famine went mad and hit the convict on the head with a wooden spoon! He shouted, 'Shut your mouth and keep mixing or I will throw you into the fire.' We had large coke-filled ovens in those days which later in my service as a works' officer I had the pleasure of replacing.

It was obvious to all by now that there was far too much water and the convicts kept adding dry material to the water making it rise ominously. Father Famine did not want the convicts to be proved right, and again would not allow for some of the water to be drained away. He ordered some of the convicts to follow him into the dry store and piled them with all sorts of dried goods to put into the pile and soak up the water. One convict whispered to me, 'It's like Noah's flood all over again!' I thought it wise not to mention that to Father Famine.

At this point I asked Father Famine if I should drain off some water. He replied in a nasty manner, 'That will only prove the convicts were right, whose side are you on and what do you know about cooking anyway? I have been doing this for thirty years so shut your mouth and supervise convicts, that's your job.' So the convicts kept adding dry goods of unknown description and the pile grew dramatically without making any difference to the water level. We just could not keep the absorption going and the water eventually won the battle. A hole appeared in the massive pile and a terrific avalanche carried most of the materials and water on one side off the table. We tried desperately to stem the flood but my uniform was covered with evil-smelling material which washed on to the floor and into the drains running across the kitchen.

Father Famine gave the order for the convicts to clean the floor and drains and save the little left on the table for the prisoners' tea, reinforcing just how appropriate the name Father Famine was. He turned to me and said, 'B_____ them, I will give the cons a bit of bully beef to make up for a small portion of fishcake.' He then bellowed to the convicts, 'Two of you fetch a couple of cans of bully beef and open them up and slice them as thin as you can.' This was the meal for a roll of about 600 convicts – a small dollop of Dartmoor fishcake in the middle of a large tray with an almost transparent slice of bully beef about two inches square. Father Famine instructed the convicts who were serving to 'spread the fishcake out on the tray to make it look more'.

Father Famine's name was brought to the fore in all discussions by convicts and staff. Convicts were not allowed to complain and if they did would be sent back to their cells and told to shut up. On the other hand, many of the cons treated Father Famine with great respect in hopes of improving their rations, and they thought it very funny that he flooded the kitchen. But needless to say some meals had, by necessity, to be smaller to compensate for all the dry goods lost in 'Noah's flood', and the thin slice of bully beef. Thankfully when another cook and baker known as TK, a superb officer and a strong disciplinarian, was on duty, meals improved dramatically all round.

It is interesting to compare typical Christmas meals some fifty years apart:

The Christmas Day Lunch 1932

12oz potatoes
4oz bully or canned corned beef
4oz bread
3oz cabbage
3oz prison-made Christmas Pudding

The Christmas Fare 1980

BREAKFAST: fresh grapefruit, cereal, egg and bacon, beans and mushrooms

LUNCH: Cream of tomato soup, roast turkey with cranberry sauce, stuffing, chipolatas, roast potatoes, sprouts, sweetcorn, gravy, Christmas Pudding, rum sauce and coffee

SUPPER: Sliced ham, cheddar cheese, beetroot, pickle, fruit salad, ice cream, individual Christmas cakes and mixed nuts, mince pie and hot chocolate at bedtime

Whenever I think of my service at Dartmoor I think of Father Famine and cannot fail to smile even after all these years. Then there was the officer named Mr Pastry by the prisoners on account of his cooking.

MR PASTRY

Mr Pastry had obviously lost all sense of taste. Many of his meals were reasonable but his pastries were abominable, they set like concrete and no amount of soaking could render them edible. Many of the convicts did not have teeth which did not help. When on discipline duty on the landings my convicts would complain to me that the pastry was not suitable for the mice and jackdaws which they kept in their cells. I would order them back into their cells and they would not dare complain to the fierce hall principal officer. The convicts would say 'it's not forever', give a sigh and return to their cells where they would slam the door.

THE ICE MAN

Another memorable character made his mark, literally, in the snow. There was often heavy snowfall on the moors especially around Rundlestone Ridge, the highest point. The prison leat was, and still is, an open ditch about four-feet wide with bog water for recesses, toilets and, indeed, baths. Whenever heavy snow fell the prison leat would become blocked which was disastrous on those landings where there were only two water-closets. The workshops, too, could not operate without water-closet facilities.

When I was in the works' department I would take a party of convicts, as usual poorly dressed for the conditions, and march them up to Rundlestone Ridge where my friend Cyril Sinclair would ask me to clear certain areas. The main problem was finding the leat as the whole area would be white with snow, but one member of the party who had been selected for snow-clearing for a number of years had a trick. He would march off across country with all of the party standing in amazement that the staff would allow him to do so. All of a sudden the prisoner would vanish from sight having found the leat all by himself.

We then hurried to the scene following his deep tracks to find the hole in the snow. Bellows of raucous laughter would be heard coming up from the depths and the convict would then be dug out by the party. He would be given a drink of tea which Cyril had made in the leat hut and told to sweep out the hut in the warm. He was named Leat Hut Orderly for the day to keep him out of the cold. The party would work hard to try and keep warm as they shovelled snow from the leat. Inevitably water would be shovelled out too and covered the convicts until their hair froze into tiny icicles which would chink together like a chandelier as they moved. The prisoner who found the leat each winter was a memorable character.

Eventually it was decided that something permanent should be done to keep the leat from blocking up. When I was deputy works' officer part of my responsibility was the leat and water supplies. So, with the correct funding, I purchased some long lengths of 12-inch wide plastic pipes which I had the leat-man bury at the bottom of the leat. In future, no matter how much snow fell, we would always have two 12-inch pipes' worth of water available.

Two 12-inch pipes laid in bottom of leat to make sure there is a water supply in blizzards.

I could not possibly record every memorable member of staff I had the pleasure of working with but here follows memories of four staff members, Cyril Sinclair, Dave Bone, Tim Easterbrook and Chilli Frampton.

THE CYRIL SINCLAIR STORY

Cyril Sinclair worked as the prison's leat-man for more than thirty years, his job being to ensure that the prison always had a supply of leat water. Dartmoor Prison is also a meteorological station and has recorded weather conditions since 1875. These were firstly passed on to the Admiralty and of late to the Meteorological Office at Bracknell. At 3.20pm on 6 July 1983, the records show, there was an incredible rainstorm with thunder and lightning.

Met. rainfall chart on the day that Cyril Sinclair was killed by lightning.

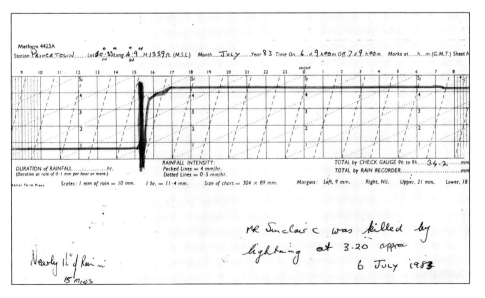

As the most senior works' officer on duty that day I received a phone call at 5.15pm from the orderly officer that Cyril Sinclair had not reported back from work and had not handed his radio in to the orderly room. Cyril was a most diligent and conscientious man who was never sick or late for work, so this was most out of character. I suspected that his watch must have stopped. I immediately despatched two of my staff to search for him, officers Baskett and Lloyd, both very experienced and knowledgeable men who knew the prison estates like the back of their hands.

Trades' Officer Baskett came back very red in the face having run two miles to the prison. He said that they had found Cyril lying injured beside the leat and requested that an ambulance be sent. I alerted the orderly officer who telephoned for one. But I drew a stretcher from the prison hospital as I knew that an ambulance would not be able to get very close to Cyril and set off with six of my staff in the prison Land Rover. At the leat we saw Cyril lying face down on the path, his face quite black. At the inquest it was established that he had been struck by lightning.

I went to Cyril's head to help lift him on to the stretcher so that we could carry him to wherever the ambulance would be waiting. Before carrying him away I pushed two red matches into the path behind his shoulders to mark where he had been lying. Cyril was carried to the ambulance which had managed to drive a little way up the track leading to Fice's Well below the leat path. His brother Bernard helped to lift him into the ambulance. A couple of days later I cut a rough cross out of granite and made it up into a horizontal slab.

Prison leat and the Cornish and Devon River Authorities areas.

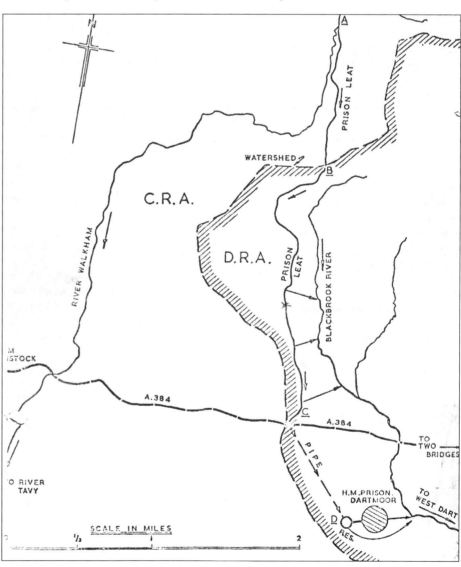

The next day I took a prisoner with me on to the leat to carry the slab out to where Cyril had fallen. He was the same prisoner who had usually worked on the leat with Cyril but mercifully had remained in the prison that day because of a family visit, otherwise he too would have been killed. We found the red matches sticking out of the grass and I personally bedded the slab down so that the centre of the cross coincided with the position of Cyril's heart as he lay beside the beloved leat which he had tended and nurtured for so many years. I was lucky to count Cyril amongst my friends, a quiet, loyal and deep-thinking man.

On checking the rainfall chart I saw that at 3.20pm, the time of the thunderclap, there had been 34.2 millimetres of rain in just fifteen minutes. There had been no other rain or thunder that day so poor Cyril must have died at 3.20pm on 6 July 1983 to the sound of the tremendous thunder.

Early on 4 September 1913 several cattle were killed by lightning at the same spot, which is the highest point around Princetown. Directly to the west the land falls to the Merivale area and the Walkham river and to the east to the Dart rivers. Water falling to the west of Rundlestone Ridge was the responsibility of the Cornwall River Authority and that falling to the east was the responsibility of the Devon Water Authority.

The exact spot where Cyril Sinclair was killed, the cross made and placed by the author in 1983.

A postcard of prison cattle killed by lightning in the same area, 1913.

PONY PATROLS

The famous pony patrols were an institution at Dartmoor, used initially just after the turn of the century. They were mentioned in records in 1902 but may have been used earlier. They were an efficient unit at Dartmoor and delighted the tourists for more than seventy years. In earlier years the patrols were

Prison mounted patrols; a superb body of selected officers who patrolled all external areas ensuring the safety of staff. They would also chase convicts who were trying to escape.

armed with a revolver, and a sabre was mounted on the saddle. On the tireless sturdy ponies an officer would patrol all areas where prisoners were working to ensure the officer's safety and to catch escaping convicts over an area which extended to more than five miles from the prison.

Tim Easterbrook who became a prison officer in 1927 and spent twelve of his thirty-three years' service on mounted patrol told me many tales of escape and capture from those days. Another stalwart was Cecil 'Chilli' Frampton who joined the service in 1932 and was a mounted patrol officer for two years. He then became stable officer looking after all the horses, both those used for mounted patrol and the farm horses. The farm horses numbered 14 carthorses and eight brood mares while there were eight mounted patrol ponies. Chilli would breed the horses and one of his favourites was a horse called Billy.

Chilli broke in Billy and trained him to jump fences, and after being sold to a man in Cornwall he became an excellent showjumper. Sadly Billy was killed by a bad fall at an event so Chilli made a memorial stone which was placed beside the stable entrance. One escaping convict was chased by Chilli who bowled him over. He was handcuffed to the saddle and brought back to the farm officers.

Another favourite horse was Blind Bob who was an extremely hard-working carthorse, guided by the reins of course. When shut in his field at night during the summertime the staff children would go to the gate, call Blind Bob and he would come to them for the titbits they had brought. Chilli became the farm manager for the last part of his long service.

Dave A. Bone was the last officer to ride mounted patrols. He was detailed main shift on Christmas Eve in 1974 which he completed at 5.30pm. Nobody has patrolled on horseback since. I also talked to Dave on numerous occasions about his pony patrol days checking on the outside parties. These exceeded 200 convicts, most of whom were on long sentences and looking for a way to escape.

The bogs were treacherous and during my time at Dartmoor, an officer on patrol radioed back to the prison that he had inadvertently gone into a bog and was up to the horse's chest in mud. Reception was unclear and the prison ordered him to go to a different location and radio in again! This remained a great topic of conversation with members of staff for years to come. The mounted patrols were on duty in all types of weather on the moors and were a credit to the service for more than seventy years.

MRS COOK'S MEMORIES

On 23 March 1989 a Mrs Cook (née Coombs) wrote to me with her memories as a child in Princetown. Here is some of the information contained in a letter she gave to me on a visit to see me at the prison.

My father Hubert John Coombs joined the Prison Service at the age of thirty in 1903 and was sent to Dartmoor, prior to which he was a Bath Stone mason working for a firm by the name of Long, they did a lot of church work also at the Roman Baths in Bath. He married my mother Alice Louisa Batchelor at Gt Cheverall, Wiltshire in 1903 and I was born in July 1904, the eldest of five children, me, Winifred Alice, then Irene May, then Ethel Elizabeth, then William John followed by Aileen Ellen. We lived at No. 8, No. 9 Block until I was four years old and then moved to 13A Quarters and from there to 12H Quarters where my parents stayed until my father retired at the end of March 1931. He would never consider having a transfer from Dartmoor as he always liked the working of the prison.

I went to Princetown Primary School at the age of two and a half years but my mother usually had to come and find me as I used to sit in the cricket field picking daisies on my way home. (Imagine allowing a two-and-a-half-year-old to walk home alone now.) Miss James was the headmistress of the primary school and Miss Day the headmistress of the girls' school. Mr Brown who lived in the school house was headmaster of the boys' school. After school and up to the age of about ten years we would either go down to the playground on the swings or the giant slide or play ball games such as rounders etc. The playground is now built on. On Bonfire Night we always had a lovely bonfire on the playground as Mr Ball the officer who was in charge of the gasworks always gave us a barrel of tar for the centre of the fire and we would also have a large cartload of old timbers stacked around so it made a lovely fire. There was always an officer in charge of the fire to see no one got burnt. As we got older we would venture further afield and on to the moor playing prisoner. One of us would play the escaped prisoner and the rest would look for you, but I always had to be home in time for tea which was 5 o'clock one day and 6 o'clock the next, and no being late, we all had to be sitting down with clean hands when father came in. Also we were not allowed out after tea in the winter but in the summer we could go out until quarter to nine and no later. My father was very strict and there was always a cane hanging by the fireplace which he would use. One night a week there was a 2d. hop at the recreation room where we were taught to dance. Then when we attained the age of sixteen we were allowed to join the whist club which was one evening a month. After school we had to do any bits of shopping also go to the spring and fill two pitchers with drinking water as the only water we had in the house was unfiltered.

In the early days of the First World War we would take a sack and go on to the moor and pick sphagnum moss which was dried and eventually made up into dressing packs for use on the wounded soldiers, also we would knit socks in the evening. On Sunday we went to Sunday School morning and afternoon would then go for a walk usually around the triangle, which was from Princetown to Rundlestone then Rundlestone to Two Bridges and Two Bridges back home to Princetown in time for tea. After tea we either went to church or a walk with our parents to visit friends who lived at a little house on the moor known as Stanlake. During the summer school holidays we usually went away to Wiltshire my mother's home but if for any reason we didn't go away we would go on to the moors picking whortleberries. We used to go out to Holmen Beam [Holming]. As we had to be around the boundary wall before the prisoners came out at 8.20am and we were not allowed to come back until the cease labour bell at 4.20pm we had a long day out but we usually managed to fill our buckets with erts and were always ready for a good meal when we arrived home.

The weather in those days was more reliable and often boiling hot so to prevent the grey flies from biting we would tie a vinegar rag to the back of our hats and that kept them away. Should any of the family be unwell the prison doctor would call and prescribe a bottle of medicine which we collected from the steps adjoining the gatekeeper's lodge inside the wooden door at the entrance to Dartmoor Prison, we also collected milk from there and on Sunday mornings, the post for the prison was

Mrs Cook with her two daughters standing in the exact spot where she used to live in No. 9 Barracks.

collected from Tavistock. Also if there were any letters for the quarters they would be brought up and we would go up to the gate after 12 o'clock to collect them. I remember a very heavy snowfall we had one night, I think it was 1917, and my father had to dig his way out to go on duty, also he came in one day with icicles from his moustache to his shoulders it was so cold. Of course we always had a snowman in the garden which was good fun. We would also go up to quarry field carrying an old tin tray which we used as a toboggan. During the Great War 1914–18 the officers were allowed to go out on to the prison Newtake and cut peat. When dried it made a lovely fire although terribly dusty because the ash from the burnt peat is so very fine.

In 1917 I was fortunate enough to pass two scholarships which enabled me to go to Devonport Tech. College. The train left for Princetown at five minutes to seven in the morning and I arrived at school at 9.20am. I left school at 4.30pm and had to walk to Millbay Station in Plymouth. The train arrived back in Princetown at 7.30pm except odd days during the winter when if there had been a heavy fall of snow on the moors during the day, they would have to put a snow-plough in front of the engine in which case we would not get home until midnight having enjoyed the experience but starving hungry. But the good old train always got us home. Also if you were a few minutes late in the morning you would give the gate at the entrance to the station property a good bang and the train would wait for you but should the train have started, Mr Cowling the stationmaster would whistle up the driver Mr Newcombe and you would run down the line and Mr Prowse the guard would help you up on to the train telling you off all the while for being late. There was nothing very exciting to do but we made our own fun and always enjoyed ourselves.

I remember a prisoner escaped once and was running over the cornfield, the officer called to stop but when he didn't the officer shot him in the leg.

There was a funny little man named Billy Setters who always carried a stick with a V-shaped top. He lived in the cottages which stood just past Albert Terrace. If there was a funeral anywhere on the moor he would walk there to head the procession into Princetown as all coffins were brought there for burial. There would be two sets of bearers and he at the head would take ten or twelve paces, stop, announce 'All change' and the other bearers would take over.

My two daughters who came with me to see you are Mrs Elizabeth Ann Brimblecombe and Mrs Diane Winifred Bennett.

The train which Mrs Cook, daughter of a Dartmoor warder, had to catch to get to Plymouth.

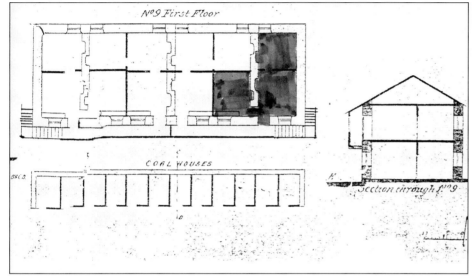

No.9 First Floor

COAL HOUSES

Section through No. 9

Above left: *Staff at the gate, 1900s.*
Above: *Mrs Cook's father, Officer Coombs, centre of photo with heavy moustache.*
Left: *The shaded area shows the complete flat of the Coombs family, (No. 8 of No. 9 barracks). Each family had three rooms only in this barrack regardless of the size of the family, which in the Coombs family was seven persons.*

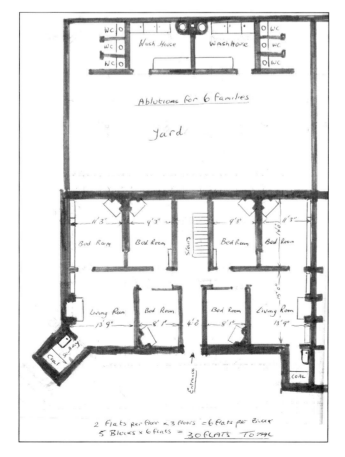

A-block, later Blackabrook House, where Mrs Cook later lived, was slightly better, having three bedrooms and a living room, a total of four rooms.

WAYCOTT'S WAY

Officer John Waycott was born on 22 May 1856 at Broadhempston and joined the Royal Navy on 20 May 1874 when he was eighteen years old. His naval papers show that he served on the following warships:

Royal Alfred	20 May 1874	Boy First Class
Achilles	22 May 1874	ORD Second Class
Warrior	1 April 1875	ORD Second Class
Duke of Wellington	24 November 1875	ORD Second Class
Malabar	15 September 1876	ORD Second Class
Malabar	1 March 1877	ORD
Malabar	10 October 1877	AB
Duke of Wellington	26 May 1878	AB
Royal Adelaide	2 June 1878	AB
Nankin	15 June 1878	AB
Valiant	10 October 1880	Leading Seaman
Valiant	15 December 1881	Quarter Master
Valiant	31 March 1884	To Naval Barracks
Valiant	4 June 1884	Time Expired

He served faithfully for ten years in the Royal Navy his official number being 86321. He was awarded his first good conduct badge on 1 January 1879 and his second on 22 May 1882. His character was exemplary.

In 1885 John Waycott joined the prison service at Dartmoor and left in 1905 after twenty years. He returned to Dartmoor during the First World War owing to a shortage of prison staff. From 1915 to 1934 he was sexton of the parish church in Princetown where he performed sterling work. John Waycott died aged eighty in 1936 and was buried in his beloved Princetown where he had lived for more than fifty years. He was a credit both to the prison service and to the Church. I had the pleasure of knowing the two grandsons of John Waycott, Cliff and Fred Waycott, who talked often of John.

Officer John Waycott (standing).

Chapter Eleven
LATER ESCAPES

In its 150-year existence, Dartmoor has housed some of the country's most dangerous criminals and there have been hundreds of escape bids, some endlessly well documented, but most all but forgotten.

Many of these escapes could have been prevented by locking up convicts for twenty-four hours a day, but the system of allowing them out to work helped them immensely, especially when a convict had many years to serve at Dartmoor. By taking them out to the open moors to work, some who had been born in cities and had never seen a cow in real life, worked hard with great benefit to themselves, and of course the prison.

At times there were over 200 long-term convicts working out on the estates doing essential works, and without these parties the prison could not have functioned. The many farm and moor reclaiming parties built up the fine, well-managed estate that exists today.

The roads and drains parties would sweep all the quarters' roads daily, the sports field party was immensely skilled in maintaining the grounds at 1500 feet above sea level, then there were the gardens' party, forestry party, external gardens' party and over 60 convicts at the quarry. The leat part ensured an efficient water supply, along with many other parties. During the refurbishment of quarters there were 25 convicts of the works' party working in the staff houses and many other small parties who did great service.

Sometimes in more recent times a convict would just walk away from his work party. The supervising officer, being on his own, could only radio to the prison that 'one was away', then take the rest of the party back to the prison. In the old days the Snider carbine would have been fired to stop him, alerting other gun guards on other parties to assist. At the same time, the pony patrol was excellent for catching convicts running across the boggy moors, far more so than modern vehicles which are often of no use whatsoever in the wetter areas. The dog section has also done sterling work tracking down escapees, often over many miles before catching them; and searching for drugs in recent years.

In the 1930s prior to having our own dog section, some ladies in the neighbourhood would assist in the capture of escaping convicts by bringing their own bloodhounds to the scene to help with tracking, with prison staff in attendance at all times.

On 24 June 1963 at about 9.30am a Bulwark oil tanker arrived to fill the oil tanks outside the boiler house at the bottom of the main drive, a regular occurrence as vast quantities of oil (which had now taken over from gas) were used to heat the prisons and to provide steam to all areas.

At that time there was no check fence between the outer boundary wall and prison buildings, exercise yards, sports fields and other areas, so the tanker would be taken straight down the main drive to the boiler house for the stoker to supervise the unloading, with discipline escort, of course.

A series of photographs from the 1920s and 1930s showing police and the military searching for escaped convicts.

Left: *Local ladies with their blood-hounds were called in during escapes in the 1930s.*

Above: *The Dartmoor Prison Dog Section, a most able body of professional dog handlers.*

Bloodhounds used to track convicts, some were supplied by civilians, some by police.

This is the story of one of the lesser-known, though no-less dramatic at the time, escape bids. At about 9.45am some prisoners who included James Henry Jennings, Raymond Ernest Charles Matthew, Leslie Anthony Moore and others, jumped the tanker just inside the main gate, pushed the driver out and some of them leapt aboard.

Off they drove to the old tea boat, then turned right and past the hospital, left down the perimeter road, then left at the sports field where they turned around and picked up speed on the grass in order to ram the double back gates.

These were duly demolished, and though some of the convicts were captured by the pursuing prison officers, the three previously mentioned escaped and made off at high speed. Their bold bid came to naught, however, as they were recaptured by police and prison officers in a wood about five miles away.

After that a temporary wood-post and chain-link fence was constructed around the entire prison from the hospital to the blacksmiths' shop. As a trades' officer, the author was involved in this. Later the temporary fence was replaced by a modern security fence.

The double back gates were bricked-up after they were rammed by the escaping prisoners in the oil tanker. A single gate remained to let convicts out to go to the prison quarry.

The temporary wooden post and chain-link fence, erected prior to the erection of the security fence. The author, with assistants, was one of many staff employed on the erection of this temporary fence.

In the above photograph the original caption states:

Farmer's clue to convict chase on 21 Nov 1932, Mr Joseph May (taller left) *the farmer of Morwellham near Tavistock who overheard a conversation alleged to have been made by the convicts John Michael GASKEN and Frederick AMEY, in a wood near his farm. As a result of information the police have surrounded the wood and their capture is expected at any hour.*

This caption turned out to be the height of optimism as the following report states:

On the 7th day of their freedom, apparently exhausted by their efforts, they gave themselves up on the Southern Railway line at Newton St Cyres, near Crediton, without a struggle to Sgt Greek and Constable Rawsel.

A friend of the author's, Officer Penny, who was at Dartmoor Convict Prison at that time in 1932 until a few years later, when he transferred to Exeter Prison, related the following story:

The year was 1940, I was coming off duty at Exeter Prison about 6pm in the black-out when I was spoken to in the Blackhall Road by an army sergeant who called me by name, 'Goodnight Mr Penny.' 'I do not know you,' I replied. He then said, 'I am John Michael Gasken stationed temporarily at the higher barracks.' I wished him well, shook hands and went on my way.

Many ex-prisoners served with extreme gallantry in the wars and many were decorated, having made a good transition from convict to soldier.

Name of Prisoner	Date and Time of Escape	Date and Method of Recapture
MITCHELL Frank Samuel	3.40 p.m. 12.12.66 Working Party	
JOHNSON John Kenneth	2.35 p.m. 26.12.66 Over Prison Wall	30.12.66 P.C. Hallett and P.C. 66 Semmens, Calstock, Cornwall
HANNEY Raymond Charles		27.12.66 P.C. 639 Jefferd and P.C. Orton, Bovey Tracey
THOMPSON John		2.1.67 P.C. 400 Walker, Ashburton
OWENS Mark		2.1.67 P.C. 400 Walker, Ashburton
MOREY James		2.1.67 P.C. 9;9 Parsley and P.C. 991 Northvist, Drumbridges
DENNIS Charles	21.7.67 Home Leave	Rearrested on 2?.7.67 in cafe near home at Enfield on information of neighbour
McCULLOCH David Bruce Stewart	3.8.67 Home Leave	Arrested in M.P.D. 30.1.68 charged with burglary at Balham on 29.1.68
LAMB Robert James	30.11.67 Working Party	Arrested by Police Officers at Dousland on information of civilian
JACK Terence Charles	17.00 hrs. 8.5.1968 Home Leave	Arrested in Glasgow on 1.7.68 and dealt with on 2.7.68 at the Glasgow Marine Court and sentenced to 4 years impris.
FLETCHER Peter John	16.30 hrs. 23.9.68 Home Leave	Arrested at Dartmouth by P.C. 759 HARDING and subsequently charged with Larceny in D/House. Using Firearm to resist arrest, (2 offences T.I.C.) At Devon Assize 4.1.69 he was sentenced to 9 years imprisonment.
PESTER Keith Gordon	3.50 p.m. 22.10.1968 Home Leave	Arrested at Lincoln on 26.2.69 for another offence
LEE Thomas	15.40 hrs. 22.1.1969 Working Party	Arrested at Clearbrook Cross Yelverton on 23.1.69 8.30 p.m. Before visiting committee H.M. Prison, Dartmoor, sentenced to: 150 days loss of remission. 28 days loss of priviliges 28 days loss of earnings 28 days non-associated labour 9 days No. 1 Dietary Punish.
DURRANT Roger Michael	As Red Band he was working in Prison Officers Mess left between 1100 hrs and 14.30 hrs. 12/4/69	

Name of Prisoner	Date and Method of Escape.	Date and Method of Recapture.
STANTON Michael	31.1.64 Attempted to scale wall	Recaptured within Prison by warders.31.1.64
SMITHSON Thomas Ernest	22.2.64 at 11.10 a.m. Through toilet window in blacksmith's shop	Caught 22.2.64 by warder in field adjoining prison
TAYLOR Ronald James	"	"
WHITFIELD Christopher	"	"
PURDUE John William	5.3.64 Failed to return from Home Leave	Surrendered to police at Bath. 18.3.64
TAYLOR, William	5 p.m. 23.6.64. Failed to return from Home Leave, Bolton	Arrested Blackpool 25.6.64
HAYLES, Peter Charles	1st June 1964. Failed to return from home leave to London	Arrested 16.6.4. London. Suspected person loitering.
FENTON, Norman	31.7.64 Escape from Prison Farm	Arrested by P.C. EVANS at Princetown on 1.8.64
PROBYN Walter	28.8.64 2.35 p.m. Outside working party	Arrested in M.P.D. 1.10.64
SMITH Robert (1) FITZGERALD Patrick Leonard(2) COOPER Benjamin(3) MANGLE Eric Samuel (4)	22.8.64 7.30 p.m. Prison Laundry	Arrested M.P.D. 31.3.65(1) Arrested by T.A. at Okehampton 24.9.64 (2) Arrested by T.A. at Okehampton 24.9.64 (3) Arrested 19.11.64 at Harrogate, Yorks. (4)
MANLEY Sydney	8.10.64 8 p.m. Fail to return from Home Leave	Arrested by police 15.10.64 at Stoke on Trent and taken to Liverpool Prison.
JOHNSON Gerald Ivan	23.10.64 10.15 a.m. From Freedom Fields Hospital, Plymouth	Arrested 25.10.64 at Swindon
MALLINSON Eric	10.11.64 at 9.40 p.m. Fail to return from Home Leave	Arrested in M.P.D. on 24.11.64
STIRLING William Joseph	2.12.64 7 p.m. Fail to return from Home Leave at Leeds	Surrendered to M.P.D. 3.12.64.

Two pages from records of the names of about 133 convicts who escaped for short periods between 1 January 1956 and 12 April 1969. There were over 200 convicts working outside during the author's time at Dartmoor and in the past there were over 500 in various areas of the estates. An officer would sometimes have six or more long-time convicts working, sometimes a long way from the prison, and if one decided to walk away, the officer could do nothing except radio in 'one away' and immediate help would arrive. Prior to 1953 a gun guard would always be with the party to fire at escaping convicts. The prisoner at the top of the left-hand page was Frank Samuel Mitchell, perhaps one of Dartmoor's most famous inmates. Dubbed the 'Mad Axeman', he was linked to the Kray brothers, but after his escape he simply disappeared, presumed dead.

Chapter Twelve
BUILDINGS

During the author's fifteen or so years spent as the prison historian, many people asked about the present buildings and, in particular, the dates when they were built. Some of these major buildings, like the convicts halls, took several years to build as all the work was carried out by men without the aid of machinery. The dates provided are those at which the author knows that building works were being carried out, not specifically the date of the start of building or the completion (see the Prison Plan page 174).

F-wing was built from 1806 to 1809 as No. 1 war prison and comprised three floors. Floors one and two were for the use of prisoners of war who all slept in hammocks. The top floor was called the 'cockloft' and was designed to be used for wet-weather exercise. Due to overcrowding it was also used for accommodation. No. 1 war prison has held over 1700 prisoners. After 1850, during the convict period, this prison was the penal prison and was known as No. 6 penal prison. Later the name was changed to D2 specials and held long-term special-stage prisoners. Unfortunately there were only 60 cells available and, as Dartmoor was a lagging station, a lot of long-term convicts were eligible for specials but had to go on a waiting list. The name changed to F-wing in the 1980s and remains so today.

War prison No. 1, now F-wing. The picture above shows how quickly grass and weeds will grow on weed-free, stony ground.

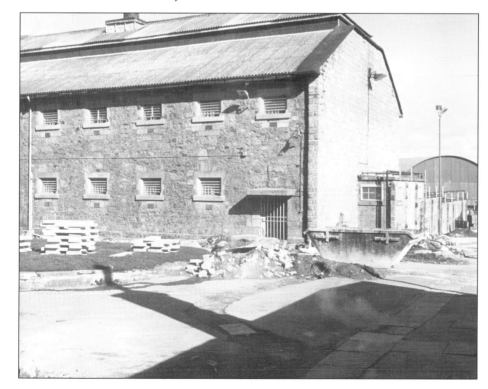

G-wing was built as an extension to No. 1 war prison around 1904. It took several years to complete and all the work was carried out by convicts and artisan officers. As with other constructions all of the stone was cut and pre-

G-wing, built by convicts around 1904.

pared by convicts in the prison quarry. It was initially called D1 hall but is now known as G-wing.

The **Church of England chapel** was built as No. 4 war prison in 1806–09 and at one time had a wall built around it to contain American prisoners of war from the War of 1812. Later Americans were held in all seven of the war prisons. When the convicts arrived in 1850, No. 4 was used for a short time for the artificer convicts. These men were to repair all of the seven war prisons for use by convicts. Soon after, No. 4 war prison was converted into the C. of E. chapel and has remained so to the present day. It has been used as a cinema as well as a church.

Interior and exterior views of the No. 4 war prison building, now the Church of England chapel.

The **old kitchen** was built in 1812 by French prisoners of war. It was No. 6 war prison which was an additional facility to help alleviate the overcrowding. It was used by the prisoners of war until 1816. During convict times it was known as No. 3 convict prison and on opening in 1850 it housed convicts in association. This means that they were open floors with hammocks, like those used by the French and American prisoners. In 1880, 136 corrugated iron cells were built in order to isolate the convicts. In about 1946 the roof of the prison was removed so that the walls could be lowered. It was reduced from a three-storey to a single-storey building and then became the new kitchen. In the 1990s a replacement kitchen was built on the old marketplace at the bottom of the main drive so this old kitchen became obsolete. It was an inglorious end for the building to be finally closed in the early 1990s after fifty-five years of porridge.

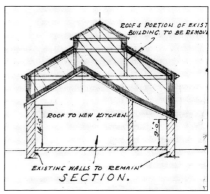

No. 6 war prison was converted to the kitchen, 1945.

E-hall was built in 1897 as a separate confinement punishment block. It had separate exercise areas with one convict per exercise yard. The strong control over the prisoners included three silent cells which were cells fitted with three doors so that the convicts could not hear anything. E-hall was known as the 'Tea Garden' to convicts; if a member of staff placed a convict on report then it was referred to as 'getting a telegram to go to the Tea Garden'. This was the place in which the cruellest of punishments would take place.

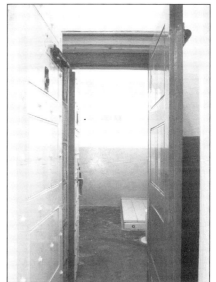

Left: *E-hall punishment block.*
Above: *A quiet cell for noisy convicts, which quickly quietened them.*

The **main stores** is another Nissen hut built post-war in 1946 on the site of the old twine shop (circa 1875). During the war there were many Nissen huts on prison land for Royal Navy storage and workshops. Indeed the US Army used some on prison land.

The **reception block** was built at the turn of the century as a hospital for warders. During the mutiny of 1932 this building was still the officers' infirmary. Officer Birch, who was slashed by a razor by convict Davis, was treated here. The gate-book records the visits that his family made to see him. In later years it replaced the old reception block in the basement of B-wing when it was closed down, and was still operating in 1998.

The **octagonal building** at the top of the main drive on the right-hand side as one travels down the drive was built 1806–09 as a lookout post or guardroom and held two small cells for miscreant soldiers. There was also a larger cell which had a Napoleonic lavatory – a slab of granite with a hole in it placed directly over a flowing leat. The lavatory was removed in the 1970s when the octagonal building was converted into the prison officers' tea boat. This also housed the heavy gang. A new refreshment room for officers has now been built down the main drive and the old lookout building has been incorporated into offices.

The **octagonal building** on the left-hand side was also built 1806–09 and was part of the old gatekeeper's house. It was later part of the Civil Guard's quarters. The Probation Service occupied the building in the 1960s until the 1990s when a refurbishment took place.

The **library** which adjoins A2 hall (B-wing) was a basic wooden structure built at the turn of the century. Despite having beautiful murals on the wall the convicts were not allowed there. Instead books were taken from the main library and distributed to the individual halls where they were handed out to the men.

The old prison library, alongside the old A2 hall, now called B-wing.

The **old bath-house** was built in 1886 alongside A2 hall (B-wing) and 700 convicts could easily be bathed there in three days. The water came from the bogs and contained flecks of metal. If one rubbed the bath while underwater a red stripe would appear. The bath-house was in daily use until the 1960s when a new version was built out of reconstituted stone. It seems totally out of place amid the dense granite of all the other buildings but is still an improvement on the old bath-house.

The **old iron chapel**, later known as the Methodist chapel, was built at the turn of the century against the wall adjacent to the gardens in the corner of what is now A-yard. Corrugated sheets were used to clad the timber-framed building, probably taken from the corrugated iron cells which were being demolished at the same time. In later years, during the author's service, it became the officers' tea boat and the heavy gang were based there. There was an indicator board in the tea boat to inform the heavy gang as soon as an alarm was raised, a device essential for the protection of officers' lives. The building was demolished in the 1970s after the new tea boat was constructed in the lookout building. This building had a lot of 'presence'. In later years the corrugated sheets began to rot and asbestos was used as cladding.

There are more buildings between the gates. The inner gate and arch were built in 1878 with the building on the left being used as the foreman of works' office. The building on the right was the steward's offices. Behind the present gate lodge was the armoury where the Snider rifles and ammunition were held. The **armoury** existed until the 1950s when rifles were withdrawn from use. Gun guards posted to outside parties would collect their guns and ammunition each day to carry out their duty of shooting at any escaping convicts.

The **security principal officer** had his office on the right-hand side. The author helped to build the concrete block extension to the gate lodge and fitted the key shutes in the 1970s with the assistance of two convicts. The whole area was roofed over in the 1970s so that staff would have protection from the atrocious weather. The building of the gate-lodge extension took place after the author transferred from discipline officer to trades' officer in 1969.

The **old surgeon's house** which is on the left in Agent's Square, is a large house built 1806–09. The assistant surgeons' houses were inside the prison wall. When the convict prison opened in 1850 the deputy governor lived here until it later became the assistant governor's quarters. At one point a basic-grade prison officer called Billy Steele had possession of a part. In the 1980s the works' department moved from inside the prison to this fine building. Many contracts were taking place so a works' conference room was fitted out for meetings.

The **old steward's house** which is on the right-hand side of Agent's Square was built 1806–09. The steward lived there until it was later changed into a staff training building. I had the pleasure of inviting Mr Tiley, who was more than one-hundred years old, to open it in its new role. Mr Tiley joined the Convict Service in 1904 and became the steward at Dartmoor until his retirement. I felt it fitting that the man who lived in the steward's house for many years should be the one to reopen it as a training building.

Mr Tiley, a marvellous old gentleman. The author visited him in Harewood House, Tavistock several times and talked for long periods about conditions in the old Convict Service. This photograph was taken in his room in 1991. At the request of Governor Kendrick, the author invited him to open the new prison officers' mess. Mr Tiley lived for many years just next door in the old steward's house which is now the training room. He joined the prison service in 1904.

The **visits waiting room** on the right-hand side of Agent's Square was built in 1870. At this time even these people were not allowed any luxuries and heating was not connected to the building until the 1970s so visitors would wait in the freezing room until called to the gate.

The **old dairy** was built after the convict prison's opening in 1850 and was used continuously for about one-hundred-and-forty years when the new dairy was built on prison land near the back gate to the prison. The old one became the Dartmoor Prison Museum in the early 1990s.

The **workshops** were originally the infirmary of the war prisons built 1806–09. Nearly 1500 Frenchmen and 271 Americans died at the Dartmoor Depot, the majority in this building. After the Napoleonic Wars and the War of 1812 had ended, the infirmary was let to a private firm, the British Naphtha Company. This did not go well and in 1850 when the convict prison opened it became the prison gasworks to supply gas to the prison and barracks.

In 1875 the gasworks outside the prison was built. Gas made here not only supplied the prison but also all the barracks and streets in Princetown. Some old officers who served in the 1930s always called the workshops 'the old gas-house'. As soon as the gasworks moved outside, the old infirmary became the convict workshops and has remained so until the present day.

Clockwise: *The old mailbag shop, with welding shop on the ground floor; the carpenters' machine shop; the TV assembly shop, blacksmiths' forges; the carpenters' TV cabinet assembly shop; the shoe repair shop.*

The **hospital/lower, upper classrooms** were built 1806–09 as the petty officers' prison, to separate non-commissioned officers from the basic seamen; this building had its own bathing place, a clean open pool of water fed by an open leat, and had its own separate enclosure walls and sentries on the petty officers' battlements. In 1850 it became convict prison No. 1 and convict hospital. The ground-floor cells still have the inner cell doors with a metal external barred door in place. It was used as an invalid prison for quite some time, and later became classrooms for prisoner evening classes. The extension to the hospital took place in 1912 as the date on the façade testifies. It is now a modern hospital.

Main entrance to hospital.

The old **visits' building**, the **blacksmiths'** and the **farriers'** shops were built 1806–09. Situated along the boundary wall just inside the main gate on the left-hand side, they were first built as the assistant surgeons' house, the matrons' house and others. After 1850 they became the Civil Guard's rooms and the gatekeeper's rooms for the convict prison. The farriers' shop was where the present blacksmiths' shop is now situated.

Left: *Former matrons', assistant surgeons' rooms, c.1809, later the old Civil Guard's quarters. Subsequently these old derelict rooms were converted into visits' rooms for relatives visiting prisoners. This conversion was carried out by the author, with convicts as assistants, when he was a junior trades' officer.*
Above: *View of the inside, with two prison officers awaiting the arrival of the visitors.*

The **old works' block** is just inside the main gate on the right-hand side and was built in 1907 as a bachelor quarters building. As mentioned before, single officers were not permitted to occupy a prison quarter. This later became the works' department until around the 1980s when this was moved to the old surgeon's house in the compound between the outer arch and the main gate which was called Agent's Square in the war prison days.

D-wing (old B2) was built in 1880 as No. 4 convict hall and later named B2 hall. After the 1980s' renaming it became D-wing and was the hall in which I commenced my career at Dartmoor. Old B2 was called 'super B' because of its strong discipline of staff and strong control of prisoners.

The former B2 hall, now C-wing.

C-wing (old B1) built in 1914 was the last hall to be built at Dartmoor – on the site of No. 5 war prison. No. 5 war prison was converted into 4A and 4B convict prisons before demolition in order to build the present C-wing. Again it was known for strict control of both staff and prisoners. The building was delayed during the First World War in order to finish the prison hospital, in case it was needed for servicemen.

Above: *Former B1 hall on the left, smooth granite walls; B2's rough granite walls are to right of picture.*
Right: *Magnificent former C-hall, built by convicts in the 1870s and demolished by convicts from 1945 to 1950. The present gymnasium was then built on its base.*

A-wing (old A1) was built as No. 2 convict prison in 1903 on the site of war prison No. 7. This was converted into 2A and 2B convict prisons before demolition in order to build A-wing.

B-wing (old A2) was built by convict labour in 1883 and is a superb example of skilled work by convicts and artisan officers. It was originally 2C convict prison with A-wing being 2A and 2B. It was later called A2 hall, until the designation in the 1980s of the name B-wing.

The former A1 hall on the left, now A-wing, and the former A2 hall, right side, now known as B-wing.

Below: *Gymnasium built on the foundations of former C-hall.*
Bottom: *C-hall being demolished (middle left).*

The **gymnasium** was a Nissen hut used as a gym, and was built post-Second World War on the base of the old C-hall. The latter was demolished by convicts between 1945 and the 1950s. The old C-hall was a huge building of over 300 cells before its demolition.

The old **dead house** was built in the early convict days as a mortuary, and was used as such until quite recent times. It has now been converted into a calorifier room for heating purposes.

The **stable block** at the farm, built at the turn of the century, is possibly the best one on Dartmoor, with plenty of room undercover.

Above: *The dead house, (mortuary).*
Above right: *Stable block, with windows being inserted by works' staff.*

The population of Princetown in the years 1809–15 largely consisted of prison staff and their families. Very few outsiders lived there and, even in the 1980s, prison employees outnumbered locals. Over 1000 soldiers were housed in the prison war barracks (down Barrack Road, opposite the church) and many soldiers' families were housed in the barracks, today known as married quarters. There were also more than 100 turnkeys and their families in the barracks.

The **officers' mess** was purely for army officers and, occasionally, their families. At the Dartmoor Depot there was the agent and his family, the surgeon and family, the assistant surgeons, and matrons, as well as language translators and various others. What can we see of the villagers not employed in the prison? Records of Duchy of Cornwall leases, dated 1810, reveal:

A lease to Mr John Wicklin for four houses up Plymouth Hill let to:
1. *John Watts cottage and garden.*
2. *Edward Vosper's cottage and garden.*
3. *Richard Underhayes' stable, cottage and garden.*
4. *Anthony Cooper's cottage and garden.*
5. *Bakehouse Mr James Cooper gentleman, three roods, three perches (next to Bolts on Two Bridges Road).*
6. *Robert Lane victualist of the Plume of Feathers Inn. [This was a renewal of lease dated 20 April 1808, the first lease presumably would be from 1785 when the Plume was built, of thirty-three acres, three roods, three perches.]*
7. *Thomas Tyrwhitt's lease of Tor Royal (1785) renewed on 15 September 1812 for 2284 acres, two roods and thirty four perches.*
8. *Butchery on site of prison officers' school (circa 1874) now Princetown Primary School. [Not much is known about the butchery except that it kept enough livestock in the fields below the butchery (now Bellever Close) to keep 12 000 hungry men fed, perhaps employing a dozen or so as herdsmen and slaughterers – all employed by the prison.]*
9. *Princetown Brewery. [Again not much known but perhaps employed a dozen men.]*

There were few outlying houses, cottages and farms and most of the residences were in the village. A likely estimate of the prison population in about 1812 would be about 10 000 prisoners, 1000 soldiers and their families, 200 turnkeys and families, prison staff about a further 100. So perhaps about 12 000 were directly involved in the prison. The civilian population of Princetown in 1812 would not have exceeded 100 people.

The **agent's/governor's house** (now part of the new officers' mess) was built from 1806–09 as the residence of the Captains Royal Navy, who were the agents (Officers Commanding) during the Napoleonic Wars and American War of 1812. When the original house became the governor's house with the opening of the convict prison in 1850, it became too small to house the governor and his servants, as demonstrated only too clearly by the disastrous fire of 1865 which started in servants' quarters built into the roof space. Extensions were added in 1872 and 1897.

In due course the last governor ever to live in the house, Governor Heald and family, obtained permission to move out. Prior to this it was compulsory for the governor, chief officers and staff to live in official quarters. In the early 1990s, this historic house was converted into the officers' mess, the lease of the Duchy Hotel having already been relinquished. During this conversion many historic features such as carved beams, built-up windows still left in situ and metal wine racks in the cellar, were revealed. It is now a fine building, considered by the staff to be what they call 'proper job' as the old mess was about half a mile away, through heavy snowfall, gales or whatever the weather chose to throw at them. Fittingly the last governor to live in the governor's house was a Royal Navy man, as was the very first one.

Governor Heald, the last occupant of the governor's house.

The agent's and governor's coachman had quarters in the coach-house which until it was demolished in 1990, still had racks for harness, saddles and suchlike. The coachman's room above the stable had the small luxury of a fire.

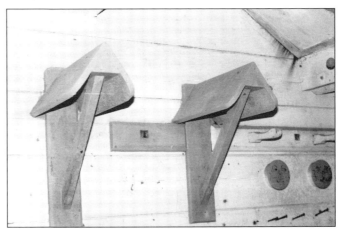

Above and above left: *Coachman's house and saddle racks in his house.*
Left: *The governor's house, c.1809.*

Demolition of Victorian extension to the governor's house enabling the new prison officers' mess to be built.
Right: *The author's last duty at Dartmoor Prison before retirement was as principal officer clerk of works on conversion of the governor's house to the mess.*

Tor View comprised six houses built for farm staff in 1910. Prison officers also occupied the houses until the late 1980s when the lease was relinquished and the Duchy of Cornwall received them back from the prison. They are now private houses.

Church Row was built around 1810–13 by French prisoners of war. When the Chapel of Ease was established in St Michael's Church this row of eight homes became **Chapel Row**, later **Government Row** and finally **Woodville Terrace**, before being demolished in the 1960s. The low wall in front of the Cornish Unit houses called Woodville Avenue was the remains of the front wall of Church Row.

Woodville Avenue was built after the Second World War as 42 houses for staff. Later, when staff were permitted to live out, the homes were redundant and all but six Cornish Unit houses were handed back to the Duchy of Cornwall. The six retained are for present staff at Dartmoor Prison. Some were demolished in 1998 and new private homes built on the site.

The bus shelter was built in a corner of the chaplain's house in 1970 by the author, then a junior trades' officer, and two convict assistants. It was very basic indeed as orders were not to make it too comfortable, to deter undesirables. No cavity walls were allowed, no doors, windows or seats. It had to be simply a roof on granite and granite concrete blocks (made at the prison quarry). But it is pleasing on visits to Princetown to see children waiting for the school bus to Tavistock, still using the shelter.

The New Villas were built in 1898 as quarters for superior staff such as the chief officer first class, the farm manager and the foreman of works. In 1980, after eighty years, it was declared no longer required and the leases were relinquished back to the Duchy of Cornwall. Again, the quarters are now private houses.

Isca was built very early on in the prison's history. It is shown as **Mr Carpenter's House** on early maps. In 1850 it came into use as the schoolmaster's house and was also used as a small school for prison staff children until the prison officers' school was built in 1874. It became the official quarters for the chief officer (class 2) for many years and finally became a basic prison officer's quarter.

Bus shelter for schoolchildren, built by the author and two convicts.

Left: *New Villas, then Isca House, across the road is Church Row.*

AMOS House (A Medical Officer's House) was built for the prison doctors in about 1859 and was used by them for more than one-hundred years before being relinquished back to the Duchy in the 1970s, later becoming a private house.

Devonshire House is a large prison building which was built in 1872 as No. 1 warders' block. Later it became E-block and finally Devonshire House before its demolition in the late 1960s. The final demolition of a small part of the basement took place in 1971 after which the area was landscaped. It was built as 30 flats for prison officers' families, each with just three rooms, two bedrooms, a tiny living room, and tiny scullery off the living room. Unsurprisingly, prison officers with large families found it very cramped. This three-storey building had ten flats per storey, and a wash-house at the back with a peat burner to heat the boiler and six troughs, one for each family. There were only four water-closets for six families! The plans were signed on 22 November 1872 by Edward Du Cane.

Blackabrook House was built in 1880 and was of similar size to Devonshire House. It was formerly built as No. 2 warders' block, later becoming A-block, then Blackabrook House prior to demolition after the Second World War. It was replaced with 30 Cornish Units for prison officers' families in 1950 which were named **Blackabrook Avenue** and are still in use by officers. The large pile of stones behind the units is Blackabrook House which was also used for storage by the Admiralty in the Second World War.

Below: *The former E-block, later Devonshire House.*
Bottom: *The former A-block, later Blackabrook House, bottom of picture.*

Burrator Avenue consists of three blocks, originally all numbered separately, which are used for warders' families and were built between 1890 and 1898. The block on the left going down was built as B-block (Blackabrook House was A-block), and was numbered 1 to 14. The block on the right-hand side at the bottom of Burrator Avenue was built as C-block and numbered from 1 to 10. The last block at the top was built as D-block and numbered from 1 to 7. Blocks B, C and D were called Garcia Avenue by the prison officers' families to avoid having a postal address which read No. 8, C-block, HMP Dartmoor. This was the author's prison quarter for ten years. The street was nicknamed Piano Street because all the warders supposedly bought pianos and kept them in their front room so that everyone could see them. It was finally renamed Burrator Avenue and was handed back to the Duchy in the 1980s.

Above: *The first of Burrator Avenue houses being built, 1890s.*
Right: *E-block, later Devonshire House.*
Below: *Prison officers' club.*

Heather Terrace was built in 1905 as F-block Nos 1 to 10, ten solidly-built houses for prison warders and their families. It, too, was handed back to the Duchy in the 1980s.

The officers' club was built in 1880 as a rest-room for officers and their families. It was extended during the author's service at Dartmoor in the 1970s. It was still the prison officers' club in 2000 and closed in 2001. Few prison officers now live in Princetown.

The ladies' club was built from 1806–09 as part of No. 1 barrack block, becoming a reading room for warders after the convict prison opened. It became the prison officers ladies' club prior to the relinquishing of the lease in the 1980s, and is now private.

Dart Cottage was built from 1806 to 1809 as No. 11 barrack block. This building was the guardroom at the entrance to the barracks compound at the bottom of Barrack Road. The barrack gate-hangers can still be seen in the old gate pillar at the side of Dart Cottage. In convict days this barrack became a staff quarter. Again, it was handed back to the Duchy in the 1980s, sold on and is now a private home.

Grosvenor House was built from 1806 to 1809 as No. 10 barracks for troops and turnkeys. In convict times it was converted into four flats for families of warders which was still the case in 2000. It had a water-closet block at the rear which was demolished when internal water-closets were fitted.

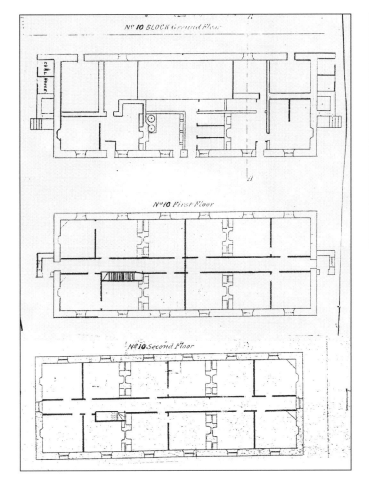

Plan of No. 10 barracks, later Grosvenor House, and outside view.

Below: *Milk cart outside Hessary Terrace.*
Bottom: *Moor View Terrace and sports' pavilion.*

Hessary Terrace was built in 1908 as G-quarters with 18 houses for warders and families, the only accommodation to be situated along the main road, where tourists visiting Princetown could stop and gaze at warders on their way to and from work. All the other prison houses were on prison land so that any wandering persons would soon be removed. In the 1980s it was relinquished. Hessary is the local dialect for 'Hisworthy'.

Moor Crescent was built in 1912 and known as H-quarters. It held 13 warders and families of fairly senior rank, principal officers and basic-grade officers of long service. Handed back to the Duchy in the 1980s after seventy years in use, it is now private homes.

The **cricket pavilion** was built adjoining the sports field in 1890, for use by warders, and was kept in immaculate condition by 27a convict party. The tennis pavilion was laid in the early 1920s as a base for the tennis court for officers and their families. It was demolished in the 1960s because of its poor state. The **bowling green** and **pavilion** were built around the turn of the century and visiting teams of prison staff played matches on many occasions. A popular annual match would be played between married and single prison warders. It was also demolished in the 1960s.

Above: *Sports pavilion.*
Right: *Single versus married officers' cricket match, 1920s.*

Above: *Remains of the bowling green.*
Above right: *Remains of the tennis courts.*

Bellever Close was built after the Second World War as 45 Cornish Unit houses for officers – again, relinquished in the 1980s.

The **Duchy Hotel** was built from 1806–09 as the army officers' mess. All other ranks were housed in barracks Nos 1 to 11 in the barrack compound on Barrack Road, opposite the church. After the closure of the war prisons in 1816 the hotel became derelict but work was carried out and it reopened as a hotel until 1940 when it was used as prison officers' mess. The author spent the first twelve weeks of his service in room ten of the officers' mess. Single officers were allocated a room in the Duchy Hotel as they were not permitted an official quarter. After the conversion of the governor's house into the new prison officers' mess the Duchy Hotel was redundant. The lease was relinquished back to the Duchy of Cornwall in 1990 and the building was converted into a visitor centre, now called the High Moorland Visitors' Centre. It is an attractive and fitting change of use, and a far cry from its old nickname of 'Heartbreak Hotel'.

The canal, now called the prison leat, was built from 1806–09 as the water supply to the war prisons and soldiers' barracks. The man responsible for the canal lived in an old hut beside the canal. The prison would later maintain a hut for the leat-man to store all his maintenance work tools, as well as being a sheltered place for him and his two convict helpers to eat their midday meal. They maintained the leat to a high standard up until the 1990s, a system which lasted for about one-hundred-and-eighty-five years until responsibility for the water supply passed to South West Water.

The prison officers' school was built in 1874 for the children of the officers only. The men had to pay for each child to attend, thus in large families it was likely that not all the children would go. Convicts built the school and carried out the daily cleaning, which included the lighting of the peat fires in the classrooms each morning. They also had to spread and rake screened sand over the playground, then called the parade ground. This continued into the 1920s. A man who was working at the prison in 1927 remembers the task taking place then.

 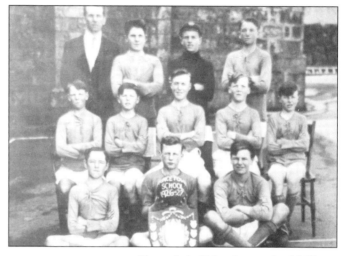

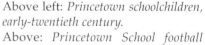

The men who cleaned the school were known as the scavenging party and would be chained together with a cart. On the back of the cart was a small box which contained the rations for the six men in each group. They were carefully all watched over by officers with Snider carbines.

Above left: *Princetown schoolchildren, early-twentieth century.*
Above: *Princetown School football team, 1926–27. Several of these schoolboys later joined the prison at Dartmoor.*

Left: *The scavenging party who would clean the school classrooms and light the fires in the classrooms in winter.*

The first parts to be built were the boys' school and the headmaster's house, followed by the girls' school and the infants' school. Teachers were evidently in short supply as the school roll was over 270 pupils, while the staff comprised the headmaster and his wife, and about six pupil teachers. Presumably these were older pupils, perhaps in their last year.

The school was handed over and eventually became the Princetown Primary School. Recent inspections have praised its excellent results, but the author is more likely to look at the stonework and praise the old convicts and artificer officers of 1874 for their workmanship!

The old **Rundlestone Inn** at Rundlestone Junction was converted into two quarters for prison officers in 1861. These were popular with staff as they were away from the prison garrison town of Princetown. It is still possible to see the entrance gate posts built into the boundary wall alongside the road at Rundlestone Cross. They are a nice reminder of all the prison officers who lived in the two houses over the years. The two cottages were two-storey buildings, each with a living room and sitting room, and lean-to scullery on the ground floor, and two bedrooms on the first floor. There were no services at all to the houses – no water, gas, electricity or mains drainage.

Other houses on the estates used for quarters were **Rookes Cottage** which was demolished and about which little is known. **Phillips Cottage** was built in Phillips Field, field 19, and later demolished. **Pascoes Cottage** was used until the 1960s when it was demolished by the prison works' department. A prison officer called Worth and his family once lived there; Worth is now a well-known name in Princetown. Pascoes Cottage was upgraded to a fairly modern standard with new damp-proof courses, new windows and doors, and extensive work to the roof, along with better drainage. The cottage, built with granite walls and slate roof, had three bedrooms, one living room, one sitting room, a scullery and a garden.

Princetown Church

Church records before the church in Princetown was built read as follows:

> *12 April 1807 (war prison well under way).*
> *Henry son of Richard Badcock and Martha his wife, living at Princehall, received full baptism. Revd Mason.*
> [This service would have taken place at Princehall as Revd Mason preached there and at Beardown.]
> *Arabella Margaret, daughter of Daniel Lane surgeon at the prisons of war, and Margaret his wife. Revd Mason.*
> [This probably would have been on unfinished prison property against the wishes of the Transport Board of the Admiralty.]
> *28 June 1807.*
> *William son of John Pryce a labourer working at the prisons of war, and Mary Love his wife. Revd Mason.*
> [Again probably on prison property and frowned upon by the Admiralty who had their own chaplain.]
> *20 December 1808.*
> *Joseph son of Edward Vosper, a mason, and Betty his wife. Revd. Mason.*
> [In the leases of 1808 Edward Vosper had a cottage up Plymouth Hill, presumably this same man.]

The agent (governor) of the war prisons was Captain Cotgrave RN and the foreman of works was Mr John Walters who was responsible for designing and supervising the building of the dreaded cachot (punishment block) at the Dartmoor Depot. The cachot was constructed from large granite blocks and was approximately 50 by 30 feet in size. There were no windows and just a single door which was steel faced on both sides. Two ventilators, each about one-foot square, were built into the gable ends of the building, while the vaulted granite roof was designed to prevent any attempt at escapes. Not surprisingly, many prisoners died here through hypothermia or starvation, a fairly inevitable consequence as they had no beds, or even straw, between them and the cold granite floors, and there was no heating, even in the grimmest of winters.

The rank of foreman of works has long existed at Dartmoor; the author was deputy senior foreman of works for many years. Any development to be carried out by our direct labour force, or by contractors, would require the drawing up of plans, specifications and bills of quantities by the author, who then submitted them to head office for rubber stamping.

The same system operated in 1812 when Captain Cotgrave received a notice from the Admiralty Transport Board instructing the erection of a church and a house for the clergyman and family. Having received the notice, Cotgrave would have handed the instructions on to foreman of works John Walters. Walters designed a simple oblong church and, with the assistance of artisan turnkeys who had instructed the French prisoners in construction, set about building it.

As the church was outside the prison the French prisoners were paid 6d. a day for six days of the week. This amounted to three shillings a week for each man. This was in 1812 and quite a sizeable sum. When the author was a junior works' officer, prisoners were paid 40 or 50 pence per week which was only about seven or eight pence a day. Bearing in mind decimalisation in 1971, it was not much greater than the amount the French and Americans earned. To gain some idea of how hard these modern prisoners worked for their money, one can look at the bus shelter built in 1972 in the chaplain's garden in Princetown. The author took the men to the quarry to get the granite stones which had been cut by the convicts in the quarry. The party then collected sand and cement which were transported to the site by handcarts. Excavation of the foundations was by hand, as was mixing of the concrete, as no cement mixers were allowed. All this for 40 or 50 pence per week. In 1920 a warder and an artisan warder were both paid 29s. per week while a principal warder got 45s. An engineer 2 received 53s. per week.

Having received the Board's order to build a church, building was started immediately, initially by the French and continued by the Americans. The wages were held for three months and then paid as a lump sum. This method of payment was for a particular purpose; if one member of a party escaped then the whole party would lose their wages for those three months. It was a forfeit of sorts and a good deterrent.

The Revd James Holman Mason MA was not a resident in Princetown as he was the vicar of Treneglos and Wardstock and had no need of another vicarage. He had been holding services, baptisms and the like for local people in various village buildings such as the barns at Beardown. This is still the case today. Eventually the church was more or less complete externally and the Revd J.H. Mason, paid by the governor, held the first Divine Service on 2 June 1814 as prison chaplain.

The first entry into the records at the new church was entry No. 29 and read as follows:

> *Caroline Mason daughter of James Broderick Esq. and Sarah his wife residing near Two Bridges received into Dartmoor Church (after Divine Service was performed therein this day for the first time). Having been privately baptised at Okehampton 15 October 1806 by me Revd J.H. Mason, Minister of Dartmoor.*
>
> *No. 30. Thomas Lukey son of Stephen Jewell Husbandman living at Princetown Brewery and Catherine his wife.*
>
> *No. 31. 27 March 1814. Mary daughter of John Wilkins a private soldier in the Monaghan Militia, now at Dartmoor Prison, and Sarah his wife.*
>
> A little later in 1815 the following entry by Revd Mason makes interesting reading:
>
> *No. 70. 19 November 1815. Catherine Elizabeth the daughter of Pascal Puchet Sergeant in the Twenty Fifth Regiment in the Service of France, a prisoner at Dartmoor, and Helen Mulder his wife.*

Author's sketch of the original St Michael's Church, built by the French and American prisoners of war. Note the short length of the church with only four windows on each side.

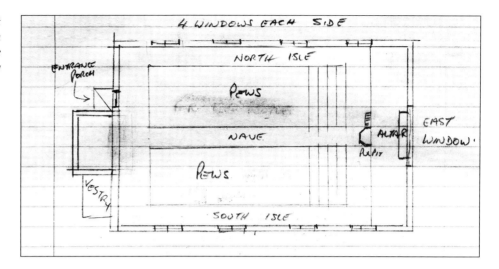

The above sketch was made at the Duchy of Cornwall Record Office. Note the vestry and entrance porch that were added later. The church would only seat 300 people so space was important. Prison staff would have taken priority.

When the war prisons closed in 1816 the church was locked up. The Government would not provide finance for civilian establishments and the building deteriorated rapidly. Quarry workers and miners occupied the derelict prison buildings and barracks. The church more or less reopened in 1831 though services were rare, perhaps not surprisingly as the floor was covered in weeds and moss and the stench of rotting timber filled the air. In 1850 things would change dramatically.

On 2 November 1850 the first governor of Dartmoor as a convict prison arrived with his staff of military guards and warders to reopen the prison. The chaplain then began his sole duty of holding irregular services in the church for the Dartmoor staff. Convicts and artisan warders worked hard to get the church back into its previous shape. On 23 April 1860, ten years after the prison chaplain conducted services in the church, it became a separate ecclesiastical chapel under Lydford.

The first incumbent was the same Revd James Mason who performed the initial service some forty-six years earlier. He had in the past been curate of Lydford Church and the Prince of Wales's chaplain in this part of the country since the early part of the century. Revd Mason was a most fortunate man although he was a non-resident. Even though there was no government building at Princetown after the closing of the war prisons, Revd Mason received £300 per annum until 1850. The parish clerk received £20 and the sexton just £10. Mason was superannuated in the early part of 1859 with an annual pension of £300. On his retirement the church was again closed for a year, causing both scandal and inconvenience. The prison chaplain with 1200 convicts and staff could no longer hold services. The first convict to be buried was William Tegg on 31 May 1851.

The Revd Morris Fuller took over the church in 1862. Fuller was a very different type of clergyman to Revd Mason and on 11 August 1860 a faculty for performing marriages in the church was granted. Fuller's work received a considerable setback on 8 March 1868 when the *Flying Post* reported that the 'church was greatly damaged by fire on Sunday morning'. The fire supposedly occurred after some wood ignited through a patent heating apparatus. The damage was considerable with the roof remaining almost intact while the interior was destroyed.

Revd Fuller saw this as his chance to alter and refit the Georgian box-shaped church to make it into something more in accordance with ecclesiological principles. The following petition was drawn up:

The said Chapel of Ease in Princetown was lately so far destroyed by fire as to render the same wholly unfit for the purposes of Divine Service. That it is proposed to rebuild the said Chapel of Ease, to erect a new chancel at the east end, to reseat the said chapel in a uniform manner throughout according to plans prepared by Mr R. Medley Fulford.

Mr Fulford, a distinguished local architect, was closely associated with some of the moving spirits of the Diocesan Architectural Association. His plan of January 1869 retains the building as it stood but adds an apsidal chancel, rather a shallow one, at the east end. Seating is provided for 257, including 40 seats for children, which was still exceedingly small when thinking of the prison staff and families of around 3000. Some of the ritual arrangements proposed by Medley the architect, or the Revd Fuller, were objected to by the Chancellor of the Cathedral W.J. Phillpotts. He was the eldest son of Bishop Phillpotts and clearly had his father's taste for enforcing obedience.

The plans had placed the altar as a free-standing structure and was annotated by Phillpotts as follows:

The Lord's table to be placed against the east wall, the reredos to be affixed to the wall, the cross attached thereto not more than one foot in height.

He was informed that the apsidal shape of the chancel made it inconvenient to place the altar against the east wall, instead it was proposed to place a reredos three feet, three inches from the east wall and position the altar in front of this. In reply he stated that he had heard that Fuller was using a moveable cross which was contrary to law. Phillpotts's fussiness is made somewhat more understandable when it is remembered that 'ritualism' was troubling the higher ranks of the Church of England at that time. He clearly did not want to leave an opening for any unauthorised practices at all. Fulford then took up the position that if the altar against the east wall be insisted upon then the reredos must be dispensed with or altered entirely.

The faculty was eventually granted on 25 June 1869. For some reason not known, perhaps due to the reluctance to abandon the cherished altar scheme, or financial constraint, Fuller had undertaken to underwrite the restoration and the new choir was never built. The Revd Woolcombe, curate of Princetown 1923–27, stated in 1926 that sufficient money for the restoration had not been collected until 1875. The building was then merely restored internally by Revd Fuller as recorded in *Kelly's Directory* in 1883.

The pulpit was stated to have been brought from St Sidwell's in Exeter and was installed at this date. The church continued in this way until 1899 when plans were drawn up for thorough rebuilding. The distinguished architect Edmund Sedding prepared the design which involved retaining only the tower and the side walls of the nave. The roof was to be raised and clerestory windows provided. The nave was to be refenestrated and new arcades installed, also a new chancel was to be added. Transept-like projections on either side of this held a morning chapel on the north side and an organ room over a subterranean vestry on the south side. A large geometrically decorated east window was the main feature of the chancel.

Again the Chancellor (Dibdin) had comments to make. He stipulated that the northern and southern positions must be possible at the altar and queried the need for a second altar. He was told that this would be most convenient for daily services and weekday celebrations, no reason for this was given. Sedding deleted the top step of the sanctuary to allow ample room for the diocesan requirements. The estimated cost of the building was optimistically set at £1200.

Just as thirty years before, the project was never carried out. The reasons for the drastic pruning of Sedding's design must have been financial. The final cost was much reduced to £2000, of which the Government would provide £450 in lieu of convict labour.

The reduced scheme produced in essence the church that stands today. The vestry and porch flanking the tower were swept away and the magnificent arcades inserted within. The chancel was added but the roof was not raised nor the clerestories added. The line of the proposed roof can be seen marked on the tower, together with the old roof line of the original church. The day chapel was abandoned and only slight projections now represent the proposed transepts. The subterranean vestry was built and the old windows of the nave were retained. This work was completed by the autumn of 1901 and the reconsecration of the Bishop of Exeter was described in the *Exeter Gazette* of 6 September as follows:

The church externally, and for the greater part internally, has been thoroughly restored, a new floor has been laid, new rectangular pillars and arches erected, the ceiling raised and a chancel added, the church being thus extended some 22 feet. The original walls retained to form the nave, the old porch removed and a new porch added to the new entrance.

Inside St Michael's Church prior to the fitting of the stained-glass window in 1910, which was donated by the United States Daughters of 1812.

Unfortunately rejoicing was to be short-lived. The Revd Woolcombe writing in 1926 stated, 'It has been so badly done that in 1905 the east wall was found to be in danger of collapsing.'

A former warder of Dartmoor Prison 1885–1918, John Waycott (church sexton in 1915) discovered and reported the commencement of the collapse of the newly built wall in 1905. Things were quickly set in place for repairs to commence. Waycott joined the Royal Navy aged eighteen in 1874 leaving after eleven years' service as a quartermaster. He joined the Convict Service in 1885 and retired in 1907. He rejoined the service at the outbreak of war in 1914 and left in 1918 on cessation of hostilities. (Incidentally, John Waycott's grandson, Cliff, was ninety years old in 2001.)

The blame for the collapse of the east wall can surely be put on Sedding who had annotated his proposal to elevate the east window, 'foundations to be taken down as far only as necessary to obtain good and solid bottom'. The east window was then built in its present form, a free adaptation of Perpendicular which fits in much better with the imaginative arcades than the original design as a consequence.

In 1909 a faculty was granted for the insertion of the glass in the east window. The donor was the National Society of the United States Daughters of 1812. It is by a firm whose work is very uncommon in England, Mayer & Co., an international firm based in Germany, with branches in London, New York and Munich. The window erected in 1910 is in itself a most interesting work to commemorate the American prisoners of war who died at the prison.

A faculty for installing central heating was granted in December 1915 and the work was carried out by the firm Richardson & Gill, financed by the Prince of Wales. The plan shows that the present porch had by then been constructed. The vestry was adapted to act as a boiler room. Further royal patronage followed as the vestry meeting agreed, in September 1915, that the Prince could move the font under the tower, using its lowest stage as a baptistry. In 1916 the tower was restored again by Richardson & Gill; the faculty application preserves an elevation and sections of the tower.

Other work, as well as turning the ground floor into a baptistry, included the removal of coping which had been placed on the tower in 1899 (in preparation for Seddings's great scheme), and placing it at the level of the old existing roof. The estimated cost was £332 which again was to be paid by the Prince of Wales. Nothing else was to be added to the fabric; the faculty for the organ loft was granted in 1920 and in 1950 one was granted for the installation of an English altar with riddel posts and hangings. This church has proved to be singularly unlucky in any proposed ritual alterations for there is no such altar now.

It is plain that this is a church with an interesting history that is well documented. Externally it still has much of the appearance of the building created by the prisoners of war, of a pre-archaeological Gothic church of the Regency period. Inside, and at the east end, there are fine examples of Arts & Crafts Gothic by a designer who, despite not attaining the celebrity achieved by his uncle John Seddings, certainly established himself as an architect of more than local importance.

The mixture of simplicity and sophistication gives the building an extraordinarily interesting character. Sadly the church closed in 1994 owing to poor maintenance of the fabric and low attendance. It was wet and cold, and on occasions the high level of internal moisture made it impossible to use the electricity. But in 2001, £500 000 was put aside by the Church Conservation Trust to preserve and secure the building. The author was pleased to be present with Prison Chaplain Captain David Swales to see the commencement of Phase One of these works on St Valentine's Day 2001.

The US Daughters of 1812 have continued to provide funds since 1910 to help maintain the church. During the author's two visits to the United States to meet and give talks to the US Daughters, money was donated for this purpose. As the prison historian the author would meet historical parties and host visits over many years, sometimes greeting visitors at Plymouth before taking them on to Princetown to see their beloved church built by prisoners of war. The church features on the letterheads of the certificates of the US Daughters.

Much gratitude is owed to Prison Chaplain Captain David Swales CA who helped the author many times over the years in allowing visitors to come to the church. The US Daughters also paid for the memorial arch and plaque at the entrance to the American cemetery on prison land in 1928. On the official visit by the Daughters in 1987 they supplied a star and anchor plaque which the author fitted to the obelisk. They also paid for the plaque to be fitted inside St Michael's to commemorate their visit on 29 May 1987, one-hundred-and-seventy-five years after the start of the War of 1812.

Ghostly figures behind the tarpaulins during the refurbishment of the tower, early 2002.

The author is grateful to former chaplain of Dartmoor Prison Robin Grigg for much of the information about the history of the church. The prison continued

*Rows of small stones in Princetown ceme-
tery mark the deaths of prisoners who died
at the turn of the century. Each stone was
cut from the quarry and bore the initals
and date of death of the prisoner.*

*The cross which was cut and erected by
convicts to commemorate all unmarked
graves, the stone which holds the cross has
the broad arrow on each corner, even in
death they cannot escape the broad arrow.*

to maintain the church and graveyard for years with grass-cutting being performed by the farms and garden party until the 1980s.

In memory of the hundreds of men buried in unmarked graves, the prison had
a granite cross cut in its quarry and installed it in the churchyard in 1912.
Prison records contain most of the names of the men who died at the turn of
the century, and a small stone was also cut at the quarry bearing the initials and
the date of death.

There are no vicars in prisons, always a chaplain. What is now the old vicarage
was built in 1813 as the **chaplain's residence**. This house remained the chaplain's house until the prison chaplain was superannuated in about 1859. Some
records suggest (Revd Woolcombe, curate of Princetown 1923–27 and Rector
Revelstoke) that three families were living in the vicarage until about 1862
when the Revd Morris Fuller was appointed by Her Majesty the Queen to the
incumbency of Princetown, and not to the rectory of Lydford.

In 1867 the Duchy of Cornwall conveyed the Feesimple of the Princetown
vicarage to the Ecclesiastical Commission to be appropriated 'as and for the
residence and site for the residence of the minister who may serve the church
at Princetown only.' In 1864 the vicarage had been put into repair by public
subscription and prison labour. This prison labour, at no cost to the vicarage,
was authorised by Sir Geo. Grey the Home Secretary at that time.

This prison labour was granted to keep the vicarage and all its grounds in good
repair on the condition that the cost of any materials did not fall on prison
funds. Bear in mind that most jobs were labour intensive and that this labour
was free. This grant of free labour was in operation until the termination of
Princetown with Lydford on 11 October 1912.

The **vicarage** has sometimes been inhabited by the rector but more frequently
by a 'curate in charge' who would be the minister serving the church at
Princetown. The curate in charge has always claimed the house under the
wording of the clause in deed of gift. It has never been held to be the property
of Lydford, but held in trust by the Ecclesiastical Commission for the minister
serving Princetown. The dilapidation report of 1901 was submitted to the
Prison Commission who carried out the work using prison labour. The vicar
advanced money for materials, amounting to £30. He then paid this money by
public subscription:

*Since 1902, until the vicar of Princetown was established on 11 October 1912, the
following funds have been spent on the vicarage. All of these were by public subscription for materials with labour from the prison:*

June	*£30.0s.0d.*	*General repairs*
October	*£10.0s.0d.*	*New drains*
February	*£11.11s.4½d.*	*General repairs*
May	*£20.0s.0d.*	*General repairs*
May	*£4.10s.0d.*	*Cost of study book case (paid by rector)*
May	*£4.8s.0d.*	*General repairs*
December	*£17.1s.0d.*	*General repairs*
September	*£7.0s.0d.*	*General repairs*
Total	*£104.10s.4½d.*	*Cost of materials*
	£75.0s.0d.	*Prison labour valued at*
Total	*£179.10s.4½d.*	

The above came from prison records, but much of the material probably came
from prison funds. There are many references which state 'repairs to vicarage
using prison labour and materials', and even in the author's time at
Dartmoor the prison farms and garden party would always cut the churchyard grass and do small repairs. This was a goodwill gesture from the
governor to the village.

In 1850 when the convict prison opened, a new chaplain was required so a new **chaplain's house** was built adjoining Church Row and was used as such right up until the 1980s, reverting to the Duchy and now a private residence. The present family has deeds dating from 1850.

The prison chaplain's house, c.1850, now a private house.

OTHER RELIGIOUS BUILDINGS

Religion is of extreme importance to both prisoners and staff, so many denominations have been catered for, especially of late. As well as the Church of England church, there is the Roman Catholic church and Jewish synagogue, as well as people coming from outside for a wide variety of services. The prison chaplain has given sterling service since the very first days of Dartmoor Prison.

Entrance to the American cemetery, dog training boxes on the steps to the Memorial Arch. This arch was paid for by the US Daughters of 1812.

Ground floor of No. 4 war prison, now the Church of England chapel.

Prison chaplain with the Bishop of Plymouth during a confirmation service.

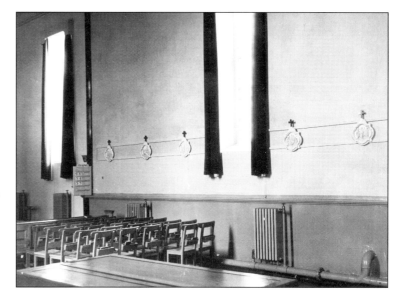

Staff have always used St Michael's Church, Princetown, since it was built for them from 1811–15 by the French and American prisoners of war. Many staff have also attended the Methodist church in Two Bridges Road.

Above left: *St Michael's Church showing how high the walls were above the windows prior to the disastrous fire, after which the roof was lowered.*
Above: *The tower of St Michael's shows clearly how high the roof used to be before the fire.*
Left: *The Methodist church, now used by Princetown, to the left of the Tea Rooms.*

The Oratory of St John Vianney, built in 1914 for the Roman Catholic priest, included a small chapel and confessional for the use of prison staff and their families. The Roman Catholic priest did a lot of work in the prison but eventually moved out, and the building's last use was as the farm manager's quarters. It was eventually relinquished back to the Duchy of Cornwall and subsequently sold, and is now a private home. Before the oratory was built, Roman Catholics used **Hisworthy House,** opposite which was the house of the priest, with its own chapel for services. The date of Hisworthy House is unknown. It is described on some old drawings as 'The Engineer III House' and some of the sewerage manholes in the garden are marked 'DP 1851' so it seems probable that it was built mid to late-nineteenth century. Some staff also used the Mission Hall at Rundlestone for their services so the prison was, and still is, able to provide religious services for all staff and prisoners.

General Booth, founder of the Salvation Army, paid at least two visits to preach to the convicts. On 30 January 1906 he preached to 900 convicts in the Church of England chapel, having travelled by motor car from Plymouth, accompanied by his Chief of Staff Mr Bramwell Booth. Villagers had assembled at the prison gate to welcome him to Princetown and he was welcomed by Governor Mr Basil Thompson. In his address to the convicts, he talked of his consecration of his life to God when just a lad of fifteen. As he left the chapel, the convicts, who were not allowed to talk, broke into spontaneous cheers. General Booth had lunch with Governor Thompson and left for London in the afternoon. He later visited the prison again on 25 January 1911.

General Booth, founder of the Salvation Army, during a visit on 29 January 1911, when he preached a sermon to about 800 convicts in the Church of England chapel at the prison.

DARTMOOR PRISON BARRACKS

The prison barracks have tended to be confused by many people over the years with the old tinners' and miners' barracks out on the moors. The barracks at Dartmoor Depot were built from 1806–09 to house the soldiers guarding the prisoners of war, both French and American. After the war prisons closed in 1816, the Sappers and Miners Regiment was housed in these barracks to try to maintain the prison building, an impossible task. On the opening of Dartmoor Convict Prison in 1950, soldiers and warders occupied the barracks, the soldiers mainly for external duties to prevent escapes, the warders to maintain discipline, not only in the prison but on all external parties. On these the soldiers would 'flank in and out', as it was described, in other words, they would stay on the perimeter of the parties to prevent escapes, opening fire on escapees who disobeyed the order to stop.

In the 1860s the soldiers left Princetown, and the gun guard duties were taken over by a highly efficient group of men to be known as the Civil Guard. They remained for almost a century. The Civil Guard's barracks were formerly part of No. 6; each barrack room would accommodate about 10 soldiers.

These barracks should not be confused with the internal barracks of the prison. When the American prisoners of war arrived in 1813, they were so troublesome that additional soldiers were required, so the petty officers' prison was used as an extra barracks; the prisoners in the petty officers' prison were sent out on parole, while prisoners not suitable for parole were put in the ordinary war prisons numbered 1 to 7. The army officers were housed in the officers' mess, later the prison officers' mess, and now the High Moorland Visitors' Centre.

Former No. 10 barracks, now Grosvenor House.

Today only three barracks remain: No. 1 barracks, later known as the ladies' club for the wives of prison officers, and now a private building; No. 10 barracks, now Grosvenor House, quarters for prison officers; and No. 11 barracks, later Dart Cottage. The little wash-house building on No. 11 plan was used by about 200 families during the convict prison days. Mrs Cook, mentioned earlier, vividly remembers using it and the problems it caused.

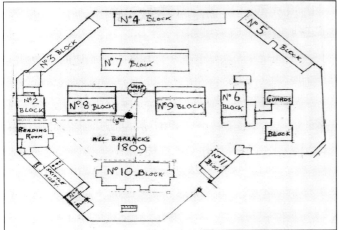

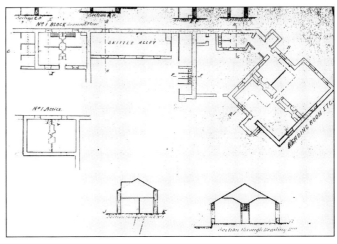

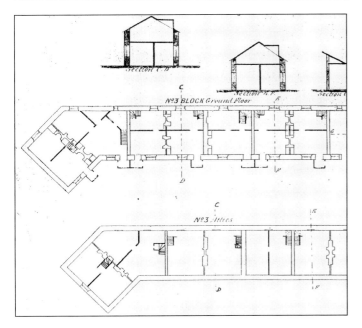

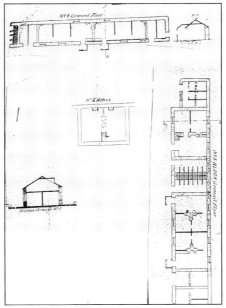

Top left: *No. 11 barracks.*
Top right: *No. 1 barracks, later the ladies' club.*
Middle left: *Plan of all 11 barracks.*
Middle right: *No. 1 barracks in total.*
Above left: *No. 3 barracks.*
Above: *No. 4 and No. 5 barracks.*

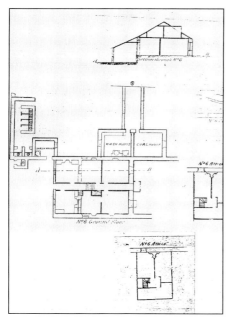

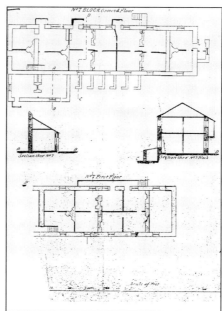

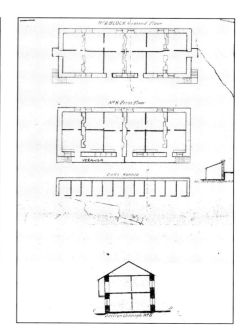

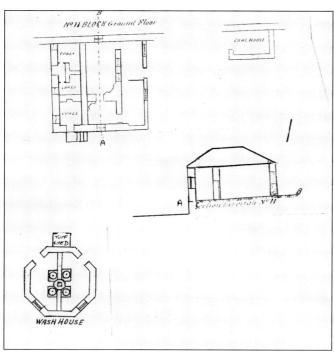

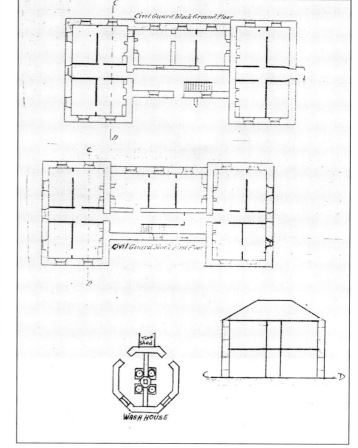

Top left: *No. 6 barracks.*
Top middle: *No. 7 barracks.*
Top right: *No. 8 barracks. No. 9 barracks (on page 125) would be the same as No. 8.*
Above: *No. 11 barracks.*
Above right: *Civil Guard's barracks. (No. 10 barracks are on page 147 and No. 2 barracks are on page 11.) The wash-house for all the barracks is on the plans of No. 11 and the Civil Guard. There was only one wash-house, described vividly by Mrs Cook who was born in the barracks.*

THE QUARRY

The quarry and its buildings, known as Herne Hole, was the source of all granite for the seven war prisons and all the ancillary buildings, and especially the mighty convict halls: A1, now known as A-wing; A2, now B-wing; B1, now C-wing; B2, now D-wing; the huge C-hall, now demolished, and the gymnasium built on its base; D1 hall, now G-wing; E-hall, the punishment hall, now E-wing, and many smaller buildings.

For a century-and-a-half, from 1850 to 2000, the works' staff employed anywhere on the estates, would take a party of convicts with their carts to the quarry to collect aggregate, sand, fencing materials or materials for maintenance works. The quarry party would extract granite for buildings, smash it for use in roadworks, and supply screened sand for putting on the children's playgrounds in the prison officers' school. In recent years they have used modern stone-crushing machinery.

All roads, including some public roads, were coated in the old days while in recent times vast quantities were produced to spread on all the prison tracks. Hard-labour convicts produced large amounts of crushed stone, so it had to be taken from the quarry and used anywhere possible to get rid of it.

Hard-labour party in the prison quarry busy with quarrying, dressing the granite and carting stone to the convict builders of the convict halls in the prison. Handcarts were used as a rule, but occasionally horse and carts were used, see bottom picture.

Modern quarrying in the 1970s, showing some of the materials made in the quarry. Convicts are shown dressing and splitting granite and sorting crushed stone aggregate for use by the works' party.

THE WORKS' DEPARTMENT – AND CONCLUSION

The works' department is a branch of the prison service responsible both for maintenance and, at times, the building of complete new prisons from green-field sites. The author is extremely proud of this department, of which he was a member for many years, and proud of the work they have carried out at Dartmoor Prison during the last one-hundred-and-fifty years. Trades' officers within the works' department are discipline officers who work with inmates, training them in a variety of skills, as electricians, fitters, plumbers, bricklayers, plasterers, painters and decorators, and welders.

As already mentioned, the magnificent wings, A, B, C, D, E, F and G (known until 1970 as halls) were built by convicts, with artisan officers supervising. In effect, the inmates received a full apprenticeship, having often spent some ten years working with these skilled artisan warders, now called trades' officers, and civilian workmen formerly called free workmen.

Left: Convicts building granite walls c.1900.
Below: Works' party on major refurbishment in the 1970s.
Bottom: Prisoner using hammer and chisel to cut up floor prior to resurfacing and tiling the cells.

The trades' officers started work at 7am on their own landing, slopping out the prisoners, feeding them, and then going on to help supervise in the exercise yard. Then at 'form up' time they would proceed to their works' duties and take their party of prisoners to work at about 8.15am.

The author worked with a party of prisoners for about seven years in the prison refurbishment section, later working out on the estates with trusted prisoners, who enjoyed the hard work and freedom of being away from the prison building, and also in the prison quarters maintaining all 211 houses. The author was promoted to engineer 2 in 1976, and in 1981 became a principal officer (works).

Part of the author's duties was to be a principal officer controlling three Construction Industry Training courses: builders' operatives, painting and decorating and plastering. Three tutors assisted in running these courses, and as a former general foreman of a construction firm, these courses were of special interest to the author. Later, National Vocational Qualifications were introduced.

The author became a deputy senior foreman of works and part of the duties this entailed was to be a clerk of works on several major contracts by outside contractors. A particularly enjoyable project was the conversion of the old 1806 agent's/governor's house to the officers' mess, an historic building transformed for modern use.

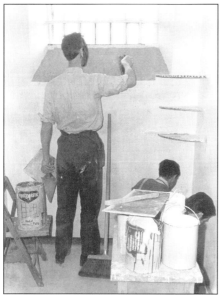

Trade training by the works' department, with trades' officer instructors teaching prisoners painting and decorating and carpentry. Building operatives' work was done in cells to brighten them up.

This book details some of the vast amount of work carried out and the role played in this by the works' department in the years since 1850. Huge sums of money have been spent on modernising the ancient Napoleonic and Victorian buildings. In 1990 there were a few problems at Dartmoor Prison, which lead to a visit by Mr Justice May, who produced a well-written report. The following are his comments referring to the works' department:

Mr Justice May's Report on the Works' Department
The basis for our proposals lies in the belief that the works' departments in prison establishments should be fully and constructively used. For too long the prison department has under-used what is, in our view, a scarce and valuable resource, namely the prison works' officer. At his, or her best, the works' officer is a multi-skilled trades professional. In the context of a Victorian prison, the judgement and expertise of the works' department could not easily be reproduced in one person by an outside contractor. In our view, prison departments should encourage governors to use works' officers for professional duties as much as possible, and to resist whenever possible the urge to redeploy them for discipline duties at times of staff shortage. When engaged upon work on Planned Preventive Maintenance, or on projects, works' staff frequently train, and use, inmate labour. If this were encouraged and developed further, specifically with regard to the provision of sanitation facilities, slopping out could become a fact of history within seven years, at a cost of up to £40 million. If this were achieved it would be one of the most important reforms of the prison system in the twentieth century. For the first time fresh thought could be given to the type of activities that should be planned for individual establishments which have hitherto been impeded by the necessary daily rituals associated with slopping out, which form the backdrop to much of contemporary prison life.

The works' department trades' officers and their inmate trainees at Dartmoor Prison were the first to commence with providing toilet facilities in the cells, a notable achievement of which the author is immensely proud. All the cells were refurbished, with newly plastered walls taking over from the previous bare granite. They were well decorated with new floors, good lighting and heating; all taken for granted today but very much appreciated by the prisoners of the 1970s.

Overall, working conditions are much improved throughout the entire prison, both for staff and inmates. Prisoners are allowed to mix more on association, radios are allowed in cells, cinema shows were held in the Church of England church which was originally No. 4 war prison. One can only wonder what the prisoners of war 1809–16 would have made of all this. Sports facilities have improved out of all recognition, with an all-weather sports field and well-equipped gymnasium, as well as televisions and videos available in each hall. Prison food, too, has changed dramatically since Father Famine's day, now being of decent quality and quantity, prepared in a purpose-built kitchen.

All this, with a more humane system of treatment for prisoners and staff, including the labour regime and better medical care, has brought Dartmoor finally into the twenty-first century, a far cry from such soul-destroying work as the old mailbags shop of yesteryear. A hostel scheme allows long-term prisoners to go out to acclimatise to the modern world.

The prison service has moved on in leaps and bounds. Indeed during the author's short service of almost twenty-five years, great developments have taken place, making one feel proud to have played a small role in the Dartmoor Prison story. Praise is due to the modern governors and their staff for its advancement from its bleak, cold days as a dustbin-cum-lagging station, to the fine prison of today.

A convict is about to be released. The chief officer with the prisoner has just given him an update on what is happening in the outside world, and advice on how to behave, before escorting him to the main gate for release. A taxi would normally be waiting at the gate to take him to Plymouth Railway Station, and he would be in possession of a rail warrant to continue his journey. This is often a traumatic time for a prisoner, especially a long-term inmate, often without any family, or a family which has chosen to forget him over a period of anything up to twenty years.

VARIOUS BUILDING PLANS OF THE PRISON

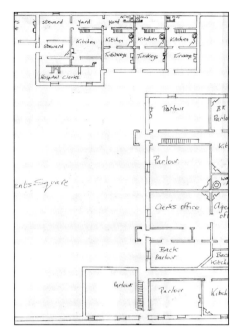
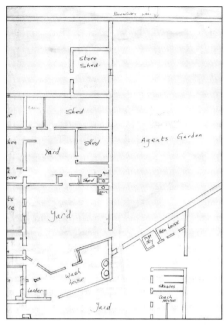
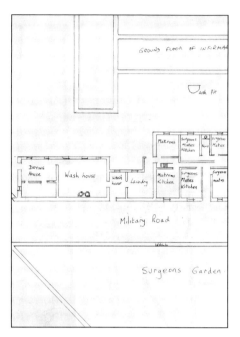
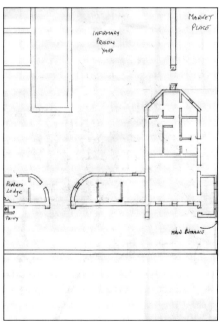
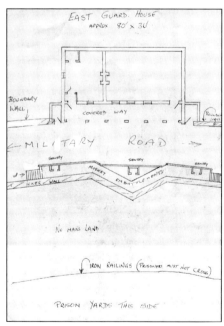
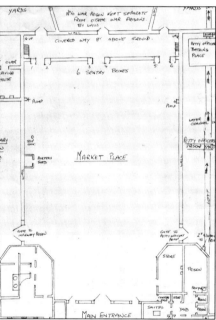

Top left: *Former steward's house.*
Top middle: *Part of the governor's house.* Top right: *Matrons', assistant surgeons' house along the Military Road.*
Above left: *Part of porter's house.*
Above middle: *East guardhouse.*
Above right: *Market Square where war prisoners were allowed to buy goods from incoming traders.*

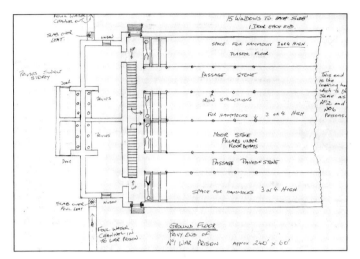

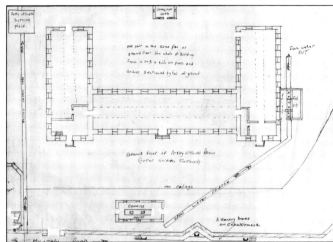

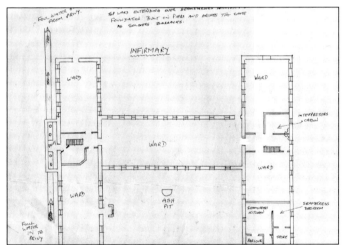

Top left: *Part of No. 1 war prison showing hammock arrangements and privies, about a dozen for the entire war prison of perhaps 1500 men. The privies would be directly over the flowing leats.*
Top right: *The petty officers' prison, with privies over the leat.*
Above: *The infirmary, again with the privies over the fast-flowing leat.*

Chapter Thirteen
FINIS

To end this story of the life of Dartmoor Prison – a progress report in many ways – it seems fitting to quote a poem written by a convict who, more than once, did time at Dartmoor. One of the sentences he was serving when he wrote the poem was for ten years. He called the poem 'The Lay of the Lagged Minstrel'. 'Lagged' is a term given to a convict who has done a 'lagging' which is a long sentence in a 'lagging station', a convict prison.

I am a lag, an artful lag, and do not care a rap
For all the D's in Scotland Yard, who are as soft as pap.
I can fake the broads and crack a crib, and never met my match
In taking down a bank cashier by what is termed the scratch
I'm doing ten long weary years at Dartmoor wild and bleak
Of what I've suffered, seen, and heard, I really cannot speak
We have to keep strick silence here, but if you please will wait
In racing phrase I'll give you all 'the straight tip' on my slate
The prison bread, like Mrs Brown, is brown, but not so nice
The skilly and the soup are made of beetles, meal and mice
They cut our hair down to the skin, moustache and whiskers too
Instead of men they make us look like monkeys at the Zoo
They clothe us in brown fustian, broad-arrowed, large and black
It is most harrowing to the nerves to have them on the back
Nine months slip by, one summer day, myself and others seven
Handcuffed and chained, we travel down for change of air to Devon
And lest some female gay and fair, should tempt us on the rail
To stray from virtue's narrow path, we go down by the mail
We get to Princetown safe and sound and there as well is known
They strip us naked just to see we're really flesh and bone
They find no stiffs, not even snouts, no readers chivs or spikes
And then we see Chief Warder H--, whom everybody likes
Next day at ten, we take a bath in water just like ochre
And then we march up to the Farm and interview the Croaker
Again we strip; he sounds our chest and chest *to make a joke*
He sounds my heart and then exclaims, 'You are a hearty bloke!'
Each morning when we've breakfasted, we march away to chapel
The Chaplain says we all are lagged because Eve stole an apple
We sing a hymn all out of tune, and then we kneel and pray
And twice on Sundays, wet or fine, the old boy cracks a lay
We join our parties on parade, each day when we have churched
And, lest a lag should crutch a toke, we're diligently searched
When all's correct we march away in hail, rain, snow or fog
To practise agricultural work in trenching on the bog
The seven tasks of Hercules compared with ours were easy
You cannot dig, you cannot stand, the peat's so wet and greasy
The God of Strength, without a doubt, had beef and beer ad lib
Poor lags get neither but they go chokey if they jib
Sometimes when things are very dull, a convict makes a dash
To gain his freedom, but the guards of him soon make a hash

Lag-shooting is such good old sport it's never out of season
But to shoot a pheasant in July is almost worse than treason
If Francatelli could but see our daily bill of fare
He'd say, 'Oui, oui Monsieur, je vois, your convicts live on air'
The bread's like asphalt, tough and black, the soup and tea's so weak
They cannot stand or walk about, in fact they cannot speak
Our Sunday dinner is a pint of pork soup mixed with peas
It's fairly good; in days gone by we had but bread and cheese
On weekdays every convict gets of boiled spuds just a pound
And five small ounces of tough beef, off anywhere but the round
On Tuesdays and on Fridays too, we have a pint of shins
We swear the cook's left out the meat; he only bows and grins
Five ounces of fat mutton is our Wednesday bill of fare
Of Thursday's duff my dearest friends, I'll have you all beware
The fame of English convict duff is known both far and wide
From San Francisco to Hong Kong, from Melbourne to the Clyde
It's utilised for building forts and ironclads as well
It's guaranteed to be bomb proof 'gainst bullet, shot and shell
When feeling sick, each day at twelve, the doctor you can see
He'll say you get too much to eat and order S and G
I'll speak the truth and frankly own that when a man is ill
He'll take you to the Farm, and there he'll cure or kill
Our conduct as a general rule is exemplary, I think
We do not smoke, we're never seen to be the worse for drink
No sporting papers do we read; such thoughts they make me shiver
We patronize the Leisure Hour, The Lamp, Good Words, The Quiver
I've often heard that honesty policy's the best
And as I'll soon be going home, I'll put it to the test
God save the Queen, and may He send down blessings on her head
She may make me Poet Laureate when Alfred Austin's dead.

Key to convict slang as used in 'The Lay of the Lagged Minstrel'. This was given to me by an old Dartmoor Prison convict in 1972, aged about 70, who had done laggings in many prisons and shall remain anonymous!:

A lag	long-term prisoner
Fake the broads	con the ladies
Crack a crib	open a safe
The scratch	forgery
The croaker	doctor
Stiffs	letter smuggled out of prison
Snouts	tobacco, usually rolled up cigarettes
Readers	books
Chivs, spikes	knives and pointed weapons
Cracks a lay	reads a sermon
Crutch a toke	hide an unauthorised article, usually in the crutch
Lag-shooting	firing at escaping convicts
Chokey	punishment block
Duff	pudding

Appendix One

GOVERNORS OF DARTMOOR PRISON

The governor's board in the governor's office up to 1990. To be added are the names of Governor Powls, Governor Lawrence and the present Governor, Graham Johnson.

1809–1812	Captain Cotgrave RN
1812–1815	Captain Shortland
1815–1850	Prison closed
1850–1854	Captain Gambier RN
1854–1864	Captain Morrish
1864–1866	G. Clifton
1866–1868	Captain Stopford
1868–1869	W. Pitt-Butts
1869–1874	Major Hickey
1874–1876	Major Noott
1876–1879	Captain Harris
1879–1890	Captain Every
1890–1892	Captain Johnson (Acting up for sick Capt. Every)
1893–1899	Captain Johnson
1900–1902	W.H.O. Russell
1902–1907	Basil Thompson
1907–1910	Captain G.H. Guyon
1910–1913	Captain G.E. Temple
1913–1919	Major Reade
1919–1921	Major Wisden
1921–1928	Captain Morgan
1928–1930	Captain Clayton
1930–1932	Major Morris (later Chief Constable)
1932–1932	S.N. Roberts (ex military)
1932–1945	Major Charles Pannal
1945–1955	Major Harvey
1955–1957	J. Richards
1957–1960	G.B. Smith
1960–1966	D. Malone
1966–1968	P.C. Jones
1968–1974	Major Golding
1974–1981	Colin Heald (Naval Officer)
1981–1982	E.R.E. Skelton
1982–1985	David Thompson
1985–1990	R.J. May
1990–1992	R.J. Kendrick (Army Officer)
1992–1994	R.J. Powls
1994–2001	John Lawrence
2001–	Graham Johnson

On the governors' board in the governor's office, it records the new incumbents from Capt. Every to Captain Clayton (1890–1929) as taking over after one year. On my list as soon as a governor leaves, his replacement is recorded as from that date. This is normal practice as there is never a period without a governor.

Appendix Two

THE AMERICAN CEMETERY

During the middle part of 2002, upgrades were made to the French and American cemeteries. This work was done on the instructions of Governor Graham Johnson, and he should be applauded for this noble effort.

The superb work done to the American obelisk, mid 2002.

Far left: *These are the gates to the American Memorial Arch, presented by members of the United States Navy. Looking through the gates one can see the flag poles and seats provided by the prison.*
Left: *Outside the new gates to the American cemetery, made and fitted by the prison.*

Appendix Three

PLAN OF PRISON 1872

This plan is dated 1872 when five of the old war prisons were still in use and north, east and south guardhouses are in use as quarters for warders.

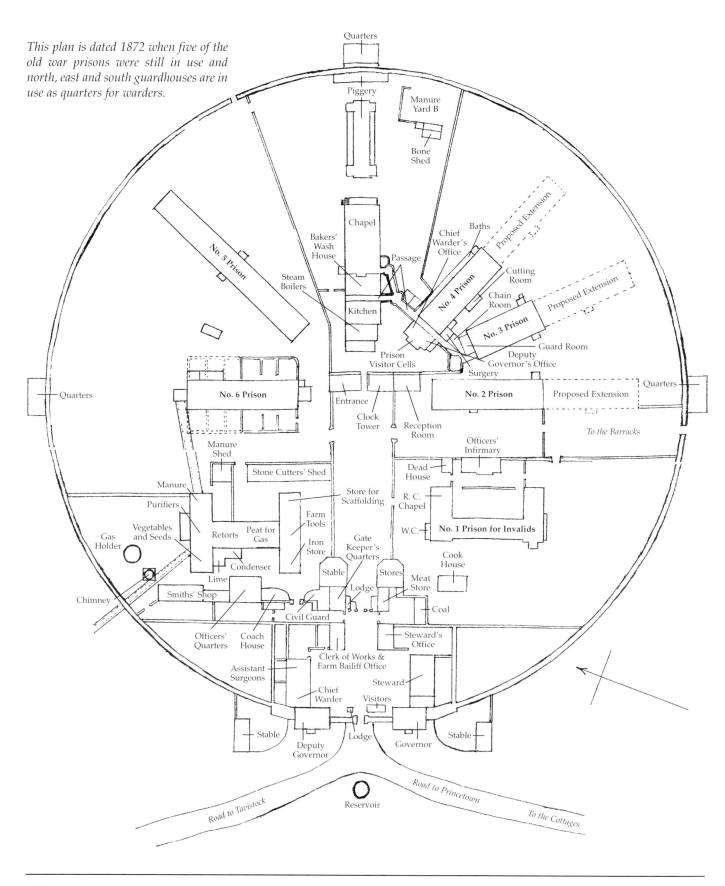

Appendix Four

PRISON CHANGES

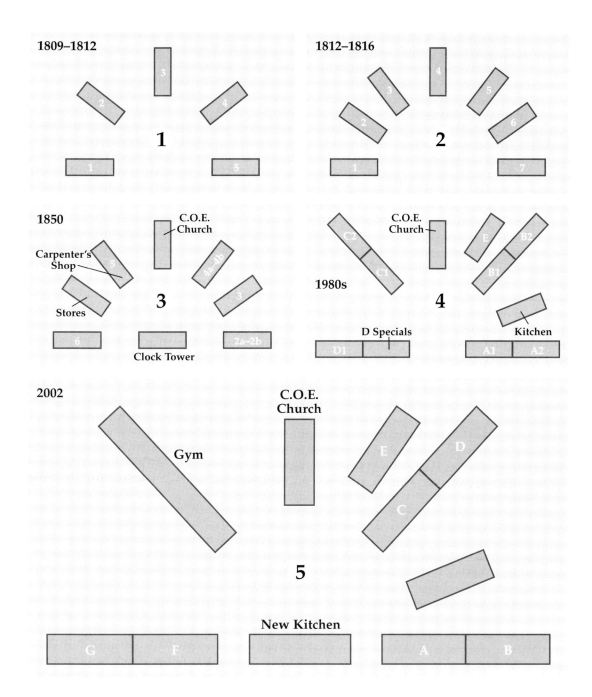

Dartmoor Depot 1809–1816 – Dartmoor Convict Prison 1850-2002

1. The 5 war prisons 1809–1812.
2. The 7 war prisons 1812–1816. Numbers 2 and 6 built by French prisoners of war in 1812.
3. The convict prison on opening in 1850; No. 2 prison had 324 cells of corrugated iron; No. 3 prison had 382 hammocks in open association. No. 4 prison held 240 cells. Total cells available about 1200; at times we held just that.
4. Turn of the century until 1980s, C-hall was demolished post the Second World War and a Nissen hut gymnasium built on its base.
5. Dartmoor Prison 2002, roll just over 600 cells.

BIBLIOGRAPHY

Abell, Francis. *Prisoners of War in Britain, 1756–1815.*

Atholl, Justin. *Prison on the Moor.*

Dartmoor Prison Works' Department Archives, various plans and documents.

Dartmoor Prison Archives, Governor Gambier's letters 1853.

Dartmoor Prison Muniments Room Archives.

Dartmoor Prison Archive photographs, courtesy various departments/author's collection.

Devon Record Office, Exeter. Diocesan Records (Chaplain's house 1813 accession 5720A/PB1-16) and Faculty Petitions 3-4-5-6-9 ref rebuilding of St Michael's Church, Princetown.

Dye, Ira. 'Essays in Maritime History', chapter in *Ships, Seafaring and Society,* edited by Timothy J. Runyan.

Ex-convict, An. *One who has endured it, five years' penal servitude 1878.*

Exeter University. *Reports of the Directors Convict Prisons,* courtesy Dr Fordyce.

Felknor, Bruce, and Kimberley Van Derveer. *Perez Drinkwater letters home,* BruceFelknor@usmm.org, USA.

Grew, Major B.D. *Prison Governor.*

Marblehead Historical Society at the Jeremiah Mansion, Marblehead, courtesy, Marion Gosling, USA.

Huntsberry, Thomas V. and Joanne M. *Dartmoor (War of 1812) Prison, USA.*

Novak, Rynell. *National Society US Daughters of 1812.* USA.

Plymouth and West Devon Record Office. Captain Hawkins' papers (accession 380–450).

Thompson, Governor 1 Basil. *Dartmoor Prison.*

Tullett, Tom. *Inside Dartmoor.*

Rhodes, A.J. *Dartmoor Prison 1806–1932.*

Webb, Major General Sir Joshua KCB 1793–1863. *Prison Service Journal,* April 1965 (IV No.15 page 26).